The Early Modern Englishwoman:
A Facsimile Library of Essential Works

Series II

Printed Writings, 1641–1700: Part 4

Volume 3

Gertrude More

The Early Modern Englishwoman:
A Facsimile Library of Essential Works

Series II

Printed Writings, 1641–1700: Part 4

Volume 3

Gertrude More

Selected and Introduced by
Arthur F. Marotti

General Editors
Betty S. Travitsky and Anne Lake Prescott

ASHGATE

Published by
Ashgate Publishing Limited
Wey Court East
Union Road
Farnham
Surrey, GU9 7PT
England

Ashgate Publishing Company
Suite 420
101 Cherry Street
Burlington
VT 05401-4405
USA

BX
2181
.M67
2009

www.ashgate.com

British Library Cataloguing-in-Publication Data
More, Gertrude, 1606–1633.
  Gertrude More. – (The early modern Englishwoman. Series II,
  Printed writings, 1641–1700, part 4 ; v. 3)
  1. Meditations–Early works to 1800. 2. Negative theology–
  Christianity–Early works to 1800.
  I. Title II. Series III. Marotti, Arthur F., 1940–
  242-dc22

Library of Congress Control Number: 2009926669

The image reproduced on the title page and on the cover is from the frontispiece portrait in *Poems. By the Most Deservedly Admired Mrs. Katherine Philips* (1667). Reproduced by permission of the Folger Shakespeare Library, Washington DC.

ISBN 978 0 7546 6309 6

Mixed Sources
Product group from well-managed
forests and other controlled sources
www.fsc.org Cert no. SGS-COC-2482
© 1996 Forest Stewardship Council
FSC

Printed and bound in Great Britain by
TJ International Ltd, Padstow, Cornwall

CONTENTS

PREFACE
BY THE GENERAL EDITORS

Until very recently, scholars of the early modern period have assumed that there were no Judith Shakespeares in early modern England. Much of the energy of the current generation of scholars has been devoted to constructing a history of early modern England that takes into account what women actually wrote, what women actually read, and what women actually did. In so doing, contemporary scholars have revised the traditional representation of early modern women as constructed both in their own time and in ours. The study of early modern women has thus become one of the most important – indeed perhaps the most important – means for the rewriting of early modern history.

The Early Modern Englishwoman: A Facsimile Library of Essential Works is one of the developments of this energetic reappraisal of the period. As the names on our advisory board and our list of editors testify, it has been the beneficiary of scholarship in the field, and we hope it will also be an essential part of that scholarship's continuing momentum.

The Early Modern Englishwoman is designed to make available a comprehensive and focused collection of writings in English from 1500 to 1750, both by women and for and about them. The three series of Printed Writings (1500–1640, 1641–1700, and 1701–1750) provide a comprehensive if not entirely complete collection of the separately published writings by women. In reprinting these writings we intend to remedy one of the major obstacles to the advancement of feminist criticism of the early modern period, namely the limited availability of the very texts upon which the field is based. The volumes in the facsimile library reproduce carefully chosen copies of these texts, incorporating significant variants (usually in the appendices). Each text is preceded by a short introduction providing an overview of the life and work of a writer along with a survey of important scholarship. These works, we strongly believe, deserve a large readership – of historians, literary critics, feminist critics, and non-specialist readers.

The Early Modern Englishwoman also includes separate facsimile series of Essential Works for the Study of Early Modern Women and of Manuscript Writings. These facsimile series are complemented by The Early Modern Englishwoman 1500–1750: Contemporary Editions. Also under our general editorship, this series includes both old-spelling and modernized editions of works by and about women and gender in early modern England.

New York City
2009

INTRODUCTORY NOTE

Dame Gertrude More's only book-length work, *Spiritual Exercises* (Paris, 1658), is a collection of her writing assembled by Dom Augustine Baker, OSB, and published some thirty-three years after her death. Some of More's other verse and prose appears in the biography that Baker composed (Baker, 2002[1]), but her *Spiritual Exercises* remains the main text she has bequeathed to her order and to posterity. One other early-modern printed book with which she is associated is a collection of devotional texts published one year earlier, *The Holy Practises of a Devine Lover, or The Sainctly Ideots Deuotions* (Paris, 1657), a work more properly classified as an anthology of devotional utterances compiled by Baker as models for those whose contemplative practices he guided. The materials included in this volume may have been in More's possession at her death, but they are not, properly speaking, her own work, although, as Claire Walker has demonstrated, both Baker's and More's writings had a collaborative character.[2]

Dame Gertrude More

Dom Augustine Baker's *The Life and Death of Dame Gertrude More* is the main source for Dame Gertrude More's biography.[3] Gertrude (née Helen) More was born in 1606 in Essex, the elder of two daughters of Cresacre More, and the great-great-granddaughter of Sir Thomas More. She lost her mother when she was five years old and was raised by her father, who provided his daughters with an intellectually substantial education. Baker describes her behaviour as a girl:

> she was of a verie good nature, gentle, affable, kinde, tractable, meerie and pleasant, verie forwarde in naturall witte and judgment for her years. Her father was so delighted in her compagnie and conversation,

that his life, that otherwise was solitarie, was the more tolerable and pleasing to him. (*Life*, 12–13)

When she was sixteen, her confessor, Dom Benet Jones, OSB, persuaded her to go to the Continent to 'make some triall of a religious life, and to proceed or not proceed, as uppon experience she should see cause' (*Life*, 13). Jones's counsel to her was part of a plan of reviving English monasticism that involved her father's providing the financial backing for the establishment of a new Benedictine convent at Cambrai in the Spanish Netherlands.[4]

At eighteen More left England with eight other young women, entered the Benedictine order and went to the new Monastery of Our Lady of Comfort, where she took the name of Gertrude, signalling her devotion to a saint whose life she admired and whose writings she studied.[5] Baker acknowledges her ambivalence about entering the religious life, but he interprets it as her inability to recognize that she had a true vocation from God:

Comming into Religion I thinke she camme as it were blindfolde ... ledde by imaginations, hearesaies, and other things. ... But yet being come on this side of the Seas ... she became much better disposed for Religion. And though as yet she could perceave no call to it, yet surelie she had a privie Call ... though she could not as yet discerne it. (*Life*, 19)

Unhappy in her new religious life for the first year-and-one-half or two years in the convent, More reluctantly made her profession as a nun in January, 1625. During the period of her discontent she changed, as Baker observes, 'from an humble, simple, obedient, gentle, quiet, and tractable nature' to one who was 'factious, craftie or wilie, willful stobborne and disobedient', living in a state he characterized as one of 'spiritual confusion' (*Life*, 3), supposedly because she had not yet found a method of prayer suitable to her. More herself portrays her early years in the convent as a time of suffering because she had not found a productive spiritual direction.[6]

Earlier, in the fall of 1624, More had been advised by her friend Catherine Gascoigne (who later became abbess) to seek the counsel of Baker, who was the convent's unofficial spiritual director, but she initially resisted his guidance. The second time she came to Baker, however, she had a conversion experience and wholeheartedly accepted the form of prayer that Baker was recommending to her. Baker perceived in her a natural ability for deep contemplative prayer, whose exercise 'in her must not be by anie discoursing of the Imagination, or by the use of anie sensible images, but must be meerelie by the exercise of Amorous affections' (*Life*, 36). Under Baker's non-prescriptive guidance, More developed the kind of prayer that suited her abilities and disposition, gaining confidence in herself as a practising contemplative or mystic. Since this form of contemplation avoided the use of 'sensible images', it was set in opposition to Jesuit techniques of meditation, whose reliance on the imagination and the analytical intellect defined that practice as markedly different.

Baker divided More's life in the convent into four 'stations' or stages. In the second stage her discovery of contemplative prayer gave her six years in which 'she founde the meanes and waie to becomme recollected, and to leade an internall life' (*Life*, 6). Nevertheless, the third stage of her convent life was characterized by 'great and extraordinarie affliction and probation in soule' (*Life*, 6), mainly because the convent's newly appointed confessor, Dom Francis Hull, OSB, opposed Baker's teachings and the form of contemplative prayer practised by him and his followers.[7] This created, for More and others, a crisis of obedience and authority. She even became the 'head of a faction of disobedience and opposition against the Abbesse' (*Life*, 48), who supported Hull.

In defence of her own spiritual practices and those of her fellow contemplatives, More stood her ground against coercion, finally writing a long 'Apology' defending Baker when he was charged before the General Chapter of the Benedictines with heterodox spiritual teaching and offering, at the same time, a justification for her own devotional practices.[8] This document, which is printed before the 'Confessiones Amantis' in the *Spiritual Exercises*, is remarkably and courageously assertive and confident. In it, More offers a clear rationale for resisting the imposition by Father Hull of Jesuit methods of meditation. In effect, she claims that the individual practitioner of devotion, with God's help, knows best what is good for her and no human authority has the right to force her in a different direction. As was the case with Protestant reformers, such a configuration of divinely sanctioned individual spiritual authority was potentially threatening to a hierarchical Church, whose Inquisition had designated 'Illuminism' as a heresy, one with which Baker's opponents sought to associate him.

The final stage of More's life demarcated by Baker in his biography is that of her last eighteen or nineteen days, in which she was ill from smallpox; she died on 17 August 1633 at the young age of twenty-seven.

THE SPIRITVAL EXERCISES. OF THE MOST VERTVOVS and Religious D. GERTRVDE MORE of the holy Order of S. Bennet and English Congregation of our Ladies of Comfort in Cambray, she called them. Amor ordinem nescit. And Ideots deuotions. Her only Spiritual Father and Directour the Ven. Fa. Baker stiled them. Confessiones Amantis. A Louers Confessions. (1658)

The *Spiritual Exercises* has several parts. After some preliminaries, it places first Dame Gertrude's most combative piece of writing, 'The Devout Souls Advertisement to the Reader. With an Apology for herself, and her spiritual Guide, and Director the V. F. Augustin Baker'. This is followed by the fifty-three confessions, the 'Confessiones Amantis' of the book's extended title, and by other materials that had been found among More's literary remains: 'Sentences, and Sayings of the same pious Soul found in some others [sic] papers of hers' (C 237–53), 'Certain other Deuotions of the same deuot Soul D. Gertrude More, which she left written in her Breuiary' (C 253–76), and 'some other Deuotions of the same pious soul D. Gertrude More' (C 277–312), the last including her responses and comments in both poetry and prose inspired by her reading of Scripture and by the works of both Christian writers and 'Heathen Philosophers' (C 312).

Like Augustine Baker, Gertrude More belongs to a tradition of mystical writers who believed in the value of the *via negativa*, a path to union with God by way of total self-abnegation and the emptying of the mind of set ideas and images. Whether in the form of the negative theology of Dionysius the pseudo-Areopagite (Dionysius, 1940) or the nescience of a text such as the medieval *Cloud of Unknowing* (1973), this mystical practice sought direct affective and spiritual contact with the Godhead without the help of the analytic intellect or the sensuous imagination.

In *Sancta Sophia*, a collection of some forty of his treatises edited after his death by Dom Serenus Cressy and published in 1657, Baker distinguishes two kinds of mystic contemplation:

> 1. *Actiue* and ordinary: being indeed an habituall state of perfect soules by which they are enabled, whensoever fit occasion shall be, to vnite themselves actiuely and actually to God by efficacious, feruent, amorous, and constant, yet withall silent and quiet, Elevations of the Spirit. 2. *Passiue* and extraordinary: the which is not a state but an actuall Grace and fauour from God, by which He is pleased at certaine times according to his free Good pleasure, to communicate a glimpse of his Majesty to the spirits of his Seruants after a secret & wonderfull manner. (*Sancta Sophia*, 2: 243)

As the mystic becomes more and more habituated to contemplation, Baker argues, 'the soule comes to operate more & more abstracted from sense, & more eleuated aboue the corporall organs & faculties, so drawing nearer to the resemblance of the operations of an Angell or separated spirit' (*Sancta Sophia*, 2: 244–5).

Dame Gertrude More's *Spiritual Exercises* are the product of her personal adaptation of the contemplative methods taught her by Augustine Baker, but they are also the fruit of her own wide reading of manuscript and printed texts, many of which were provided to the community by Baker, who had gathered medieval and post-medieval mystical and devotional literature for his own and others' edification. Baker mentions that More spent time 'reading of bookes, that either were spiritual, or contained good or tollerable matter, of which sorte were the saiengs and doengs of Philosophers and other wise men, and secular stories judiciouslie written' (*Life*, 87). This reading included not only the work of religious mystics and saints such as St Augustine, Thomas à Kempis, St John of the

Cross, and St Teresa, and 'all St Gertruds workes' (*Life*, 87), but also the histories of Tacitus (*Life*, 100), writings of pagan philosophers, and the poetry of the Protestant Guillaume du Bartas in Joshua Sylvester's translation (*Life*, 87).

In her *Spiritual Exercises*, More seeks the kind of passive union with God that Baker defined as the highest form of contemplation, but to prepare herself to be open to this experience, she engages in repeated expressions of mortification and self-abnegation. She says in her first confession that 'losing of ourselves' involves a 'most sweet and happy exchange' in which we can discover 'the greatest *liberty* in this world' (C 2–3). Justifying her own abandonment of the world for the confines of the convent, she happily accepts leaving 'freinds, riches, honours, pleasures ... and euen (which is most of all) our very selues' (A 21–22). She accepts afflictions and sufferings as beneficial, 'to the end that we being proued or tried, as gold in the furnace, should thereby become capable of *thy* pure *loue*' (C 130). In the last instalment of her confessions, the fifty-third, written some two weeks before her death, she writes 'Let me dy to al created things that I may liue alone to *thee*' (C 236), a statement that, in context, seems to be part of her effort to practise the *ars moriendi* (art of dying).

More deals repeatedly with the sensitive issue of obedience to superiors: on the one hand, she accepts humility and subordination to them as part of her submission to the Divine will, but, on the other, she is careful to distinguish between true and false authority. In her twenty-second confession she addresses God:

> a Superior reflecting on his own authority, rather than on what in *thy* behalf he ought to exact ... rather gouerneth in his owne power then in *thine*, and the effect ... will consequently be more human than *divine*; and the Superiors while sensible of their honour, abusing the power giuen by *thee*, doe yet loose what they would haue. (C 113–14)

She does finally accept the need for obedience to superiors for the sake of social harmony within the religious community (C 190–91), very much aware of the scandal that might result from a religious house's internal struggles becoming known to supportive fellow Catholics beyond its walls and to the world at large.

The supplementary material following the confessions also deals with the problem of authority within the convent, framing it ultimately within the context of larger internal Catholic conflicts. More observes that those who live within cloistered communities 'do easily fal into occasion of iars, and differences with others, whilst euery one pretends the truth, and holds the best to be of her side, howsoeuer it be indeed' (C 242). Misunderstandings can account for some of the hostility between contemplatives and others: '*Those that liue an internal life* do so withdraw al natural inordinate affection from creatures, that they often therfor are censured by superiors & equals to neglect others out of pride' (C 244–45). Having in mind the contemporary competition and conflicts of the Benedictine, Franciscan, and Jesuit orders, she idealizes early monasticism and argues that internecine Catholic struggles harm a Church that was attempting to win back Protestant defectors (C 249–50). She looks beyond the local struggle between Hull and Baker over the proper method of prayer for the nuns at Cambrai to consider the larger framework of the English and Continental Catholic world, in which religious orders, by their conflicts with one another, both created a kind of scandal and diverted energies better used for purposes of conversion.

More's confessions repeat a limited set of basic themes: the value of the method of contemplative prayer; the necessity of humility and obedience; the problem of relating to superiors who abuse their authority in impeding the course of prayer that enriches the contemplative's relationship to God; the liberty to be found in complete self-abnegation and submission to God; the dangers posed by the sin of pride; the benefits of afflictions and tribulations; the importance of rejecting worldly attachments; the need for discretion; and the memorial function of writing. More sometimes autobiographically alludes to the history of her own vocation, her resistance to the requirements of convent life, the dramatic change effected by her discovery of contemplative prayer through Baker's guidance, her struggles with just and unjust superiors, and her attainment of peace of mind through total devotion to God and humble acceptance of her situation. Though she emphasizes her one-on-one relationship with God, she does acknowledge her devotion to saints and angels as heavenly mediators and role models: Mary, St. Augustine ('my deare Patron' [C 300–301]), 'Saint Michael ... Saint Raphael ... Saint Gabriel ... S. Benedict ... S. Scholastica ... S. Joseph, S. John, S. Thomas, and S. Gertrude' (C 133–4). She treats St. Mary Magdalen as a model mystic who abandoned the world of the senses to pursue contemplation (C 196–9).[9]

Occasionally More expresses herself in verse. In the first confession, she has a long poem on the theme of the superiority of the way of Mary (the contemplative life) to that of Martha (the active life) (C 5–9).[10] In the seventh confession she cites a long passage from St. Thomas à Kempis and, after providing an English translation, puts it into verse form as the longest of her poems in the book (C 46–52). In the supplementary material to her confessions, other examples of her poetry are included: a sixteen-line psalm-meter poem, 'A short Oblation of this smal work by the writer gatherer thereof to our most sweet and Merciful God' (C 277); a poem 'To ovr Blessed Lady, the Aduocate of sinners' (C 279–81); a fifty-eight-line poem 'To our most Holy Father Saint Benedict' (C 281–3); and an untitled poem of fifty-two lines following 'An acte of Contrition, partly taken out of the words of blessed S. Augustin' (C 285–7). Though this writing might seem to be devotional doggerel, its deliberate artlessness and avoidance of imagery, of ingenious language, and of literary complexity are part of a strategy of self-effacing religious plain-speaking consistent with Baker's and More's ideals of contemplative prayer, which included an avoidance of distracting sensuous particularity.[11]

More's writings are private, but within the social world of the religious community in which she functioned and in the context of the larger world of the early modern English Catholics living on the Continent, who retained important real and symbolic ties to the home country, they express a kind of social agency. Although feminist historical scholarship has been slower to recover the devotional writing of early modern Englishwomen than to rediscover the more obviously transgressive, though sometimes quite atypical, texts of such women as Eleanor Davies, Anna Trapnel, and Margaret

Cavendish, who functioned more boldly in the public sphere, scholars are beginning to see the value of studying the religious writings of other women, especially Catholic nuns, both within the context of gender politics of the time and within the large cultural processes of early modern England and Europe.[12] Dame Gertrude More's work is the product of an independent intelligence and courageous temperament. She herself was at once humbly pious and boldly assertive, exploiting the surprising possibilities for personal freedom and independence that were possible within a rule-bound, cloistered way of life.

The publication of More's *Spiritual Exercises* in 1658 had a double context – first, of a renewed attack within the Benedictine order on Augustine Baker's teachings, and, second, of the instructive use within the convent and beyond of the personal devotional writing of nuns. In 1655 the president of the Benedictines, Father Claude White, ordered the Cambrai nuns to hand over the treatises and papers of Baker's held in their possession in order for him to censor, if not destroy, them as dangerous and heretical. The Abbess, Catherine Gascoigne, refused, White soon died, and the controversy ended. Putting Baker's treatise *Sancta Sophia* into print in 1657 and publishing his disciple's *Spiritual Exercises* in 1658 appear to have been attempts to preserve devotional teachings in the face of their possible destruction at some future time.[13] In addition, as Claire Walker points out, both Baker's treatises at Cambrai and Gertrude More's devotional writings represent the kind of shared authorship that developed between Baker and the nuns he instructed: his texts took shape in response to the nuns' contemplative experiences and their writings employed materials, ideas and models he developed with them. The texts produced by both Baker and the nuns were shared in, and owned by, the Cambrai community, but they were also disseminated to other religious houses and to a larger Continental and English Catholic community. The situation is one in which the writings of a spiritually empowered More, who had lived within the bounds of a cloister, had an impact well beyond the convent walls, in both manuscript and print (Walker, 2004, 247–53). Father Serenus Cressy, OSB, commented on More's influence when he wrote:

> She proved, as it were, a Domestick Mistresse after her Death, to All the present, and Succeeding souls in That Convent. Yea, Many others, of divers Conditions, have not only Received much Edification, but Great Profit, by the sight of the said Writings, in being drawn and Encouraged by them, to Give themselves very seriously to prayer; as her Example and Counsell, when Living did worke the like Effects in Many.[14]

What was written in the nun's cell exploded into the wider world.

No additional early-modern edition of More's *Spiritual Exercises* followed its 1658 publication, but the work was edited by Dom Benedict Weld-Blundell as the second part of *The Writings of Dame Gertrude More* (1910). A more recent edition of *The Spiritual Exercises* is based on the manuscript text of the work, Bodleian MS Rawlinson C.1581 (Baker, 2007), which has four poems prefaced to the work missing from the 1658 edition, along with another poem left out of the printed version of the thirty-eighth confession.[15] Other pieces of Dame Gertrude's writings are found in Baker's biography of her.

One of the interesting physical features of this book is the presence in it of manicules or the pointing finger images that are put in the margin next to some of the passages in the volume. Kitty Scoular Datta argues that

> passages marked in the 1658 volume by a small pointer-hand are the most radical. Since Baker's posthumous reputation in the Benedictine Order was cleared only three years before the volume's publication date, the volume may be seen as part of a campaign by Baker's disciples in his exoneration and for the spread of his ideas which Gertrude's own writing exemplified. (2002, 50).

Dorothy Latz suggests an additional context with regard to the 1658 volume's place of publication, Paris, where 'Queen Henrietta Maria became a donor and protector' of the Benedictine convent (1989, 30). The insertion of two 'Approbations' in the volume, instead of one simple 'imprimatur', suggests the potentially controversial nature of the work. Thus, the second 'Approbation', by the Benedictine prior assured readers that More's work is not only free of doctrinal error, but that it is basically an elaboration of the spiritual practices of Thomas à Kempis's *Imitatio Christi*.

Copies of the *Spiritual Exercises* are found in The British Library; Dr. Williams's Library, London; the London Oratory; Longleat House; the Bodleian Library, Oxford; St. Mary's Seminary, New Oscott; Downside Abbey, Bath; Ushaw College; The Folger Shakespeare Library; The Huntington Library; St. Louis University; The University of Texas; Sterling Library, Yale University; and Bibliothèque Nationale, Paris. Some of these, including the Downside Abbey copy, put an address to the 'Deuout spiritual Reader', 'The Approbation' by Hen[ry] Holden, and 'The Approbation' by 'Fr. Walgravivs Doct. Theol. Monachus & Prior Benedictinus' on sigs. *i and ii at the start of the volume, followed by a poem in praise of Sir Thomas More (sig. *ii^v), possibly by Dame Gertrude More, and an engraved portrait of her (sig. ai^r);[16] other copies of the book place these items after the long address to the reader.[17]

The facsimile reproduced here is of the Yale University copy. This source was chosen because other available reproductions of this small (duodecimo) text either lose some letters in the gutters of the tightly bound copies used for filming or show excessive bleed-through that distorts the images.

The pagination of the 1658 edition of the work has some peculiarities. The title page, dedicatory letter, and 'Apology' consist of sigs. a–d i–xii and 'c' [e] i–viii. Arabic number pagination begins on sig. a ii^r with page 3 and concludes with page 112. The second major part of the book, 'Confessiones Amantis' (the fifty-three confessions More completed), along with other materials from her literary remains, is found on sigs. A–N i–xii. On these signatures the printer begins the arabic pagination anew as pages 1–312.

Acknowledgements

For providing a microfilm of its copy and for permission to use it in this edition, I am grateful to the Yale University Library.

Notes

1. I cite this within the text as *Life*. When, in the notes, I am quoting the Introduction, I cite the book as 'Wekking'.
2. For a discussion of the ways in which Baker's writings were, in a sense, co-authored by the nuns whose contemplative practices he guided and of the sense in which the nuns' writings were also collaborative, see Claire Walker (2004). Both Baker and More also absorbed into their texts the writings and insights of previous contemplative writers whose works they read.
3. Wekking, lxxvii, points out that a poor assemblage of manuscript material for the *Life* was published in the late nineteenth century as *Life of Dame Gertrude More, Order of S. Benedict. From Ancient MSS* by Rev. Henry Collins (1877). This was followed by an editing of manuscript materials by Benedict Weld-Blundell, OSB, *The Life and Death of Dame Gertrude More* [1910]. I draw also on the article on Dame Gertrude More in the new *Oxford Dictionary of National Biography*, ed. H.C.G. Matthew and Brian Harrison (2004) and on material found in Wekking's introduction to Baker's biography. In his biography of Augustine Baker, Serenus Cressy also has several pages devoted to More and to Baker's relationship with her (Cressy, 1997, 108–13), using material drawn from Baker's biography of her and citing some of More's writing from her 'Confessions'.
4. D. Shanahan states that this amounted to £500 (1974, 19 n.15).
5. Baker, *Life*, 12, notes that her younger sister Bridget also avoided marriage and joined her at Cambrai once she turned eighteen.
6. See More's account on pp. 90–91 of the 'Apology' section in *The Spiritual Exercises*, 'The Devout Souls Advertisement to the Reader. With an Apology for herself, and her spiritual Guide, and Director the V. F. Augustin Baker'. Since the 'Apology' and the 'Confessions' sections of this publication have separate arabic pagination, I shall distinguish the page numbers with a prefatory 'A' or 'C'.

7. For a discussion of the Baker–Hull conflict, see Wekking, xiii–xiv. See also Anthony Low (1970, 43–5).

8. This 'Apology' is printed on A 7–112 of the 1658 edition. Although Baker was exonerated before the General Chapter of the Benedictines following this inquiry, he was removed from Cambrai and his accuser treated more kindly. See the comments of one of Baker's biographers, Leander Pritchard (1933, 119).

9. See also the fifty-second confession, written on the feast day of St. Mary Magdalen (C 231–33).

10. Baker alludes to the Mary/Martha contrast in *Sancta Sophia* (Douai, 1657), 2: 247. On the use of Mary and Martha to refer to the different activities performed by cloistered nuns see Claire Walker, 1999.

11. Dorothy Latz collects all of More's extant verse (1989, 23–57).

12. For a recent study that recognizes the political and cultural importance of early modern English nuns, see Claire Walker (2003). See also Heather Wolfe (2004, 2007); the anthology of religious writing by early modern English nuns edited by Nicky Hallett (2007); and the essays in Dorothy L. Latz (1997).

13. Walker (2004, 250), suggests that White made his move to confiscate the Baker manuscripts at the time he did, before they could reach a wider audience, because Serenus Cressy was already editing some of them for the volume that finally appeared in 1657. She also discusses White's actions in the context of the tricky subject of the Cambrai convent's property rights to Baker's manuscripts (238–39). David Lunn (1975) discusses further complexities of the situation.

14. BL MS 1755, fol. 182, cited in Walker (2004, 247).

15. These are, in their manuscript source: 'Which to attempt if it seem much' (fols. 2v–3r), 'Who be ador'd by auncoents all' (fols. 5r–6r), 'For as thou knowest, all othere loues' (fol. 7r–v), 'My God the *summum bonum* is' (fols. 10r–v) and 'O Lord my God, to thee I do aspire' (fol. 95v). The Rawlinson manuscript, however, does not have the poems to St. Augustine and to St. Benedict found in the printed text.

16. The Huntington Library copy (reproduced in the UMI and EEBO versions of this title) and two of the three British Library copies (4401.C.10 and G.19720) place the More poem and the engraving of Gertrude More (by 'R. Lochon') at the start of the volume. The BL copies, however, are in modern bindings and these items may have been moved from their original positions.

17. See, for example, one of the three British Library copies, 1418. a.29.

References

Wing M2632

Baker, Augustine OSB (2002), *The Life and Death of Dame Gertrude More*, ed. Ben Wekking, *Analecta Cartusiana* 119:19, Salzburg, Austria: Institut für Anglistik und Amerikanstik Universität Salzburg

———— (2007), *Confessiones Amantis: The Spiritual Exercises of the most Vertuous and Religious Dame Gertrude More*, ed. and introduced by John Clark, *Analecta Cartusiana* 119:27, Salzburg, Austria: Institut für Anglistik und Amerikanistik Universität Salzburg

The Cloud of Unknowing and The Book of Privy Counseling (1973), ed. William Johnston, New York: Doubleday

Collins, Revd Henry (1877), *Life of Dame Gertrude More, Order of S. Benedict. From Ancient MSS*, Derby and London

Cressy, Serenus (1977), *The Life of Father Augustine Baker, OSB (1575–1641) by Fr. Peter Slavin & Fr. Serenus Cressy*, ed. Dom Justin McCann, OSB, Salzburg, Austria: Institut für Anglistik und Amerikanstik Universität Salzburg

Datta, Kitty Scoular (2002) 'Women, Authority and Mysticism: The Case of Dame Gertrude More (1606–1633)', in Supriya Chaudhuri and Sajni Mukherji (eds), *Literature and Gender*, New Delhi: Orient Longman, 50–59

Dionysius the Areopagite on the Divine Names and Mystical Theology (1940), trans. C.E. Rolt, New York: Macmillan

Hallett, Nicky (2007), *Lives of Spirit: English Carmelite Self-Writing of the Early Modern Period*, Aldershot, UK, and Burlington, VT: Ashgate

Latz, Dorothy (1989), *'Glow-worm Light': Writings of 17th Century English Recusant Women from Original Manuscripts*, Salzburg: Institut für Anglistik und Amerikanstik Universität Salzburg

————— (ed.) (1997), *Neglected English Literature: Recusant Writings of the 16th–17th Centuries*, Salzburg Studies in English Literature, Elizabethan and Renaissance Studies, ed. James Hogg, 92:24, Salzburg, Austria: Institut für Anglistik und Amerikanstik Universität Salzburg

Low, Anthony (1970), *Augustine Baker*, New York: Twayne Publishers

Lunn, David (1975), 'Augustine Baker (1575–1641) and the English Mystical Tradition', *Journal of Ecclesiastical History* 26.3: 270–71

Oxford Dictionary of National Biography (2004), ed. H.C.G. Matthew and Brian Harrison, 60 vols, Oxford and New York: Oxford University Press

Pritchard, Leander (1933), *Memorials of Father Augustine Baker*, ed. Dom Justin McCann, OSB, and Dom Hugh Connolly, OSB, Catholic Record Society 33, London: John Whitehead and Son

Shanahan, D. (1974), 'The Descendants of St. Thomas More in Essex: Dame Gertrude More, OSB', *Essex Recusant* 16

Walker, Claire (1999), 'Combining Martha and Mary: Gender and Word in Seventeenth-Century English Cloisters', *Sixteenth Century Journal* 30.2: 397–418

————— (2003), *Gender and Politics in Early Modern Europe: English Convents in France and the Low Countries*, Basingstoke, UK, and New York: Palgrave

————— (2004), 'Spiritual Property: The English Benedictine Nuns of Cambrai and the Dispute over the Baker Manuscripts', in Nancy E. Wright, Margaret W. Ferguson, and A. R. Buck (eds), *Women, Property, and the Letters of the Law in Early Modern*

England, Toronto, Buffalo, London: University of Toronto Press, 237–55

Weld-Blundell, Benedict OSB (ed.) (1910), *The Life and Death of Dame Gertrude More*, London: R. & T. Washbourne

Wolfe, Heather (2004), 'Reading Bells and Loose Papers: Reading and Writing Practices of the English Benedictine Nuns of Cambrai', in Victoria E. Burke and Jonathan Gibson (eds), *Early Modern Women's Manuscript Writing: Selected Papers from the Trinity/Trent Colloquium*, Aldershot, UK, and Burlington, VT: Ashgate, 135–56

——— (2007), 'Dame Barbara Constable: Catholic Antiquarian, Advisor, and Closet Missionary', in Ronald Corthell, Frances D. Dolan, Christopher Highley and Arthur F. Marotti (eds), *Catholic Culture in Early Modern England*, Notre Dame, IN: University of Notre Dame Press, 158–88

ARTHUR F. MAROTTI

THE SPIRITVAL EXERCISES. OF THE MOST VERTVOVS and Religious D. GERTRVDE MORE of the holy Order of S. Bennet and English Congregation of our Ladies of Comfort in Cambray, she called them. Amor ordinem nescit. And Ideots deuotions. Her only Spiritual Father and Directour the Ven. Fa. Baker stiled them. Confessiones Amantis. A Louers Confessions. (1658; Wing M2632) is reproduced, by permission, from the copy at the Beinecke Rare Book and Manuscript Library, Yale University (Call number: Mhc5 M812 Sp47). The text block of the original measures 130 mm × 67 mm.

Words or passages which are difficult to read:

aviii^r.31	reasons
bvi^r.26	[f]eare w[hic]h [instead of "seare w.h"]
bviii^v.30	welminded
dvii^v margin	This Sir Thomas More the famous Lord Chancellor of England Blessed, and renovvned Martyr of Christ IESVS vvas her great, great grandfather
*i^v .4	and vertuous
Ci^r.27	sing
Cii^r	page number 51 unclear
Nix^v. 18	intention
Nx^r.17	this
Nx^v.16	vanity

Additional notes:

Ev^v	Marginal reference to Psalm should be to Psalm 87 not "187"
Iv^r	signature incorrectly identified as "Gv"
Iix^v–Ix^r	Page numbers given as "110" and "111" instead of "210" and "211"
Kx^r	Page 235 incorrectly numbered as "225"

Renowned, *More* whose bloody Fate
England neer yet could expiate,
Such was thy constant *Faith*, so much

Sir
Thom.
More,

Thy *Hope*, thy *Charity* was such;
As made thee twise a Martyr proue;
Of *Faith* in Death, in Life of *Loue!*
View heer thy Grandchilds broken *Hart*
Wounded with a *Seraphick Dart.*
Who while she liu'd mortals among
Thus to her *Spouse Divine* she sung.
Mirrour of Beauty in whose Face
The essence liues of euery Grace!
True lustre dwels in thy sole spheare
Those glimmerings that sometimes appeare
In this dark vayl, this gloomy night
Are shadows tipt wtih glow worm light,
Shew me thy radiant parts aboue,
VVhere Angels vnconsumed moue
VVhere amourous fire maintaines their line
As man by breathing Air, suruines.
But if perchance the mortal eye,
That views thy dazling looks must dye
VVith blind faith heer ile kis them & desire
To feele the heat, before I see the fire,

D. GERTRVDE MORE.

MAGNES AMORIS AMOR.

P. Lochon sculp.

THE SPIRIT·VAL
EXERCISES.

OF THE MOST VERTVOVS
and Religioũs D. GERTRVDE MORE
of the holy Order of S. Bennet and
English Congregation of our Ladies
of Comfort in Cambray , she called
them.

Amor ordinem nescit.
And Ideots Deuotions.

Her only Spiritual Father and Directour
the Ven. Fa. Baker stiled them.

Confeßiones Amantis.
A Louers Confessions.

Amars Deum anima , sub Deo despicit vniuersa.
A soul that loueth God , despiseth al things
that be inferiour vnto God. *Imit.l.2.c.5.*

❦

Printed at Paris , by LEWIS DE LA FOSSE ,
in the Carme street , at the signe of the
Looking Glasse. M. DC. L VIII.

VVith Approbation.

3

TO THE R. MOTHER.

The R. Mother Bridgit More of Saint
Peter and Saint Paul moſt vvorthy
Prioreſſe of the English Benedictin
Nunns of our Lady of Hope in
Paris.

REVEREND MOTHER,

*This deuout Book comes to
you of right being your na-
tural ſiſters excellent Goods, and there is
no other heire left to it but your deſeruing
ſelf beſids I know few or none do any way
pretend to it, but you and your Religious
flock who exactly trace by true practice
(o Practice, diuine practice the only
means) the ſame holy paths this booke
treats of. Take and acccept of it therfore*

a. ij

R. MOTHER: *I gueſſe I need not much inuite you, for I dare ſay it wil be moſt deare to you, and moſt highly eſteemed by you, and yours. If it chance to fal into the hands of any ſuch as may reiect, or cry it down: (as ſome few did the Ideots Deuotions of the ſame Spirit lately ſet forth) it wil (as that did) but receiue the greater luſter thereby, and be more highly priſed, by how much it may be miſpriſed by ſuch ſenſual perſons as relish not the* Spirit of God, *or whoſe vain and flashing wits as it were ſpurn at the* Diuine, and true heauenly Vviſedom. *That it hath ſome hands ſet in the margin, and diuers characters in many places to point out certain matters, and make them more remarakable, is not but that in a maner euery line and ſyllable is moſt remarkable and worthy to be obſerued. And that ſome places of Scripture are quoted in the margin, and not al, is becaus thoſe be the more cleare plain and vnmingled texts, though the whole Book hath nothing in it almoſt but Scripture.*

And if there be somewhat in the latter end the very same with what is said in the preface, it wil not much annoy since good aduise cannot be too often rtpeated.

I will say nothing of the admirable graces and guifts of the Authour (let the Book speak them) becaus I should seeme thereby to praise, and extol you (her natural Sister, and imbued with the same natural and supernatural guifts) then which nothing would be more Vngratefull and distastfull vnto yon. Howsoeuer R. MOTHER giue me leaue to inuite and incite you and your Holy Company to go on cheerefully and couradgiously in these sacred and secret Paths of Diuine Loue. VVith your Beauty and Fairnes intend, proceed prosperiouslv and reign. *Let the wisemen, or rather wits of the world laugh at you.* They senseless think your life Madnes, and your vvaies dishonourable. *Be not I say dismayed.* For your Truth Mildnes, Iustice; and your Right hand (*which is is your Spiritual Traier*) vvil marueilloufly conduct you. *So*

defirous to be partaker of yeur holy Prayers , and committing you to the Diuine
Protection , I reft euer

R. Mother,

Your moft humb'e feruant and
faithful friend in our Lord.
F. G.

THIS DEVOVT SOVLS.

ADVERTISEMENT
to the Reader.

VVith an Apology for herſelf, and
her ſpiritual Guide, and Director
the V. F. Auguſtin Baker.

*VVherein is excellently deſcribed a true
interne, contemplatiue Spiritual life;
and the maner how to liue happily in
it, with right, and true Obedience to
God an man.*

T may ſeeme very ſtrange (and
that very iuſtly) that I ſhould
write what heere I haue written; But when I haue heer declared my reaſon for it, I may perhaps pas
with this cenſure only of being a little pre-
ſumptuous. Yet *God* (who is my witnes in
al, and my *deſire aboue al*) knoweth vpon what grounds I haue done *it*; And that
it is but for mine own priuate comfort, and
helpe, and to be ſeene by no other, but

a iiij

againſt my wil, my ſuperiors only excepted, from whom (as they ſhal require) I
wil not conceale the very ſecrets of my hart
much leſſe this which I haue written to lye
by me, wherein there may be what they
may miſlike and correct, to which I ſhal
moſt willingly ſubmit my-ſelf. Yea and
though it ſeeme to me to be a great help to
me to haue that which I haue writ in more
light to read when I am either in obſcurity of temptation, or other bodily indiſ-
poſition to which I may be often incident.
Yet I wil ſuppreſſe it at their command and
good pleaſure, and put the want thereof
willingly to the hazard : out of confidence
in the aſſiſtance of *God, who* is a louer, and
rewarder of *Obedience.* VVhich vertue
(howſoeuer it may be otherwiſe thought)
I honour from my hart, and beleeue verily that nothing that I do which doth not
pertake of that is of any regard at al with
God.

V. F.
Aug.
Baker   This I haue thus affirmed becaus he who
hath been my Maiſter, and Father in a
ſpiritual life : and hath brought me into a
courſe, which much ſatisfieth my ſoul,
and conſcience between me and *God* : (It
tending to nothing but *to loue God* by ſeeking *him* aboue al Graces and Guifts : And
by withdrawing all inordinate affection
from al created things to become free to

loue and praise *God* in as pure and perfect
a maner, as this life wil admit. And also
to true submission, and subiection of my-
self for *God* to whomsoeuer *he* puts ouer
me in this life, with as great a contempt of my-self as my frailty can reach
vnto.

Is notwithstanding taxed now by the
same words in a maner which were al-
leaged against our blessed Sauiour. *VVe
haue found this man subuerting the people,*   'Luk.
and forbidding to giue tribute to Cæsar.   20.23.
VVhich though none can iustly say of
him ; Yet it hath pleased *God* to honour
him so much as to haue him euen in a
publick instrument (which I haue heard
read) couertly pointed at, taxed and ac-
cused of this maner of proceeding.

They taking for their ground, the imperfections of some through meere frailty
committed in this kind. As also becaus
some who are of other wayes, and vnderstand not this, affirme it may be inferred
out of his books that subiects (in what
they pretend to haue *a diuine cal to*) may
resist contradict and disobey Superiors.
VVhich that it may be inferred I cannot
deny ; since a meaner wit then he that affirmeth this may draw strange consequen-
ces out of any booke in the howse, if he
wil looke vpon them with no other in-

tention, but to carpe. But if they wil ta' e
one place with another and confider what
we beleeue , and practife alfo , according
to our imp rfection and frailty , they wil
fee and find in practife the quite contrary.
And what was allowed by Fa. Baker concerning fhifting to get time and meanes for
our prayer , was but in cafe that Superiors
did account it but an vnprofitable exercife.
VVhich was the only thing I haue often
heard him affirme in which he would
euer allow a foul to deale in any fhifting
maner with their Superiors vnder what
pretence foeuer.

And this in it-felf was neuer held to be
a finne , but an imperfection , which he
alfo thought it to be. But his reafon, for his
as it were winking at their imperfection ,
was to make fouls that were apt for praier
to make the higher efteeme thereof, and
perceiue the neceffity of profecuting it daily and diligently too , if they euer defired to
arriue to any perfect degree in the loue of
God. VVhich *efteeme* if it had not by fuch
meanes been brought into the howfe : It
would haue been hard for him to haue
made a foul beleeue and acknowledg the
neceffity , and nobility of it. For it may
be practifed by fome a long time before
they find any extraordinary benefit by it,
and til they find the effect of it in their

owne souls they may be apt to neglect,
and make no esteeme of it in these days
when al most euery one of esteeme inuaigh
against it as the most dangerous or vnprofitable exercise in the world.

For some hold one of these opinions,
and somo hold the other, to wit. Some
hold it only vnprofitable. Others say it is
very profitable if one could auoid the pe-
r'ls of it, which yet in women they hold a
thing almost impossible. VVhich opinion
of the two I most feared, becaufe those
that hold it pretend by their obiection to
haue some experience in a spiritual life:
And therefor their words are the apter to
make in a soul the greater impression:
but as for the former it plainly sheweth a
meere ignorance in the affirmers.

To by carryed away therefor with this
opinion and errour of the dangerousnes,
of a spiritual life. Is that which by these
writings I intended, and desired to auoid
by the helpe, and *Grace of Almighty* God.
And therefor when I was cleare and not
obscured with feare (which I am very
subiect to) I set down these things to be a
helpe, and comfort to me amidst the oppositions to that which I haue found and
experienced so proper and good for me.
VVhich yet whether it be or no my Superiors wil be better able to iudg, seeing not

only what I beleeue in al , and my opinion in thefe things they fo much feare
our errour in ; but alfo my practife in a
particular manner.

Now as for the shifting about our Prayer , which is the cheif ground of the forfaid publick inftrument before mentioned, that wholy tendeth (fuppofing our beleif , and practife to be according) to the
difgrace of thofe who are in that cours of
prayer,and to affright thofewho come after
from following their aduife in any thing.
They being there painted out in plaine
tearmes to be enemies to the gouuern-
ment of Superiors , as hauing had their
inftructions by a ftrange , and indirect
way , and meanes. I fay for al that hath
been faid in this kind of following our
prayer, (come on it what wil through oppofition of Superiors) I dare affirme that
opinion of Fa. Bakers hath to ys been recalled by him long before the publishing
of the inftrument. For it was only for
an entrance; uot for a continuance fince a
foul wel fetled in prayer would not need
it-though at firft for foure or fiue years a
foul by being hindred from two ferious
recollections in a day by her Superiors,
would haue perhaps been in great danger of inconueniency to her progres , and
alfo neuer haue been able to haue obeyed

as she should. VVhich is a certain effect
of a truely profecuted courfe of prayer :
(fuppofing it be one who is fit for it ;
for otherwife it may be very conuenient
for her to be put into fome other cours
more proper for her , and if she refift Su-
puriors in it , she wil be in danger of great
inconuenience , if not errours by her mif-
vnderftanding , and mif-applying that wch
was not for her turn , and this we haue in
this very howfe feen and known) which
if by vntimely hindring (a foul apt for it)
a Superior procure , he wil alfo incurre
an inconuenience though not fo great as
hers. VVhich js that she who would
(by profecuting d fcreatly a courfe of
Mental prayer) haue become fubiect if it
were neceffary euen to a very dogg ; becometh for want of that ftrength ; and
helpe which therein shee got , to be almoft impoffible to be ruled by the wifeft
man in the world.

For liuing in Religion (as I can fpeake
by experience) if one be not in a right
courfe between *God* and our foul : Ones
nature growes much worfe ; then euer it
would haue been , if they had liued in
the word. For Pride, and felf loue which are
rooted in our foul by fin findeth meanes to
ftrengthen themfelues exceedingly in one in

Religion ; if she be not in a courſe that
may teach her , and procure her true
Humility. For by the corrections , and
contradictions which cannot be auoided
by any liuing in a Religious community,
I found my hart grown (as I may ſay) as
hard as a ſtone , and nothing could haue
been able to haue mollified it ; but by being
put into a courſe of prayer ; by which a
ſoul tendeth towards *God* ; and learneth
of *him* the true leſſon of *humbling* her-ſelf.
VVhich effect I finding by following Father Bakers plaine, ſimple . eaſy and ſweet
inſtructions , I was loath to change them,
for them I could not vnderſtand. And for
this reaſon by al the meanes I could imagin,
I haue endeauoured to ſtrengthen my-ſelf
by writing , gathering , and thus (as in
ſome part of my papers it wil appeare) ad-
dreſſing my ſpeach to our Lord. This way is
ſo plaine, and eaſy that as long as the ſoul
holdeth *Humility*, it is impoſſible for her to
erre to her great incoueniency, at leaſt in her
main point which is the *loue of God*. For it
leſs importsforſmaler ſins, her imperfectiõs,
and errors or bangers, (ſpeaking of ſuch
as are accounted ſuch by ſome preciſe and
exact perſons) as to ouerſhoot herſelf in
that in which another wou'd haue come
off with honour, or ſome ſuch point, no
way greatly to the purpoſe, as to any hin-

derance to her courfe. Yea by.thefe things
(I. fay.) she rather gaineth then loofeth
fince many times they are a great occafion
of *Humility* to her foul, which much ad-
uanceth her, and is aboue al cheifly neceffary for her. For *loue to God*, and true *Humility* increafe the one the other and are
infeparable companions.

In fine as to the point of following Prayer, when the Superior as that time would
otherwife imploy her which I was fpeaking of before. I fay that after the foul hath
been fome good fpace practifed in that
exercife. The Superiors cannot hinder her
in it by impofing that which to them feemeth fit : And the foul wil haue no defire
to refift them neither can shee do it without a check from *God Almighty*. For no
imploym nts which Religious women haue
in Religion can hinder them (after they
haue had a good entrance) that the Superiors can impofe vpon them , for if they
pray not at one time thy can eafily pray
at another , or beft of al pray with the
work it-felf , and make the work their
prayer.

This therefor being fo that Fa. Baker
did this at fift , but as a shift in the beginning, there is no iuft caus to find fuch
fault with it , he doing it for thefe two
reafons. Firft , becaus fome cheife Supe-

riors had so poor an opinion of *Prayer*,
that they thought they did *God* good seruice when they hindered them, who seeme to make esteem of it. The other reason, becaus those he gaue his instructions to, and seemed to him most fit for
them, were likly to come into place of
Authority; and thereby were not only
themselues to suffer much by the continual
oppositions they were like to find; but also
were to beare a great part of the others Bur-
dens which were more feareful, and had
been a lesser time practised in the course:
who yet were likely (if they were encouraged) to prosper very wel in a spiritual, and
internal life. These two were I say in part
his reasons, which made him go so far in
this point. And yet we that had these instru-
ctiós deliuered by him, had them with such
circumstances that we could not possibly
take liberty in any thing that was contrary
to our Superiours minds by his Books, or
words.

  And verily I may with a safe conscience affirme, that if I would neuer so fain, I
could not find any thing in his bookes,
nor in any of this iustructions, on which I
could ground my-self (without a check
in my conscience, for doing the instructions wrongs) to neglect, omit, shift of,
or sheightly to performe any thing of my

Superiors commanding, or ordaining. Nor
could I euer inferre any thing out of them,
but that they tende only , and wholy to
humble the foul ; and vrge her to feek,
defire , and reft in *God alone*. And this I
dare affirme vnder al the Oaths in the
world, if Iuftice by lawful authority should
exaɗ the fame of me. For not any book
which he hat writ hath euer tended to
any thing els , then that we should liue
with al fubmiffion and fubieɗion *to God*,
and our Superiors. And if he had taught
the contrary , an extraordinary effeɗ of
it would haue appeared in vs before now,
we hauing been dealt with (being our-
felues in authority) as we haue been ; And
indeed in fuch maner that no humain in-
ftruɗions could haue inabled vs quietly to
haue fupported the fame The grace of
God only , and tending to *him* by the way
of *loue* could do it ; which fo *humbleth* the
foul that no difficulty , or difgrace can
ha pen which she expeɗeth not , and
therefor is abled willingly to embrace the
fame.

Verily I can affirme this by mine own
experience that a croffe word , or a flight
reprehenfion before I was in this courfe
was more infupportable to me , and did
more difquiet my mind, then al the difficulties and difgraces , which haue faln vp-

on me since , haue done. For now me thinks though I be neglected by the whole world : By flying to our *Lord ne* easeth me of al my burthen. And as I haue desired to haue no friend, or comfort but *him* so it plea-seth *him*, neither in doubts, feares, payns, dis-graces, nor any other miseries (whereunto this life of ours is so subiect)to rejectme. Only *he* exacts of me that in al the con-tradictions *he* sends me I *humble* my-self, and be confident of *his* help ; which, if I do so , I shal be much more sure , then if in mine own hands I had a most absolute power to help my-self.

And this *humble* confidence maketh ones way so cleare that the soul hath few, or no questions in many years, though they haue such very neere that are neuer so wel able to resolue them. This want of questions is almost al the ground of diffi-culty between these souls and the Con-fessor , who thinks himself neglected to ☞ haue souls haue no more busines with him then in meere confession. But I know not how the souls can helpe it , though there-by they should offend the whole world. It seemeth to some a great presumption, that the soul seemeth to think her-self fit to guide her-self , and also by it they in-ferre that she sleighteth others though her Superiors as not fit to gouern her, so igno-

rant do they think shee doth esteem them.
But *God* and her own conscience knoweth that none of these things are the cause
of her being so reserued, as indeed she is,
vnles she be asked by them : which if she
be they wil see that she doth not in any
kind sleight, or neglect them ; yet in speaking she vseth discretion where and to
whom (for one Superior may be fit to be
treated with in one point, and another in
another) which none can iudge or tearme
a breach of Obedience, and yet this is the
furthest that euer Fa. Baker taught.

And who would not think it a meere
folly ; if I out of pretence of Obedience,
and greater Perfection should treat with
one in matter of conscience (in which I
were doubtful) who had such difficulty
with me in his nature that he were as little
able to iudg in my case as I were in mine
own. For my part our Congregation giuing
leaue for it, and wanting those who are
able to iudg aright in my case ; as wel as in
others. I should do not only my-self an iniury thus foolishly to go to work, but also
him, whom I should thus treat with vpon these tearmes. VVhich foolish proceed-
ding is not a proper effect of true Obedience, but rather a phansy, and meere
folly.

O how far is it then from Fa. Bakers

meaning to teach , or allow of any thing
which may fauour of difobedience : It is
true that that which thofe tearm Obedience, who draw it to nothing, but a meere
politick courfe (that leaueth by the practife
of it in a foul a poor effect in comparifon
of that which by the vow of Obedience,
God and the Church intendeth) ferueth
where it is practifed to keep better order
then where there is no Obedience at al
(which *God* knows in thefe dayes is too ordinary:) for oppofing againft Superiors is a
courfe which cannot ftand without great
inconueniences For if *God* require that
feculars fhould obey the Prince , and the
Laws of the Realm, fo far as it may be
done without offence to his own Laws:
and if it be required of them that they pay
taxes which are by the King vniuftly exacted : What fhal Religious perfons alleadg
for their defence, if after the vow of Obedience they refift, and withftand their lawe
ful Superiors in what they may iuftly exact
(as we ought to iudg al to be that is not
apparent fin and offence to *God:*) and better it is to obey in neuer fo imperfect a maner , then to contend , and withftand Superiors vnder what pretence foeuer. For
though it be true that fome great faints
haue afflicted their fubiects, and mif-vnderftood their proceedings ; yet we fhal

always read that the good fubiect neuer
fought for other remedy then Patience expecting (for their clearing in the matter) *God
Almighties* good *wil,* and pleafure *who* per-
mitteh this often to hapen without the fault
of the fubiect much leffe of the Superior
who may do that in iuftice which we fubiects are not able to comprehend the caufe
off. Neither need we trouble our-felues
with thinking of that, but regard *God*
in all and walke folicitoufly with *him* :
and then wil al turn to our good, and *God*
wil infailibly teach vs true *Obedience*
which is a vertue that maketh our life in
fome fort to refemble the life of the Saints
in Heauen. For they in al regard *God,* and
are totally fubiect to *him.* They greiue not
to fee others in higher degree then they,
but fee it is iuft it should be in al things as it
is they praife *God* in al the fins they fee committed in the world & are refigned, though
they hate fin; And wonder to fee fuch a
Goodnes as *God* is fo forgotten by men,
and fo litlefought after by afpiring through
loue towards him. This they fee, and yet
they remain in *Peace* ; and fo shal we
(thongh in a far inferior maner if we per-
porme *Obedience* as we ought, and obey
God as readily as the shaddow followeth
the body ; by which courfe we shal become truly happy. And this is our end

of coming to Religion, and if we do comply with our obligation in this kind we shal liue quietly and dy confidently ; for the *Humility* that is in this practise wil carry vs through al things. *This way of true Obedience*, and subiection to *God* in al things, is a way which though we walk as it were vpon thorns by reason of the contradictionss, temptations, pains, and afflictions with which those are tried that must be *his* true friends : yet the regard that the soul in al hath of *him*, and the *loue* which by al increaseth in her, maketh it seem to her that she walketh vpon Roses in comparison of the difficulties she suffered when she sought her own wil, by following iit, and seeking her own ease, and honour.

This is that Obedience which Fa. Baker so much commends, and wishes souls to make right vse of in there Obedienco to Superiors which is so immediate a disposition to it, and so great a help to strenthen, and perfect it : aud which if we neglect in vain do we pretend to practife that towards *God*. For their ordinances, and orders are a most certain argument of *his* wil : And nothing wil *he* bid a soul do contrary to them.

And if it should seeme otherwise to the soul , yet by *his* own words she would know that she were to stand to their iud-

gement til *he* altered their minds, which
he always doth, if it be according to *his wil*,
and neceſſary for *his* honour that) the Superior condeſcend. This I am confident he
doth teach, and hold ; and neuer other doctrin did I euer hear him affirme, and what
might be conſtrued in a contrary ſenſe was
but to condeſcend to the imperfection of
beginners : who if they had been held to
ſuch preciſe Obedience, as ſome would
exact of them, they would haue been in
great danger neuer to haue obeyed rightly
at al. For by exacting vertue and the practiſe thereof aboue the Grace and ability
of a ſimple beginner ; they make Obedience and other vertues ſeeme to be by
practiſe an intollerable burthen, and they
by this means alſo faint in their way e-
uen in their firſt beginning. VVhereas if
they had been to do things with diſcretion they vould haue been able to go faſter
on euery day then other. And this one
point is of ſuch moment that for want
of the true practiſe thereof, it commeth
many times that the burthens of Religion
ſeem ſo heauy to good and wel meaning
ſouls.

And in this point do moſt men differ
from Fa. Baker in their direction of ſouls
more them in any other point. And if this
courſe had not by him been held with me

in an extraordinary maner; and that he had
not daily for a long time encouraged me not
to be daunted with my fins, and imperfections, (affuring me that it would al turn
to my good, if by prayer I would endeauour to tend to *God*, and vfe the beft
means I could (yet with al poffible patience with my-felf for my defects.) to reforme my-felf in al inordinate affections
to created things and this more by quietnes then extraordinary force.) I know not
what would haue become of me. By this
means (I fay) diuers imperfections to
which I was fubiect (and which I defired, yet could not at firft reforme) fel of by
little, and little : when *God Almighty*, did
(as I may fay) fee *his* time. VVhich was
a quite coutrary courfe to that which was
extolled by al that euer I met with before:
Who can giue for the moft part no other
aduife then to ouercome al things by force,
and violence.

But *God did shew* to me plainly in reading Fa. Baker Books that my way was to
ouercome my-felf as I could, not as I
would; but expect *Gods* good pleafure in
it. And then when *he* pleafed if I did my
beft, I should by *his Grace* get the better of
that which with al my induftry I was not
able to ouercome. VVhich made me fee
clearly my own frailty, and how little we
                                             are

are able to do of our-felues ; yea indeed euen nothing that is good. For when I haue been able to overcome my-felf in a thing many a time, yet when I haue thought my-felf thereby fecure that I was able to do it again, I haue failed more then euer before, which maketh me neuer dare to prefume of my own ftrengh in any thing how little fo-euer it feeme : for if I do I am fure to fail

Another thing befides this point of Obe-dience (by a certain perfons means) is much feared in vs by our Fathers : And that is that we fleight, neglect and contemne al books , and inftructions but Fa. Bakers; (VVhich is as God knows) quite other-wife. For though (as may be gathered by what I haue heere collected and noted) I do arme my-felf by al the means I can ima-gin againft thofe Obiections which are made by thofe of contrary ways that I may hold on my way which feemes to be fo proper, and fit for my defired eftate which I haue taken vpon me by my profeffion; I haue no reafon to alter for ways I am not able to vnderftand ; my confcience being fatisfied with this I am in: and my Supe-tiors neuer yet condemning the fame. Yet as I fay I am far from fleighting other in-ftructions; but hold they are very good for them for whom they may be proper, which

b

they do not feeme for me. Becaufe the more I read, or hear of them the more confufed, & without coherence they feeme to be. For I find nothing but faying and vnfaying as it feemes to me, as in one place vrging moft vehemently the neceffity of mental prayer, and in twenty other places making it a moft impoffible thing to giue ones felf to prayer without more endangering our faluation, then before.

And where they treat of Obedience, they treat of as it feemes to me in fuch maner that it is almoft impoffible to find out how, or which way one may performe it in any certain, or quiet maner. But the more they fpeak of it, the more impoffible thing they feeme to make it. And verily I could neuer put it together to make other fenfe of it do what I can, then to draw it to this: (as they expres it,) that it is a moft feruil thing and much like that where with feruants are fubiect for fifty shillings a year in the world, and no further effect could come to me by the practife of it (as they feem to meane) as to any true knowledg of *God*, or my-felf, then would haue come by my being a feruant in the world, only forfooth by reafon it is performed by vs in vertue of our vow of Obedience, which makes them acts of greater perfection and confequently of much more merit. But this is a subtile point fitter to be disputed then neceſſary to be beleeued. For I know, and that by experience that it is poſſible to comply with our external Obediences and performe them ſo that the Superior shal haue one in good eſteem, and be able to diſcouer no great defect in our performãce of them: And yet the ſoul as far from knowing what true obedience is, as she was when she came into Religion, performing them al that while but in a natural maner, of which proceeding nothing can be expected but a natural effect. Pride and diſobedience encreaſing daily in the ſoul, which is an entrance (if God preuent it not) to vnſpeakable inconuenience. But yet though I could draw no ſure, and ſolid ground, for a ſoul by Obedience according to ſuch inſtructions, yet the defect may be in me as to thoſe ways, and not in the inſtructions. For ſome haue affirmed they find much good by them; of which I am exceeding glad. For ſo ſouls may liue *Quietly, Obediently, and Humbly* in the howſe, it is al one to me by what meanes, or by whom *God Almighty* doth it. And there are ſome in the howſe that I should aduiſe rather to read ſuch inſtructions then Fa. Bakers (if I were worthy to giue aduiſe,) And this I would do if they were both priuate men, but much more now theſe inſtructions are deliuered by the Confeſſor whoſe place deſerueth an extraordinary reſpect which to my powre shaLeuer be giuen him, or any other in his placewhoſoeuer he be. But yet I muſt needs ſay that of al in this howſe I could neuer ſee, but one who could diſcourſe, and diſtinguish his points in, and of Obedience, and draw out of them a ſetled quiet, and ſatisfactory courſe; but that when he is gone they be as far to ſeeke as they were before in the vnderſtanding of it. For another wil expres it in another maner, and ſo vnder al while they liue they muſt as it were begin again.

This therefor was that which made me ſo affect F. Bakers inſtructions at firſt when he deliuered them; becauſe I ſaw they were grounded vpon *God*, (not vpon him) *who* could neuer fail whatſoeuer became of him. And by this regarding *God* in al, and doing al out of *Obedience to him*; our ſoul becometh ſo humble, that it liueth in a maner, as ſubiect to al she liueth with as any one can be to any Superior in the world. She troubleth not her head diſputing how, which way, and in what maner she shal obey in this, or that: but she ſimply obeys in al as far as her frailty wil permit, and as willingly would she be the moſt abiect, and moſt neglected in the howſe as euer she was willing to do any

thing in al her life. For hauing recours to
God maketh her infensible to thofe things
fo fat as may ftand with flesh and blood.
And God doth fend, and giue a foul that
feeketh nothing but fincearly to *loue*, and
pleafe *him*) fuch occafions to humble her-
felf (which to none can be feene; becaus
the knowledge, and caufe is wholy within
herfelf) that it is of more force to humble
her then her being neglected of al the
world would be ; though that be alfo a
great help and a great fauour of *God*. For
her foul can neuer be pure , and free for
the afcending to the praife of *God*, til it be
very humble, which the more a fonl endeauoureth to be, the more *Peace* doth she
enioy, and the freer acceffe doth she find
to *God*, and the leffe impediments between
him and her foul.

For this true *Humility*, and *Obedience* to
God which Fa. Baker doth fo vrge a foul
to in al his Words and Books is an immediate difpofition to that which S. Paul wished to vs. VVhich is *that our conuerfation
may he in Heauen*. And neuer was there
fuch perceptible friendship *loue*, and cor-
refpondence between any in this world
(how great foeuer their *loue* might feeme)
as there is between thofe fouls , and our
Lord, and *his* Angels, and Saints in Heauen.
VVhich though it be not fo perceiuable to

sense as the other which is founded vpon
that alone ; yet by *Faith* , and *loue* the soul
doth more plainly , and certainly enioy it,
then we , can be certain of any thing which
with our corporal eyes may be seen : and
such a confidence doth accompany his *loue*
that she desireth not to be more certain of
any thing. She can wish , then that she dependeth wholy of her *God* alone : *whose
wil* is aboue al maft deare to her , and to
whom she often cryeth out in her soul with
the glorious S. Augustin, saying : *That al
that aboundance that is not her very God
him-self is to her , but extreame penury.* And
therefor she feareth not any want of temporal means. For she accounteth it too
great an happines , and honour that by
the want of that which is necessary for the
suftenance of nature, she should haue the
occasion the sooner to enjoy *him* her only
desire, whom while she liueth here she cannot fully enioy : *Becaus none can see God,
and liue* , til which be granted her al things
seeme as nothing to her. For she longing
and sighing only after *him* nothing can
comfort,or satisfy her soul while *He* giueth
not him-self to her. Yet in this banishment she remaineth content , becaus *His
wil* is by her euen in this life preferred before her owne.

Although those inftructions before by

me mentioned do much feeme to be like
the Iefuits as I gather by their books, yet
I hold them to be nothing fo intelligible as
theirs, but more confufed by reafon he
would bring thefe, and Fa. Bakers into one,
& make a copleat life for a foul out of both.
VVich if he (to wit the Compiler of thofe
inftructions she much miffiks for contemplatiue fouls) can do for his own vnderftanding, and practife : yet I shal think he
wil find few that wil be able to do in it as
he doth ; but wil confound one with another ; and he able with quiet and fatisfaction to practife neither.

For thofe that cannot vfe any difcourfe
to be held to it , it doth them little, or no
good. And thofe that can do nothing but
by the means of difcourfe wil profit as little by other ways. Now for my own part
I do profes I could neuer find good : by
difcours neither did I ftand in need thereof. For it was an eafy matter for any that
could haue giuen me inftructions for the
way of *loue* (which is by the exercife of
the wil) to perfuade me that to *loue God*, &
feeke after *him* alone was a moft happy
thing, and that it alone was able to make
me truly happy: for I did defire this exceedingly of my-felf, and was very defirours to
difpofe my felf for fuch a courfe betwixt
my foul, and *God* as might make me moft

pleafing to *him* : and make me not as I then
was fuch a ftranger to him. And this I
thought was by me to be brought about
by a means which I was very defectiue in;
And that was by asking of queftions of
thofe who were moft likly to tel me what I
fhould do to compas this my defire. Which
I, failing in, and when I did ask was yet
as far from knowing as I was before, I
thought to get it by reading, and the more I
read the les I did vnderftand : which made
me almoft quite out of hart. But going to
Father Baker almoft in a defperate cafe :
He told me my way muft be by *Prayer.*
for which he gaue me fome inftructions according as he deliuereth them in his *Ideots
Deuotion* , and referred me for the reft in
that point to *God.* VVhich he doing, and
giuing al other inftructions for other things
futable : I found prefently that courfe of
loue which I fo much defired. And though
I went fo fimply to work that I defired to
know nothing, (for curiofity in reading
thofe things which help to this courfe is
very dangerous though in themf.lues they
feeme but fimple,) yet *God* did make al
things to me fo plain that was neceffary for
me to know, that I wondred to fee fuch an
alteration in my foul. Yea by may faying the
diuine office (of which meerly by my extraordinary, memory I had gotten a little

vuderſtanding) *he* did ſo enlighten and inſtruct me, that no induſtry of mine own
could haue attained ſuch knowledg (for
this my only purpoſe of *louing God*, and
humbling my-ſelf) as I had euen thus for
nothing ; for my pains, and induſtry was
ſo little that it was not ſo much as to be
eſteemed. And thus *God* of *his* meere Mercy dealeth ſtil with my ſoul ; for which if
I by not humbly grateful, no puniſhment
is ſufficient for me. But I hope though I
be ſo frail and weak ; yet *his Grace* wil in
al aſſiſt me which I beſeech you to begg
of *him* for me.

It ſuſſiſeth not for the ſoul that there is
in *God himſelf* whom the ſoul ſeeketh after)
Simplicity, or *Vnity:* but there muſt alſo be
al poſſible *Simplicity* in the ſoul herſelf ; for
the making her fit to treat with *God*, and
thereupon become vnited to *him*. The more
ſimple or *one* that the ſoul is (which is that
the more ſhe is free and rid of al thoughts
of creatures which cauſe multiplicity) the
liker is ſhe to *God who* is ſimplicity itſelf, &
the more apt, and worthy to become vnited
to *Him*. And therefore al the cunning, and
induſtry of a ſpiritual maiſter ſhould euer be
by al lawful means to rid the ſoul of al multiplicity incombrances, blocks, and al o-
ther things that are enemies to the forſaid
Simplicity in ſoul. And indeed every image

b v

of a created thing is an impediment to the said simplicity ; And therefor is to be re-iecte d at such time as the soul is in case to apply it-self immediatly to *God*.

He that is a true spiritual Maister wil in such a case take great heed how he lay any thing on the soul least it caus the forsaid impediment. Euery soul of her own na-ture is apt to contract multiplicity, and im-pediments enough : and if she haue with-al a Maister to deuise, and lay more on her how can she be but held back, and be in-disposed for the said perfect immediat trea-ty with *God*. And one only impediment is impediment enough, and hinders al.

The *spirit* of *Simplicity* doth bring , and caus much *Peace* in the soul for tending wholy towards *that one thing which is on-ly neeessary*; It maketh the soul as insensible, as it can towards al other things digesting and passing ouer with patience vnkindnes, & iniuries, whereby her life becometh pro-perly a life of *Patience*. Also as this *simplicity* is grounded vpon plain, and simple instru-ctions, so is it, and must ir withal be as wel founded vpon simple , and plaine dealing with *God*, and Man. Simply intending *God* and auoiding al double dealing, and al vn-due intention.

A true spiritual life should be one long continued thread lasting from the time of

his conuerſion to the end of his life. Saint
Paul reprehendeth thoſe *who are euer lear-*
ning, and neuer come to the perfection of knowl-
ledg. Such are they who yelding to temptations looſe their ſupernatural *light,*
and fal into a ſtate of leſſe light which is
more natural then ſupernatural and therefore is but darknes in compariſon of the
other *light,* and always is deceitful and
erroneous as to the finding of the right way
towards *God.* Whereas the other ſaid internal *light* within then proceeded from a
Superior caus or guift that is more ſupernatural.

The things abſolutly neceſſary for thoſe
who ſhal begin , and proſper in a
true ſpiritual courſe are theſe
that follow.

1. INſtructions proper for a contemplatiue life.

2. Secondly , an aptnes to vnderſtand,
and practiſe the ſaid inſtructions aright

3. Thirdly, a great couradg to withſtand
al temptations come they from within, or
without that might draw her into multiplicity from *ſimplicity* : & eſpecially fears w.h

soon draweth one into the most pestilent
multiplicity that is maketh one more blind
euery day then other; and consequently
into more diffidence, whereby they are
made almost wholy incapable of conuersing with *God*, vnles *God* shew them their
errors, and they begin again : which is a
hard matter to do, if a soul haue once lost
her *light*: which *God* I beseech *him* deliuer
al capable souls from doing : For it is the
greatest ingratitude that can be offered to
God, and none but *God* can tel the miseries, perplexities, and difficulties that attend on such a soul al the days of her life,
as Saint Angela doth testify with terrible
words.

4. Fourtly there is necessary in the soul
a good, and right iudgment for the vnderstanding of things a right For els the soul
wil erroneously vnderstad al things though
neuer so plain. The more she knows the
farther she is to seek, and the more errors
she falleth into. Aud better it were if such
souls could be known (which is almost
impossible til they haue had some knowledg of a spiritual life : for many times they
seeme to haue a greater aptnes then the
most capable souls, and a greater inclination towards *God* then others ; and
yet run into errour, and are in danger
(do what they can, that haue the care of

them) (to breaks their brayns, or ouer-
throw their bodys) that they neuer had
fpirituall inftru&ions further then for the
Adiue life.

5. Fiftly , a great capacity of tending
towards *God* by the exercife of the wil :
which being profecuted together with true
mortification of themfelues wil bring , faith
Blofius , to a *myftick Vnion* , and perfection
in time conuenient.

Of thofe that haue al thefe conditions
there are yet great difference : for fome
haue more aptnes , and find les impediments then others , and fome haue more
light , and others les , as it pleafeth *God*.
Yet thofe that are moft *humble* , and *faithful* to *him* though they feeme les cleare are
the moft pleafing to *God* , *who* be bleffed
by al. *Amen*,

The Obferuing of the diuine cal , which
indeed should be , and is the very life of a
fpiritu.l life , is by moft fpirituall Maifters
now a days turned into a fcorn , or fcoff.
And therefor no meruail that true fpiritua-
lity should in thefe dayes be fo rare , and
almoft vnknown. Nay if a foul giue but
her-felf to prayer she shal haue an hundred enemies one obie&ing againft one
point, another againft another of her proceedings.

Euery one (according to their fpirit, and

humour (defiring to reforme her in they
know not what themfelues; which if she
be moued with, no other effect is like to
come of it, then happened to the Painter
who altered his work fo long, and often
that at laft it had neither forme nor fashion;
And al other that had procured this alteration in the picture (which at firft was a
very good one) called the workman fool
for his labour.

The Application whereof is very plain
and proper to our purpofe.

1. Firft. There is difference between
Vnity, and *Vnion*: for as *Vnity* is but one
thing, fo *Vnion* is a coupling together at
laft of two things.

2. Secondly, fimplicity is a finglenes, or
being alone, and fimple is fingle, that is a
thing alone. And therefor *fimple*, or *fingle*,
and one or *fimplicity*, and *vnity* is but the
felf fame thing.

3. Thirdly, multiplicity is a manyfold-
nes of things and two, or more diuers
things do make a multiplicity; but one
thing, & les then two wil not make a multiplicity, *God* and a creature both thought
of together as diftinct things are a multiplicity: not becaus the apprehenfion of *God*
being apprehended but accoding to *Faith*
but becaus of the thinking of the creature,
not as in *God* (for then it would caus no

multiplicity) is a thing diſtinct from *God* ; and a creature alone thought of without any apprehenſion withal of *God* if it be not to be tearmed multipli*city* (which it is in the takings of myſtick Authours) yet is it not moſt certainly the *ſimplicity* in ſoul that is required for vnion with *God.*

4. Fourtly, *God* is but one rhing, or an *Vnity,* ſimplicity, or a ſinglenes. For though al things, and al diuerſity of things be indeed in *God* ; yet they are al of them but one thing in *him.* Yea whatſoeuer thing, or things be in *him* they are *God himſelf. God* was, and is *that one thing (* which our *Sauiour* defending S. Mary Magdelen ſaid to be *) only neceſſary.*

The imperfect Contemplatiue ſpirits, who commonly in their external buſineſſes are in their interior ful of multiplicity ; do yet for al that when their buſineſſes are laid aſide , and they betake themſelues to their recollection at the ſeaſon proper for it, (in regard they haue as it were a natural , and habitual *propenſion* towards *God* , and *his* immediate preſence with a loathing , or at leaſt neglect , or diſeſteeme of al creatures as to any affection to them) eaſily ſurmont al multiplicity of images that could be occaſioned by their precedent imployments , wherin their ſouls had neuer fixed their loue : as who were not,

nor could be fatified , or much delighted
with them.

☞　Al the fpiritual men in the world are
not able by their inftructions to make another that yet of herfelf it moft apt for it to
become truly fpiritual , without the fchol-
lar herfelf do withal carefully obferue , and
purfue the forefaid *Lghts* and *Cals* , as her
primum mobile , or firft mouer. And to fay,
Take al your inftructions from without , is al
one in effect as to fay ; *Tend not to Contemplation.* For *God* , and none but *He* is
the true,and immediate Teacher , and Directour in the moft obfcure and fupernatural way of Contemplation. Yet here I
would be vnderftood that vnder thofe
tearmes of diuine interior *Lights* , Motions , and *Cals* which I take to be the root,
and caufe of al her true Obediences , and
other good needs : I intend , and com-
prrhend al *Cals* through other obligations,
as when they are otherwife commanded
by the vniuerfal diuine Law natural , or
pofitiue : by the Church , or other human
Law , or by the wils of Superiors. And a
true fpiritual Man should do nothing but
out of the faid root , or caufe which is the
diuine Cal.

　A fupernatural Difcretion is miparted by
God to a welminded foul that difpofeth
her-felf for it , which difpofition confifteth

chiefly in the vſe of abſtraction;and praier.
This is the *light* by which *God* guideth
ſouls which *he* leadeth to Contemplation,
and thereby teacheth them what is neceſſary for them to know, or do externally
or internally : ſo far as conduceth to the
ſaid end. Simple, and vnlearned ſouls by
the ſaid *light* come to find out thoſe internal ways moſt obſcure of themſelues;
which no man though neuer ſo learned
and acutely witted can diſcerne, or find
out of himſelf.

The moſt ſpiritual man in the world
cannot inſtil this *light* into another. Al he
can do is exteriorly to teach a ſoul how to
diſpoſe her-ſelf for it. And as a ſoul that
hath neuer ſo great a capacity for it (ſpeaking ordinarily) cannot find it out without
the help of ſome experienced perſon ; ſo
one that hath no aptnes for it, al the tea-
chers in the world cannot put it into her.
And thoſe that haue the aptnes can neuer
find true comfort, and ſatisfaction, but in
contemplatiue inſtructions, and being once
wel inſtructed wil find al things preach
them to her in their kind, nor wil she
vnderſtand any thing she reads, or hears
but in that ſenſe, if it be to any purpoſe.
Finding that to be her only ſecure way,
and al things to helpe her thereunto, if it
be not her own fault, how much ſocuer

the fore mentioned medlers miſlik of her
proceedings, and misinterpret them. So
one that hath not that aptnes wil miſvnderſtand al, or moſt of thoſe inſtructions,
and wonder how they can be practiſed
without falling into this, or that error,
and taking this, or that liberty by them;
thus meaſuring others by their own vnderſtanding of things.

This was always thus, and euer wil be,
be the perſons neuer ſo holy, *God* permitting it for the exerciſe of both. I meane
only amongſt women: for men though they
should be defectiue in practiſe yet they
haue it by ſpeculation if they be ſchollers.
And verily I am of Saint Tereſaes mind
that learned men are not ſo apt to put ſouls
out of their way, as the vnlearned are.
For if the vnlearned be ſpiritual, and not
truely ſpiritual : it is ineredible the Martyr-
dome that a Contem latiue ſoul hath to
vndergo being vnder his chardge, and a
young miracle it wil be for her (if she haue
not many to encourage her) to hold to
the inſtructions proper for her, and in
which only she can proſper : and out of
which if he should put her, he would be
the firſt but only her-ſelf that would be
weary of her. But if she hold patience it
wil faire with her as it did with S. Mary
Magdalene, that our *Saviour* wil anſwer

for her, as far as it is conuenient for her obtayning *the best part*, *which shal neuer be taken from her.*

Nothing is more improper for a Contemplatiue soul then to contend, complain, or iustify herself, al her remedy for the most part being to come from Silence, Patience, *Humility* and Resignation. I except where iustice doth require a simple relation of the *Truth* to Superiors; when the good of her own, or other souls in the howse requires it. And that she must neuer do suddenly, or out of passion, or auersion, but it behoueth her to consult the matter often and seriously with our *Lord*, and in the meane time to behaue her-self humbly to the party, or parties aud do them both with *God*, and man al offices of true charity she can.

The supernatural light, or discretion is to be nourished, and encreased by al the external helps that can be afforded. And great heed is to be taken that it be not obscured, or destroyed: as *God* knows it may easily be, if we look not wel about vs. And the least mote of darknes defeats the whole *sight*, *God* permitting it for our sinnes, and negligences when it happeneth.

This light is commonly neuer giuen but where the internal senses are naturally adapt-

ed, and made proper for the receiuing, and
vſing of it. And therefor extrauagant imaginations though otherwiſe neuer ſo deuout,
or of neuer ſo retired natures are vncapable
of it : yea are in manifeſt peril to miſtake,
at leaſt of making right of vſe of it, miſap-
ply , and miſvnderſtand (to their great
preiudice, and others great inconuenience, and trouble!) this doctrine of the *diuine
Cal.* And better it were, if it were poſſible , that ſuch ſouls should neuer ſo much
as heare of the *diuine cal.*

　　This confirmes that old prouerbe which
ſayeth , *one mans meat is another mans poy-
ſon*, and ſo it is in this. For a ſoul truly apt
for Contemplatiue inſtructons can neuer find any ſolidity , or certainty in any
other thing then this of *obſeruing of the
diuine cal* in al things ; and finds that it is
at hand at al times, and al occaſions to be
her guide, and directrix ; (ſuch a capacity
is there in our ſoul to haue relation to G*o*d
in al caſes, and in particular it is neceſſary
in doubtful caſes. For where he determi-
neth it by Obedience, or neceſſity, it were
to tempt *him* to deſire *Him* otherwiſe to
declare *his wil* to vs,) ſo as I ſay that as
the ſoul can find no comfort, or certainty
in any other inſtructions ſo on the other
ſid nothing is more perillous to be miſ-
vnderſtood by thoſe that haue not an apt-

nes for a Contemplatiue life, or the internal exercife thereof, though otherwife neuer fo good fouls, and of neuer fo good
meaning.

None are capable of rightly vnderftanding and practifing this inftruction of the
diuine cal, but they who are refolued to
deny themfelues in al things, and who
wittingly, and willingly adhere to no created thiug : for if the foul do willingly retain an affection to any thing fhe is at a
ftop, and can go no further. For *God* muft
be fought, and *loued* wholy if we defire
and endeauour to arriue to perfection.

This obferuing the diuine cal was that fu-
rely which S. Auguftin fpeaketh of in his
Confeffions, where he lamenteth his cafe
of darknes, and blindnes before he had
giuen himfelf wholy, and ferioufly to the
feruice of *God*, and to obferuing, and liuing according to his Iuftice. Thefe are his
words. *And I was not then acquainted with
that true interior Iuftice which iudgeth not by
cuftome, but by the moft righteous law of Almighty God.* And certainly the better difpofition the foul is in of liuing and walking in this *light*, and according to this Iuftice, the better wil fhe profper in a fpiritual life, and the more cleare wil her way
be, and the les peril of erring; for it is the
way of *Humility*, And noue but the hmu-

ble can walk in this *light* long, or find any gust therein.

They wil either leaue the *light*, or the light wil worthily leaue them if euer they had it.

Thaulerus saith that God rewardeth no works but his own, the purer our inten, tion is in doing suffering, or forbearing, the more is it *His* own, and the more perfectly a soul complieth with her duty towards God (in that maner that he exacteth of her, and is proper to her state, and the grace giuen her) the more she pleaseth *God*. And in this respect it is truely said that *Obedience is better then Sacrifice*: for we do neuer so much, if it be not that, and in that maner *God* requireth it of vs; we shal liue in blindnes and find no peace in our soul: for *God* hath ordained a certain way, and means for euery soul, for her walking, and profiting in the way of Perfection; And in that only wil they find their progres to consist, to obserue what it is God exacts of them, and enables them to; and not what others do or can do, or haue done. For as we al differ in face so do we differ in the manner of our exercices that are interior. As for example if one who is of a free nature, and can endure, little abstraction should force herselfe to as much as those who are of staid

and retired natures, and to recollect her-
felf in time of work, and other times,
in which by order of the howfe she is to
keep filence (which exterior filence she is
to obferue shee would but hurt her
health, and it may be her lead, and not
wel be able to recollect her-felf then, nor
at the time proper for Recollection, and
fo loofe al for want of difcretion. Whereas if she should do what she is able, and
no more, and abftract her-felf by little,
and little as *God* shal increafe *his grace*, she
wil in time be enabled to that which wil
be fufficient for her, and *God* wil require
no more but what *he* hath giuen, which
how little foeuer it be, we ought to account it more then we deferue, and em-
ploying that wel *he* wil increafe it, *who*
is more willing and defirous to giue then
we can be to receiue. If we liue fo reti-
redly as *he* wil enable vs, we shal eafily
perceiue what *he* doth require, and exact
of vs in euery thing : for we being Religious are by Obedience, and neceffity for
the moft part difpofed of; and for the reft
we haue *God* always prefent to confult
with, and when we cannot by that means
be refolued *he* wil shew vs how, and where
we shal otherwife be refolued. But thofe
th t go the way of true *Humility*, and
Mortification wil haue few queftions after

they are wel grounded, and inſtructed in a ſpiritual life. For, for the moſt part our queſtions do but tend to the winding our ſelues out of ſome Croſs or Mortification, or eaſing our mind of ſome difficulty: which wil if we yeeld thereto but put out our eyes, & conſequently put vs out of our right way. Yea though thoſe we conſult with be neuer ſo ſpiritual, or vnderſtand our caſe neuer ſo wel, and of theſe I haue been moſt affraid of al : for from other; we can eaſily reſtraign our-ſelues, but from them vpon pretence that we may eaſe our minds, and at leaſt do our ſelues no harme if it do vs no good, we often cauſe great prejudice and obſcurity to our ſouls : and yet when al comes to al we muſt ſuffer that we do, if we wil be the faithful ſeruants of *God*, and profit in a ſpiritual life. If euer *God* do ſtand to *his* promiſe (as euer *he* did, and wil to al *his* promiſes) *or granting when he is aſked, and of opening to thoſe that knock :* where, or when wil *he* fulfil ſuch promis more truely and certainly then in the caſe where a ſimple, and ſinceare meaning ſoul out of neceſſity, and with al reſignation, and humility begs at *his* hands the ſolution of that, that concerns her for *his* ſeruice and honour, and the ſaluation, and perfection of her-ſelf in *his loue.*

The

The more a soul holds her-self to this *light*, and walks by, *it* the more her *light* encreaseth; and the more she leaues this *light* and walks by another seeming *ligh*, the more her darknes encreaseth. The cleerer this *light* is in her soul the better able she is to iudge what is the iust and most righteous wil of *Alm*: God in those things which *Faith*, and Obedience hath not determined: for what one is bound to beleeue, and do for saluation the Catholick Church, doth determine; but what we are to do for perfection there be many different opinions; yet al agree in this that it must be the way of *Abnegation*, but for the rightly applying of Spiritual and contemplatiue instructions to ones own particular. *He* is the only able teacher who is the most true *loue, and light the holy Ghost*, of *whom* the Authour of the scale of perfection writeth to his scholer being a woman thus. *For grace* (*which Fa. Baker tearmeth a cal*) *shal euen teach thee by it-self if thou wilt but obserue it, and follow it til thou come to the end, al that is necessary for thee from time to time, for God alone can only teach this way.*

And of those who giue themselues seriously to walk in the way of Perfection, Saint Iohn speaketh thus. *But you haue the vnction from the holy one, and know al things, and the vnction which you haue receiued from* 1. *Io.* 2. 20. 27.

c

*him let it abide in you; and you haue no need
that any man teach you, but as this vnction
teacheth you of al things, and it is true, and
it is no lye. And as it hath taught you abide
in him.*

There are two reasons, or necessities
why God himself should take on him, and
performe the office of a Contemplatiue
Maister.

1. The *first* is because he can and none
but he can; for though the soul may haue
an instruction from another, yet is she
to make vse of it but according to her internal Maisters direction, and as if he, and
none other had giuen it her.

2. The second reason of Conueniency,
or necessity of Gods being the Teacher
is, that though man also could resolue al
doubts, and giue al directions both internal and external; yet were it not only in-
conuenient, but euen impeditiue to her in
her way to Contemplation, by reason of
the solicituds, and distractions the soul
would incur by such occasions as causing
a life meerly of distractions. For in some
souls there do occur to be resolued fre-
quent, and daily, or howrly passages in
the forepart of a spiritual course (especially in the interior) which of themselues are questionable: but such going
forth for resolution would mar al in a con-

templatiue fpirit , as caufing a life meerly of diftraction , and multiplicity , and thofe the moft profound, and pernicious diftractions, as being vpon meere internal matters : for folicitudes about the interior are the moft preiudicial that are as to tendance to cotemplation : becaus they moft obfcure the foul, and yet this is the miferable life of fcrupulous perfons. VVhereas the foul hauing always her *Maifter* at hand , and that neerer to her then fhe is to herfelf, and *He an infallible one* , and a moft quick *difpatcher* , al the mifchiefs of the precedent cafe are auoided, and fhe fatisfied in her queftions with al fufficience, and *fecurity*. Neither wil it be fufficient for the foul in this excurfions that it is iudged a reafonable occafion to aske a queftion by him fhe confulteth : for if it were a thing wherin *God himfelf* would haue refolued her, if fhe would haue had patience, or els that it were a thing that for her mortification *he* would haue had her ignorant in : fhe wil perhaps incur much obfcurity for fuch going forth without her internal *Maifters* leaue, and liking, and withal fuch a check in her confcience, that fhe could with more eafe haue endured the difpleafure of al the world : then haue thus difpleafed her *beloued*, *whom* alone fhe defireth, intendeth,

c ij

& thirfteth after, and to *whom* to adhere,&
in here she putteth al her côtent& happines.
Al *he* doth and permitteth feemeth moft
iuft, and reafonable to her, and to liue in-
teriorfly, and exteriorly according to the
right Rule of his iuftice, is al she defireth.
Thefe are they which (our Sauiour faid)
should *Adore him in Spirit, and Truth,*and
of whom it is faid, *Al the glory of the foul
is within, for the Kingdom of God is within
vs*, fuch a foul may truly fay. *I wil heare
what my Lord God faith within me.* This
my moft fweet *Lord* God be euer adored,
and praifed, and fought after by vs al, and
bliffed, and praifed by al in Heauen, and
earth for euer, and euer. *Amen.*

Thaulerus faith that it is as eafy for one
that hath an aptnes for an internal life, and
wil be diligent, and obferuant in it; to
note, obferue, and difcerne the *diuine cal*
within him, as it is for one to difcerne his
right hand from his left. And it is plain in
our rule, that our holy Fathers defire is
that fouls should obferue their interual *cal,*
and the *tracts* of the diuine *fpirit* who is the
proper Maifter of the interior. And it is
but a meere natural courfe that we can run
by the meere inftruction of man, from
whom only we haue our firft help, and
inftruction, and then the fouls capable of

liuing a true internal life are to be referred
to *God* the only Teacher of the way of
spirit.

And where it is obiected by those who
pretend to be spiritual that following the
diuine Tracts, Motions and Cals is perilous
dangerous, and without al warrant, or security. It may be answered (supposing alwayes an aptnes in the party that hath the
instructions) that as the power of *God* sur-
passeth the power of man; so the warrant,
& security of *God* which a true internal liuer
findeth from *God* is far beyond the warrant
of a mortal man: the warrant of one man
being contradicted by another: that from
God is able to stand in al the contrarieties,
changes, and oppositions which happen
out of the differing of al men in indifferent things: for as for other things *God* referreth the soul to the ordinary means *he*
vseth in those cases. As for example for
confession of mortal sins she most confesse
them to a Priest who hath iurisdiction ouer
her, and for a true doubt she must not presume that *he* must resolue her by him-self,
but she must aske according to *discretion,*
and obedience; and for her rule, and other
obligations of Religion she must obserue
them out of Obedience to *God,* and superiors, which being done, and also going,
and walking the way of the cros, what

warrant I pray you wil she need (after her
conscience is once wel setled) from confeſſor or Superior. Wo be to thoſe, at leaſt
wo in this reſpect, that haue a confidence
rather in men then in God. And thoſe that
praiſe ſo much the ſecurity of a ſoul that
hath no other confidence in God at her
death but ſo far as she is warranted by her
Confeſſor : for she cannot but by this
means dy perplexed, and troubled. For to
day I haue a Confeſſor which wil warrant
me, and to morrow another who wil doubt
of my caſe. To day I haue one ſo preciſe
that he wil warrant me in nothing, and to
morrow I haue one who thinketh he can
pearſe ſo far into al things that if I wil adhere vnto him , and no body els he wil
anſwer for al. He goes away ; and another
who muſt aſſiſt me at my death cometh
who is of a good meaning , but cannot
pearſe ſo far, as the other : He at firſt finding vs to feare, feareth too : We haue for-
got our couradg vpon the others warrant
going before , and fal into feare with him at
the preſent : And yet our ſoul doth not alter
before God according to euery ones apprehenſion we meet with : if it did , or if this
were al the certainty that were to be found
between God, and our ſouls in Religion, we
might bid al true confidence à *dieu* (I meane
thoſe only who are apt for an internal life :

for as for others I do not take vpon me to
know their cafe) and place our *peace* vpon that which is as changeable as the moon:
to wit, the humours, and opinions of men
in indifferent things. I haue had my-felf a
Confeffor who though he had the largeft
confcience that euer I knew good man haue
in my life, in what he pleafed, yet out of the
difficulty he had with me in his nature, and
out of his aptnes thereby to take al I did
and faid in another fenfe then I meant it:
he could, and did turn twenty things,
which my other Confeffors made no great
matter of, into horrible mortal fins, and
would haue frighted me from the Sacraments til I had fetled my confcience according to his wil, and mind. VVhat was
I to do in this cafe? I had been warranted
by three former Confeffors two of which
were my cheif Superiors & Doctors of
Diuinity; and now this prefent wholy
doubted my cafe: he had (as he pretended) a greaer reach into my cafe then al
the reft, and they were fimple to him in
difcouering truely the ftate of my foul But
fhould I in this cafe put my foul into his
hands, who defired to know al that had
paffed in my life to informe him in fome
things he defired to know out of pollicy
thereby alfo to tye me to him felf more
abfolutly? Verily if I had thus put my felf
c iiij

on him, I had done great wrong to God:
and I might haue bid farewel to al true
peace hereafter: but standing to my former
warrant, and giuing him the respect was
due to him, and being referued towards
him, I haue hitherto *God* be praised kept
my-felf out of his fingers. And alfo by the
grace of God hope to hold on my way in
tendance towards *God*, thereby raifing
my-felf (according as *his diuine Maiesty*
shal vouchfaf to enable me) out of my
natural feare to the *loue* of *God*, *who* is
only able to fatisfy, and fatiate our foul.
And not as this my Confeffor would haue
had me to plunge my-felf by reafon of his
words, and threats of my miferable ftate:
which notwithftanding his apprehenfions
is-fo much, and no more, as it is in the
fight of *God*, *who* changeth not his opinion of vs, as the humour of the Confeffor
may be : but imagineth vs according to
what we really are in very *truth*. But thefe
fpiritual men of this kind would be fo ab-
folute that there is no power left in the foul
thus vnder fuch to haue relation, or confidence in *God*, whereby thofe for the moft
part vnder them, if they be poor fimple
women, of how good *fpirits* foeuer, liue
miferable deiected liues : for it is their only way to bring their politicke, and abfo-
lute gouernment about. And ordinarily

vnder this pretence they do it; saying that there is no way to make this, or that soul humble, but to bring them into such feare, that they neither dare speak, think, or do any thing without their approbation. At least so far they must haue relation to them, as it may serue this turn to informe them of what is for their purpose: and then that soul is happy in their eyes, and they wil declare that they are so to others : that they may follow their example. Then the perplexity the soul suffereth they tearme a profitable pil to cure their disease with al. And the confusion they suffer to see themselues disloyal to God and man, to serue their Confessors turn; he tearmeth a suffering for Iustice, and warranteth them, what harme, disquiet, or confusion soeuer cometh by this their doings to others, or themselues out of Obedience to him, he wil answere for it, and therin they haue done God, and their Congregation great, and faithful seruice.

O misery, that al this should be fathered vpon holy Obedience the most noble of al vertues! who sees not that this is a turning of religious Obedience (in those that simply desire to performe it) to a policy abominable to be thought or named. O my God was this *thy* meaning when we vowed our selues to *thee*! Or rather didst not, *Thou* say, *be as wise as Serpents, and simple as Doues* ? *Thou* didst not, say, be so foolish vnder pretence of blinde Obedience, that thou shalt not know thy right hand from the left. *Thou bidst vs giue to Cæsar what is Cæsars, and to Thee what is Thine.* By truly obeying *thy* wil, Law, and Euangelical counsels we grow wiser. But by pretending to practise Obedience, Charity, Humility, Patience, &c. in perfection before we be ripe for it ; (through perseuerant prayer, and concurrence of *thy grace* which doth not such things suddenly) we loose al, and liue in blindnes, and the highest we come to, is seruile feare, and meere folly. O happy are they to whom

☞ *God* giueth an aptnes for all internal Contemplatiue life, and withal some one who may instruct them in it. Verily the most part of souls in this howse, who haue been fit for it, haue been satisfied with so few instructions that in a maner they might be expressed in fiue liues. As for example that they Transcend Feare, and Tend to *God* by the exercise of the wil, by which in time (as pleaseth *God*) al impediments shal be remoued between *God*, and their souls. VVhich Blosius warranteth a perseuering soul in his Institutions very confidently.

But alas those that are not in this simple way haue such an apprehension of a spiri-

tual internal life, and make it seeme so perillous, and dangerous, that souls would be
frighted exceedingly to read their books,
and hear their Sermons (which cannot be
auoided possibly) if they were not armed
with armour of proof by *God*, and those
who liue in, and walke this happy way of
simplicity: Which whosoeuer truly walketh
wil not condemn much lesse contemne those
who speake against it, but humble themselues in al things : knowing that others
who liue extrouerted liues may be more
pleasing to *God* then they, & that for many
reasons which they may easily conceiue.
And yet it doth not hinder these, at least
it ought not, from prosecuting their ways
to which they are called; and in which by
God Almighties : infinit mercy they haue
so many bookes of Fa. Bakers own writing,
and transcribing to encourage, and comfort them in al the opposition which G d
doth permit only for our exercise, and not
by it that we should be put out of our way
through our defect in patience; which the
very exercisers of vs would for the most
p rt be very sorry for; if it should so happen, howsoeuer the publick instrument and
other speechs do sound to vs. For who can
doubt that is a wise man that a soul that hath
a good, and sound natural iudgment, solid
Contemplatiue instructions, many in the

houfe that practife the fame doctrine aright,
and a quiet nature feconded with concurrence of *God Almighties* Grace, and goeth
in al the way of *Abnegation*, and *Refigna-*
tion, should paffe many years without caufe
of queftions about her interior. For who
doubteth, but the foul may *loue God* more
and more euery day, and extend her wil as
infinitly towards *God* as she can, and beare
al occurring difficulties with as much patience as she can, and performe her ordinary obediences by the orders of the houfe, and particular ordinances of Superiors
with as much relation to *God*, and out of
Obedience to *him* as she can: and al this
without any great queftions. Yea, the
forfaid courfe of fpirit, in a manner taketh away al occafion of queftions at leaft
of intricate queftions, which drawzth
the foul out of her interior more then into
it. And by the way I fay this, that thofe
fouls who are apt to aske queftions though
they be neuer fo quiet, deuout innocent
natures, or haue neuer fo much wit, and
iudgement they wil neuer profper in a contemplatiue courfe, and in thofe inftructions.
And therefor wil do wel, and much better
to take the ordinary inftructions of thefe
days: and it were wel if fuch fouls neuer
heard nor read contemplatiue books, and
inftructions; becaus they mif-vnderftand

ing them wil make both them-felues, and
others alfo with them, to lay the defect
which was only in them vpon the vnfitnes
of the inftructions for woman : for it wil
feeme to them that they cannot poffibly be
practifed by women without perils, and
dangers vnfpeakable ; which wrong done
to fouls put out of their way by this means
(who would haue happily profpered therin (redoundteh to the dishonor of Almighty *God*. But yet as it feemes to them that
they cãnot be practifed without great danger : So thofe on the contrary who are fit,
and capable for thefe ways fee and experience how little peril there is in them :
for can a foul be too *humble*, and *loue* God
too wel ? No certainly. And this is al the
courfe of this internal life, and to this only it
tends, *to loue God, and to humble our felues.*

Let vs therefor make that benefit *God*
willeth we should by thefe oppofitions,
and contradictions we find and feel from
our Order, to wit. To *humble* our-felues
in al, and behaue our felues with al refpect, and Obedience to them, as if they
had done nothing. Let vs encouradge
one another to this, and let vs not think
God cannot be wel ferued by any other
courfe then *this*. For certainly the Iefuits
who haue the perfection in their inftitute
of the Actiue life, are in a very proper courfe

for their kind of life : for that spiritual exercife which they yearly take doth them much
good , and maketh them deale with the
more pure intention in their actions , and
affairs being alfo ftrenthnedwith a daily recollection wch maketh them forefee many
inconueniences, and thereby preuent them
better then they who do giue them-felues
to no fuch thing : for who can think but it
helpeth a man much to proceed with the
more prudence , when by a certain retired-
nes he hath fo much forefight of his bufi-
neffes, and occafions. They haue alfo a fetled forme or fashion in al their proceedings, and exercifes which thofe whom they
take into their order muft conforme themfelues to , how apt or vnapt foeuer they be
for it in their nature. And they hauing indeed the choice in a maner of al the prime
wits of their fchooles , are eafily able to
find thofe, who are able to vphold , and
maintain that politick maner among them.
The main point of vpholding and maintaining of it being the exact Obedience
which they require of al , and which al
with one vniforme confent ftanding vpon,
and performing, they thus as they do, vphold the fame forme, and grow in al too
hard for al other orders ; they being al in
a manner diuided amongft themfelues, and
thefe of al nations ftanding againft al the

world for themselues. Besides the subordination is also much strengthned with the feare they haue, who desire to make any resistance how litle soeuer, of being put out of their order to their perpetual infamy and shame, and want with al of that which is necessary: which they are incident to who leaue this order.

This I say helpeth them to the powre of disposing without any resistance of any vnder them according as it may be most for the temporalities, and honour to the order. VVithal they haue a great regard to the imploying of men according to their abilities hauing almost al the best imploiments at their disposing: (and that is a great matter to the maintaining of their order in greatnes, for if they wanted aboundance of action their order would quickly fal into great desolation. And this is the reason as I conceiue which maketh the Nunns of Contemplatiue orders prosper so il vnder their hands; Becaus they put them into Exercises of discourse, and yet withal do not go about to bring their houses into that subordination which they haue amogst themselues. And besids they can not find these poore women sufficient action to imploy themselues in: and therefor out of the Aboundance of wit which they get by that superficial recollection; they deuise,

and make for themſelues vnneceſſary, and
vnprofitable action. And this was in the *light
of Truth* certainly forſeene by their founder
Saint Ignatius., when he abſolutly forbad
them the care, and gouernment of Religious women : and with this his foreſight I
wiſh he had ſo prouided that they indeed
had neuer medled., or vndertaken in this
kind : for better it is for women to be kept
in their ignorance whereby they would be
themore eaſily ruled ; then to be puffed vp
with knowledge ſo little for the good (and
ſo far ſhort of what is neceſſary for the
perfection) of their ſouls. Yet Hoſpital
Nunns make a good ſhift with their inſtructions : which ſheweth plainly that
thoſe who follow their kind of ſenſible
exerciſes without going further, or looking after a more *ſpiritual prayer* of the *wil,*
muſt be held in much Action, or els they
wil be apt to make a great ſtir. But in in-
cloſed Monaſteries action ſufficient in this
kind is impoſſible to be had, or found. And
therefor I wiſh with al my hart that either
this courſe were not amongſt ſuch, ſo much
as known, or els that they reſted not in theſe
firſt exerciſes, but proceeded to the moſt
noble , yea as Seraphinus Firmanus ſaith,
to the *Omnipotent exerciſe of the wil.* Which
if it were now practiſed in our, and other
contemplariue Ordets as it ſhould, quickly

would they surpas in knowledg , and al
moral , and diuine Vertues those whose
furthest pretence in these sensible exercises
is but to do their actions with the more
deliberation , and consequently with the
more humain discretion ; which it gaiueth
indeed ; but it is but in a maner a meere natural proceeding : only so far as it may be
grounded in Faith , and Charity, it deserueth both more praise , and reward then a
meere natural action. But how far those
proceedings are from leading a soul to perfect Charity which is the end of our coming to Religion may be seene by the few
saints wch it now produceth. And though
they haue a great aduantage by their vni-
formity in exercises , and their agreement
among themselues ; yet this being generally
accounted to proceed, and to be vpheld by
policy ; it worketh no great effect for the
most part , further then by it with al others,
and against al others to serue their own
turn : which is a quite contrary effect to
that, wch that Order produced when it was
in its prime, by hauing in it some great Con-
templatiues, and when they did so much
good and were so beneficial to the whole
world. And different also from that which
our order and others were , when in like
maner thay flowrishd with Saints. For
then the honour of God was sought, and al

Orders with one vniform confent did concur to the aduancement of that alone They
then applyed themfelues to feueral exercifes in the exterior euery one according to
his inftitute; fome more eafy, fome more
ftrict; fome of more action, and fome ofles.
Yet interiorly their end was al *one* , that
was *to find God in their fouls.* And out of
that, *perfect Charity* did grow in them by
thofe *internal exercifes :* They did euery
one (not out of cuftome, or becaus he was
of fuch , or fuch an order) as *God* did require , and enable them imploy part of their
time in gaining and doing good vnto fouls.
Then there was not fuch follicitous , en-
tangling, and as I may fo fay fole care of
temporalities , *God* taking care of them,
and cafting them on them. Then there
was indeed , perfect amity without intereft , or fond affection to their impediment
of *louing* , and feeking *God alone* , *who is
that one thing which is only neceffary.* Then
there was no exceptions of perfons , but
they were contented fo *Gods* honour were
aduanced by any as wel as by their own
order or themfelues. *O Lord my God* , if
this *fpirit* might be reuiued again how
much would my foul reioyce ! If S Benets,
S. Auguftins, S. Francis, S. Ignatius Children were al (as perfectly as this life would
permit) vnited together , and did with one

hart, and consent seek and labour to aduance *thy* honour, and praise, as our Foun-
dersdo wish in heauen,then would the *spirit*
of the *primitine Church* florish, and *thy*
torne, and mangled members of *thy Church*
be healed, and perfectly set together again;
Then sinners, and hereticks would easily be conuerted by them to thee.Then there
would be another learning then now there
doth florish in our order, and others; for
thou by them would speake *who makest
the tongues of infants eloquent.* Then they by
prayer conuersing in a familiar, and tender maner with *thee* would speak so that
none would be able to resist thee in them.
Then their iudgment would be so cleared
that they would vnderstand most hidden
mysteries. Then an howre of prayer would
instruct them more fully, then an hundred
years study ca do if they haue not in al things
relation to *thee* the only true *wisedom*, and
in *whose light*, is *true light* only to be seen.
By louing *thee*, and dying to them-selues
in al things they would become maisters of
themselues, and al the world. Then nothing would moue them, nothing would
affright them, becaus,*thou* wouldst be their
cofort,and stay in al things. Certainly there
is a wonderful difference between theObe-
dience which a soul that liueth an internal
life giueth to a Superior, and that which

we giue out of cuſtom. The former is ſlow
at firſt and ſeemeth very defectiue therin;
the other ſo violent many times at firſt
that it cōtinueth not longt;he former groweth more ſtrong, and firme euery day then
other, and the later groweth oftentimes
a greather burthen euery day then other.
Certainly a ſoul that pretendeth to liue an
internal ſpiritual life, and yet hath not a
great eſteeme of Obedience, is much to
be feared, and in great peril of errors;
yet that which in theſe days is tearmed
Obedience, I do not mean : for I knew
one who hauing a Confeſſor that had much
difficulty with her, though he affirmed that
it was a great breach of Obedience to haue
relation (while he bore that place) to any
other, yet ſhe made vſe in caſes of difficulty
(with leaue of an higher Superior) of
another, whom ſhe thought more able to
iudge in that which concerned her ; and
yet ſhe hopeth this was no breach of Obedience : for if ſhe had thought that *God* in
this caſe had exacted of her not to haue
gon to another, ſhe would (what difficulty ſoeuer ſhe had endured) haue made
vſe of no other : But this ſhe thought was
not *his* pleaſure : becaus ſhe was in a pro-
bability to fal into great inconueniences, if
ſhe treated with him in an inward maner.
VVho profeſſed by his deeds, and words

to take aduantage of any thing she could
that might serue his turn as far as he could
in conscience; beside the difficulty he had
with her in his nature made him incapable
of iudging aright in that which belonged
to her : for that difficulty of his made him
misapprehend al she did, or said. If she held
her peace she neglected him, if she spoke
she did it to sound him to serue her own
turn ; if she was compassionate towards
him in his infirmities , she flattered him;
if she offered him not that which he stood
need of , she was auerted from him. And
thus it passed between them which made
her haue as little to do with him as Obedience to higher powrs would permit her:
for by their order she was to confesse week-
ly to him which was no smal difficulty ro
her: but she knowing it to be *Gods wil*, did
it out of Obedience to *him* to *whom* if we
do as we ought we must be subiect in al
things without exceptions.

And this is the benefit of an internal life
that makes one capable of seeing , and
knowing of *Gods wil*, and also most ready
to performe it which way soeuer *he* signi-
fies it to them ; and makes them obey as
readily and willingly a simple impertinent
Superior, as they would an Angel, or the
wisest creature in the World. Yea if a worm,
or any creature were orda ned by *God* to

rule ouer them, they would see, and embrace with al their harts *his wil* by them,
for without this total subiection to *God* it
is impossible to become truly *spiritual* ;
for if we resist *his wil* in our Superiors
in vain do we pretend to please *him.* We
must learn therefor this vertue of him, that
true *Humility* and Obedience may be our
stay in al ; which tvvo vertues together
vvith the diuine vertue of *Discretion* , he
vvil teach vs , if vve labour to become
more and more *humble :* for seeing that it
is *his wil* vve should obey, and become
truly *humble.* Hovv can vve doubt but he
vvil giue vs the *Grace* , if vve *humbly* , and
perseuerantly beg it of him , and practise
them vpon occasion as vvel as vve can ?
for he *him-self* saith ; *VVhen we aske our*
father bread he doth not giue vs a stone , nor
if we aske him a fish he doth not giue vs a
serpent : much les wil he deny vs vvhat is
necessary to make vs pleasing to *him ;* if we
seek , or desire nothing but by true *loue* to
be faithful to *him.*

   O *Prayer, Prayer* able to obtain al things !
O hovv cometh it to passe *my Lord* that
this *Omnipotent prayer* , as some of thy
deare seruants stile it , should be so vn-
knovvn ; yea euen by them vvhom *thou*
tearmest the salt of the earth contemned,
at least as to the practise of poore simple

vvomen; for vvom they hold it aboue al things moſt dangerous euen to mine ovvn knovvledg, as I haue knovvn affirmed by Superiors of ſeueral Orders! O miſery to be lamented moſt hartily by thoſe that haue a taſt in Praier, and by the effect therof knovv, *how ſvveet a thing it is to attend only, and vvholy to the prayſe, and loue of God* ? Surely the vvant of the *vviſedom* vvhich by praier the Saints did gain, is the teaſon vvhy cuſtome in al things doth take place (for the moſt part in the world) of *true reaſon.* The vvorld ſurely vvas neuer reformed of ſins, and errors, but by the *vviſedom* vvhich cometh from *God,* and is far different from that vvhich is accounted vviſedom by the vvorld vvhich is as S. Paul ſaith , *foolishnes vvith God*: for the vviſedom of *God* proceedeth out of *humility,* and perfect Charity. This vviſedom did Saint Francis enioy, vvhen yet by the vvorld he vvas deſirous to be accounted a foole; vvhich opinion thongh many had of him, yer the effect of his vviſedom vvas euidently ſeen by the great reformatiõ he made in the vvorld.

It vvil neuer go vvel, and peaceably in the vvorld as long as they are only imployed, and haue the ſpiritual gouernment of ſouls, vvho take policy for their cheif ground next to Faith; vvhich in the order

and maner of their vvritings in thefe days
me thinks they feeme in al to pretend : for
they prize that moft which may ferue their
turn, and fuppres al orders but their ovvn
(though not in plain tearmes) as far inferior to them in al things. And that indeed
it is not fo to me feems euident; for I know
none, but may be compared to them in al
things, but policy. This is my fimple opinion. If the foul hath not fo much vvit, or
difcretion vvhen she knoweth for certainty
or els doubteth of the certainty of a thing
that cocerns her: or knovving the certainty
vvil go, and aske, it as a doubt; or taking it
as a doubt feeing need to aske vvil not put
her-felf to aske, I may vvarrant her from
euer coming to contemplation. *VVhofoeuer*
are lead by the fpirit of God, they are the chil-
dren of God. As S. Paul faid : If vve vvere
the perfect children of *God his fpirit* vvould
liue, and reigne in vs. But for as much as
yet vve are not : vve are ferioufly to labour
to be; and that he may be *Al* in *Al* vvith
vs, and in vs : and *his diuine voice and wil*
only regarded, and executed and none but
his. And let vs take the greateft heed that
can be of leffening the vvorthy eftimation
of the *diuine cal* that in it-felf is the *prime*
verity, or *diuine way* proceeding from it.
Let vs extol and commend it as vve vvould
do *God him-felf*; and difpofe vs, and al
others

others as much as we are able that in al things it may be obserued, and fulfilled by vs al.

But *O Religion* , No Religion where the knowledg of the *diuine cal* is as it were vnknown vnles it be in speculation : or perhaps through ignorance is persecuted, depraued, obscured derided, banished, and sought to be pulled vp by the roots, and kept out of the harts of those that desire it, or are capable of *it* ! Surely *God* wil take al this as done to *him-self,* and reuenge it in an extraordinary maner : except where inuincible ignorance excuseth this proceeding. But yet for the *verity* of this *doctrin,* or the general practise of *it God* wil neuer permit the gates of hel to preuail so far as to be able to extinguish *it.* Becaus *it* is the root, and caus of al *sanctity* in *his Church* : howsoeuer *he* may permit *it* to be lost out of the harts of some particular persons through their frailties, and the working of others. And surely, *Nisi quia Dominus erat in nobis ; Vnles that God had been in vs* , and holpen of late more then man did, or could ; *Obscuratus penitus fuisset pusilus noster sol , & versa in densissimas tenebras tenuis nostra lux :* Our litile sun had been wholy obscured, and our smal light turned into a thick darknes by the late procee-

d

dings, by writings, preachings, speakings, threatnings, libellings, and other actings of some persons the *Diuine cal* had been exploded cleane lost and abandoned.

The Religious Fa. whom she cheifly points at for opposing the free following of the diuine cal and Fa. Bakers doctrin, did vpon his death-bed repent him of it, and was very sorry he had done it, profes- sing him-self neuer to haue been any true practiser of such spirituality, and that he had taken vpon him that which he could not iudg of : and he further declared that he much liked, and ap- proued al entierly what Fa. Baker had written, and taught.

BVt *God* would not suffer it neither wil he : yet far be it from any man to say, or think that it was directly intended, or malitiously done ; It was at the most, but indirectly at sine *omni praua voluntate*, and without any intention. But *God* only, and their own consciences know what hath passed therin by the occasion of the said late proceedings. I mean what fears, what doubts, what perils, what shakings, what

internal probations, explorations, purifi-
cations, &c. *Sed benedictus es Domine Deus
meus, Qui adinuisti nos, & consolatus es nos;
Qui ex magna tentatione magnum fecisti pro-
uentum, Qui ex tenebris lucem creas, & veritatem ex erroribus & falsitate facis magis
clarescere. Mane nobiscum in æternum. In-
strue, conforta, stabili, veritas tua maneat in
æternum, spiritus tuus bonus nos instruat, di-
rigat protegat, & ducat in via quæ ducit ad te.
De nobis cæci sumus, & lux non est in nobis;
Viue, regna, & splendesce intra nos dissipe-
tur, & in nihilum redigatur nubes tenebra-
rum, & ignorantiæ. O vere, & sole sol! ado-
ramus te orientem, fruamur lucente, Quia
deficimus deficientes. In te, & per the spiremus,
respiremus, & expiremus.*

Superiors in my poor iudgment after
they haue granted, and declared most am-
ple, and almost al possible authority to their
deputies (for the gouerment of poor fear-
fulfouls that might haue been ruled according to *Gods wil* with les then a beck)
haue need to haue an eye, and good respect to matters : and not expect that *God*
must always do for their safe-guard, that
which them-selues might do.

They speak with little consideration,
who say it is enough to do what a Coun-
seller aduiseth, especially in vertue of his

place, or office: vnles they regard withal
that the soul hath been so taught by *God*
or man that she knows how to vse such
counsel for her profit, and namely for contemplation. For if this were so there would
not be such scarsity of illuminated persons
as there are; and I haue known some who
haue been so obedient that they neuer did
any thing contrary to theire Superiors wil,
nor refused to do any thing that was en-
ioyned them by their Superiors: yea further were so inward with their Superiors
that they seemed one hart, and one soul
with them, and yet for al that they haue
affirmed in my hearing, that they were as
ignorant of *God*, and as great strangers to
him as they were when they first tooke the
habit: yea not altogether so feruerous and
deuout as when they entred into Religion seuen yeares before. So that it seemes
either the Superior must be spiritual to
make his subiect so; or the subiect must be
so spiritual as to know how to benefit
him-self by his obedience, and other exercises, or els he wil neuer come to perfection, let him haue neuer so great aptnes
to a spiritual life, or read, or heare neuer
so much to that effect. For where we read
of great supplies on *Gods* part for, and in
works of Obedience; either the subiect,

or Superior was an illuminated perſon, and had a great regard to *God* in that which was done, or commanded, that it was *his wil*, and what *he* would haue to be done in it, he did clearly ſee in his interior. For if ſome diſpoſition, were not required in the party, or parties, for God to do, and ſupply great matters in the ſoul by that bare word, *do it for Obedience*, a Superior might by the command haue *God* ſo at his command and at a beck that he commanding his ſubiect to come to perfection, or to do ſuch or ſuch a work in ſuch, and ſuch perfection, *God* ſhould preſently enable the ſoul to do it ſo; Though neither the ſubiect, or Superior knew what perfection were further then by ſpeculation. But the expecting of ſuch miracles is abſurd: for *God* hath ordained another way to come to perfection. And neuer any by this courſe come to find out the right way, or euer attain to that degree of perfection which is ſo much ſpoken of, & euen out of ignorance exacted, & expected the firſt day of taking the habit, to wit of *blind Obedience.* VVhich yet in ſome ſort, ſome who haue good, and quiet natures attain to (but the cleane contrary way to that which they ſhould do) to wit to a blinde Obedience without ſenſe, or reaſon: neuer going further in it or by it then to a natural perfection: which

though it be much extolled by thofe that
fee her, and is better for her foul then to
obey only in what she lift, and no more,
which is another extreame : yet she growes
but by this into fauour with Superiors, and
into credit with thofe with whom she liues,
& into a certain natural perfection of mortification which little benefitteth her foul,
and for which if she look not wel about her,
she wil receiue her reward in this life, to
wit by fatisfying , and contenting her-felf
with the good liking, and applaufe of her
Superiors, and companions, and thinking
that if she can pleafe them she difchargeth
her duty to *God* as to her obligation of tending to perfection. But if there wete to be
no other effect of al our mortifications, and
abftractions, and other Obediences in Religion; I should fay , Wo is me that I was
Religious, But to this may be anfwered
that by our vowes and vertue of our profeffion we haue a double merit for al that
we do : whereas if we were not Religious
we should haue but a fingle reward , and
this the Church by her powre and the fu-
peraboundance of the merits of our *Sauiour*
(of which she hath the diftribution by way
of Indulgence : or by vertuc of vows made
by fouls that are in the fauour, and *grace of
God*, and confequently her deare children)
imparteth to vs that are Rel gious. But to

this I reply that if this were fufficient the world would neuer haue been fuller of Saints then now, for there were neuer more Religious ; and yet none wil deny that the world was euer fo, without Saints as it is at this day fince *Chrifts* time. Which playnly sheweth that there is to be fome other dif-pofition in the foul for her aduancing by the exercifes of Religion. And that the ha-uing made the Profeffion, and liuing lau-dably therin in the fight of others, is not fufficient for her before *God* ; nor the pre-tended examples of former times : nor that blind Obedience which is fo much extol-led, and commended by al to be exacted in perfection of her before she haue found good entrance into her interior by prayer and abftraction, and can regard *God* in that which is to be performed by her, and by the good difpofition that is in her foul turn it to good, and not to the obfcuring of her foul. For otherwife it wil be blinde Obe-dience indeed and obfcure her foul fo that she can neither perform that nor any thing els as *God* doth require she should ; which if she do not, it wil little auail her that others like of it.

By which you fee that only liuing in Re-ligion and pleafing our Superiors wil not aduance vs in the way of perfection, nor practifing a blind Obedience which hath

in it neither reason nor discretion ; and presuming to practise vertues in perfection before we are come to any perfection is to
break our necks for euer coming to perfection. Can a soul of a years standing in Religion take vpon her to become to Abrahams perfection ; surely if she do, I should
hardly expect to see *God* prosper that her
presumption with an Abrahams reward.
It is plain therefor that we may very absurd-
ly oftentimes apply the examples of Saints
to our poor imperfect case , and get little
by it. Yet this is not to disapproue of a souls
prompt Obedience , for that is most lau-
dable. And those souls who are in a contemplatiue course, and end eauour nothing
but by entring into their interior to be able
to regard *God* and *his wil* , or *cal* in euery
thing they do or omit , wil grow more
obedient, & submissiue euery day then other
and perform that which is said ; *that they*
should be subiect to euery liuing creature for
God. VVhich those other hasty, and inconsi-
derat persons who wil practise euery thing
presently in its perfection wil neuer arriue
to : but rather for their hastines (if there
natures be not the better) they wil be found
more stubborne, rebellious, and more hard
to be ruled fiften , or twenty years after
their coming into Religion then they were
the first day. And then they wil looke for

thefe, and thefe priuiledges; their Anti-
quity forfooth muft be refpected; they muft
be exempted from proftrations, and if they
haue behaued themfelues more fubmiffiue-
ly, and obediently then others though it
were but meerely out of the quietnes of
their natures; they muft be obferued, refpected and preferred in Office before al
others, or els they haue infinit wrong; and
they pretend if they be neglected, it wil be
a caus of others leffe Obedience, and refpect to Superiors: who they fay wil rather
prefer others that wil not take it wel tobe
thus humbled then one who may be made
a fool of as I haue been al this while, and it
feems euer shal be. Had not Superiors better wink at a little want of too much for-
wardnes in an imperfect foul who doth it
meerely out of confideration of her own
frailty, and that she may not obfcure, or
put out that little light which by much labour, care, and induftry she hath through
Gods grace, and affiftance gotten in her foul
for the finding out, and walking in the way
of perfection, and contemplation? Yes certainly: it were far better for Superiors to
paffe ouer fome fleight imperfections which
haue no fin in them, in a foul who ferioufly
laboureth for perfection. *For fuch a foul wil*
giue, as it is giuen her: that is to fay, that as
God of his mercy, and godnes by her con-

d v

uersing with *him*, by her suffring that *he*
layes vpon her with the best resignation
she can , and by obseruing the *diuine cal,*
and wil , and liuing according to the Iustice of *God* , shal strenghten her soul , and
purify it in *his loue*; and so much the more
prompt , and ready to obey wil she be, and
giue euery day more and more respect to
Superiors.

And there is one thing in this vertue of
Obedience principally to be obserued, and
practised to make it pleasing to *God* , and
an aduancement to the soul : and that is
that the thing commanded , and done , be
according to the *Iustice of God*. But to this
may , or wil be answered that al that is not
a sin , if it be commanded vs by our Superiors is according to the *Iustice of God*. But
if this were so, so many more would come
to perfection, then do : And it would be
far more easy to come to it then it is ; But
perfection, and sanctity must be gotten by
othersmeans then by persuading our selues,
that wee shal come to it by simply doing , from time to time what our Superior
willeth , or biddeth vs. If with al we do
not in our interior regard *God in his Iustice,*
as wel as the exterior bidding of Superiors , and do it more out of the regard of
that then the other : yea as much as is possible (if we wil do it wel) we are to do

it with a simple pure regard of *God*, *and
his cal* ; for though the interior *cal* neuer
contradicteth the exterior , (for if it do, it
is to be strewdly suspected) and that for
the most part of things to be done in Religion *God calleth* the soul by exterior Obedience ; Yet it is his wil that in al those
things as wel as in meere internal, the soul
should simply regard *him* , and that as absolutly as if *he* by *him-self* had bidden , or
commanded her. Neither doth such a soul
regard who, or what, or in what maner
God requireth it at her hands, but it suffiseth her that it is *he* that exacteth it of her,
whom she in *simplicity* of *spirit* endeauoureth
to regard in al things with out any mean
of creatures ; Which maketh the soul indifferent whether she were commanded by
an Angel, or a worme if it were *Gods wil* :
rather to command her, and signify *his wil*
to her by the worm ; not that she esteemed
not of the Angel in a far higher degree,
but becaus she would not make any thing
her obiect , or do any thing out of any
other respect then to conforme her self to
the *diuine Iustice* in al things , and regard
him alone in al she did, or omitted. And
certainly let a soul be persuaded , or per-
suade her-self what she wil as a means to
arriue to perfection, she shal neuer find true
peace (if she be of a contemplatiue *spirit*,

d vj

and be not defectiue in her natural iudgment) but by following the *diuine cal*, and
regarding that in al she doth, or omitteth:
and though she do al that Superiors command, yet to do it with as little regard of
them, and as much of *God* as if *he* had immediatly commanded her by *him-self.* And
so much as *God* shal by *his grace* (concurring with her care, and diligence) enable
her to work in this obseruation of the *diuine*
cal, so much the more *light*, she shal haue
for the obseruing of *it*, so much the more
profit, and peace wil she find in her own
soul: and so much the more shal she walk
according to the *Iustice of God*, of which
how much the more our works do pertake, so much are they worth and no more:
for as Tau'erus saith, *God rewardeth no works*
but his own.

VVhere it is said in our Constitutions
that after our profession we haue not so
much as powre ouer our own bodies, or
souls. I vnderstand it that by the very nature of our profession we are so bound to
tend to *Perfection*: that we should do nothing but in regard to *God*, *whose wil* we
haue there professed, to choos for our own,
and whose Iustice we wil with al diligence
perform, let *him* signify it by what, whom,
and in what maner *he* please: without any
regard of our own profit, or commodity

for time, or eternity ; and certainly in this
fenfe *Obedience* cannot be too much commended . But let our actions be neuer fo
much commended, and applauded by our
Superiors, and al others : if it go not right
between *God , and our fouls* , it wil be but
little to our comfort , or profit . And if
we reflect vpon the circumstances of the
Superiors command whereby wee may
obfcure that regarding *God* in our fouls we
shal neuer become perfect in Obedience.
For as S. Paul faith, *Powre was not giuen
for diftruction , but for edification* , and applying it , performing it , and exacting it
in an other maner then as it was meant,
and ordained by *God* in and by our Religious Profeffion : is the reafon that fo few
become perfectly Obedient : for by making our Obedience to regard Superiors in
the firft place ; for example to trouble , and
perplexe our-felues in thinking it muft be
done with this circumftance , and this maner , and at this time , and diuers other circumftances little to the purpofe , or els I
shal not performe my Obedience in perfection. This is to tire out my-felf, and make
my-felf weary of Obedence , and not to
ferue *God with alacrity , and chereful wil-
lingnes.* This is to find his *yoke intollerable,
and not fweet and eafy ;* which certainly ifit
be not to vs it is our own fault, and not *his.*

For *he* hath set such order, and measure in
al things, that the more they are done ac.
cording to his will the more easily are they
done ; for he is far from being the Author
of disquiet , and confusion , *His spirit is
Iustice, and Peace, and Ioy in the holy Ghost.*
And it is we that by our preposterousnes
do peruert *his Iustice* , and cause that effect
in our souls by that which we pretend *he*
exacts : And so (as sir *Thomas More* saith)

This Sir
Thomas
More the
famous
Lord
Chancel-
lor of
England
Blessed,
and re-
novvned
Martyr
of Christ
I E s v s
vvas her
great,
great
grand-
Father.
☞

the vrchin wench goes whining vp , and
down, as if nothing she did , or could do
(for some circumstance , or other which
was wanting in it) did please *Him* ; *VVho
yet indeed is so easily pleased by those of good
wils , and who intend, or desire nothing but to
please, and content him , and seeke him simply , and purely, not any guift , or grace, but
according to his will:* that if there were no
world but this and that my soul were to
dy with my body yet I would choos to
serue , and please *him alone* , and none but
him ; rather then by doing the contrary
haue al others my friends , and haue al the
honors , pleasures , and in fine the whole
world at my command ; and this though I
were also to suffer , and subiect my-self for
his sake to euery liuing creature whilest I
liued. *For in this kind of life lyeth hid the
greatest Heauen that can be enioyed vpō earth.*
And though *he* try the souls with diuers

temptations, yet *he* doth it with much regard of their frailty, & doth so accommodate *his grace* to that *he* layeth vpon them: that they find *he* reserues that for to morrow which the soul was not able to haue borne with profit to day. And the soul so plainly sees that she of her-self is able to do nothing: so that if she had ouercome one difficulty or temptation a thousand times, she dareth no more confide in her being able to ouercome it again then if she had neuer done it yet in al her life. And yet she is so confident in *God*, that if it were pronounced vnto her by *God him-self* (who can not deceiue or be deceiued) that there were infinit disgraces, pains, temptations, pouerties, and confusions hung ouer her head; Al the care she would take would be to beseech *God* continually that as *he* prouided those troubles for her, so *he* may enable her to beare them without offending *him* therin; and in that maner for *his glory* that *he* intended by sending them: for of herself she willingly acknowledgeth that no feather is more easily carried away with a violent wind, then her soul would be carryed to hel by the least temptation the diuel could suggest vnto her if *he* did not in al things by *his grace* protect her. And the longer, and the more faithfully a soul hath serued our *Lord* the cleerer doth it appeare

☞ to her, that whatſoeuer is wel done by
her it is ſo wholy to be attributed to *God*,
that she deſerues moſt iuſt puniſhment if
she take any part of it to her-ſelf; or preſume by what she hath done by *his powre*,
to be able to endure the leaſt croſſe that
can befal her of her own ſelf.

☞ But to return to that I was ſpeaking of,
I meane *Obedience*. I ſay (in the words of a
moſt learned man Albertus Magnus Maiſter to the diuine Saint Thomas of Aquin)
that ſo far as any vertue pertaks of *diſcretion* ſo much of vertue hath it in it, and no
more. So that if a ſoul practiſe Humility,
Charity, Obedience, and in fine any other
vertue without *diſcretion* it wil more pertake of folly, then true vertue as the effect in
the practiſer wil shew. This *diſcretion* is the
pure *gift* of *God* the which *he* neuer ſo
aboundātly beſtows vpon any but that they
are al their life to haue relation daily, and
☞ howrly to *him* by *praier*, in which *he* teacheth them as far as it is neceſſary for them
what they are to do, or what means they
muſt take to know what is beſt to be done
in al that they doubt of. For whether *he*
reſolue them by *him-ſelf*, or by others, they
acknowledge it to come from *him*, neither
do they deſire to be their own chooſers in
this, or any thing els, and ſo it comes al to
one paſſe, as to them; for they regard *him*

a likein al things. Neither can one generally-
lyfpeaking, apply anothers cafe to oneſfelf
without danger : becaus the circumftances
may much differ, and ſo make that in them
a folly, which was in another *Perfection*.
VVhich many times we blindly do, and
no wonder if we profper accordly. For in
al things we are to haue relation to *God*,
and do what *he* exacts, and not what is the
cuſtom or what this, or that body hath
done in the like cafe. And if we do otherwife we shal be as blind as beetles, and
neuer profper in *a true internal, contempla-*
tine, ſpiritual life. And for want of wel
practifing this point many get no entrance
into their interior al their life, though they
haue in them a very great aptnes for it.
And this point I haue before touched in
one place of thefe my notes for mine own
remembrance, which I haue written down
either as I hard them from Fa. Baker, or
as they came into my head when I was leaft
obfcured with the paffion of feare, to be
a helpe to me, or at leaft ſome little light
when I was not ſo wel able to help my-
ſelf.

And reafon I had hauing ſo many occafions to try me within and without, and
to put me into perplexity, and feare. For
one in eminent place did labour by his obiections to divert me though not with il

intention, but out of a pretence of putting
me into a courfe more proper for me , as
for example , becaus I was ful of imperfections *he* pretended that contemplatiue
inftructions were no way proper for me,
and that I took too much liberty by them,
they being proper for thofe of more tender , and fearful confciences then I was.
And in fine gaue it me vnder his hand very
refolutly as a determination from my Goft-
ly Father, as in the place of God *Almighty*
that thofe that gaue me contemplatiue inftructions , and applyed the liberty that
was neceffary for contemplatiue fouls (of
which he faith there are not two in al the
howfe) to me , *might giue me peace , but
neuer true peace in God.* Thefe were his
words which did fo much aftonifh me
that it made me puruay for al the inftructions that I could that might vphold me
in that which I found was the only way
that I could profper in , or be able to find
*onr Sauiours yoke fweet , and his burthen
light* : for I had fuffered fo much before
God did beftow the fauour vpon me of
being put into a courfe that was proper
for me , and this for neere fiue years after
my coming ouer, and had faln into fo many great inconueniences and miferies that
noue could beleeue it , but I that felt it.
And though I made a shift a days to fet a

good face on it, yet in the night I bewailed my miseries with more then ordinary
Teares of which *God* and our blessed Lady
were Witnesses of, though few others on
earth. And I did rowse vp al the books in
the howse, and whatsoeuer I found that
any had done to please *God*, I took notes
of it and did it as I could. And this course
I always held since I came into Religion:
as also to consult with al the men that any
had found good by in the howse, and yet
al this would do me no good. And me
thought I Was as great a stranger to *Almighty God* as I was in England when I
scarse thought (as to any good I did) whether there were a *God*, or no. And being
thus perplexed, and tossed with a thowsand
imaginations, and ouerwhelmed with miseries, yea almost desperate through the
feare, and consideration of my sins; My
Mystris aduised me to go to Father Baker
telling me that fowre, or fiue in the howse
had found good by him, and that at least
it was no harm to try, and it would do
me no harme though it did me no good;
for he was a very graue man, and one that
was much respected in the Congregation,
such like words as these she vsed to me
and I in my nature being not very hard
to be ruled (though I remember I had no
great mind to it of my-self) did as she bid

me which being done I found my-self in
fifteen days so quiet that I wondred at my-
self : the which was so soone as I had receiued from him some general instructions.
As that I must giuo al to God , without any
reseruation wittingly, and willingly of any in-
ordinate affection to any creature : the which
I found my-self willing to do. *And that I*
must vse prayer twise a day , which I found
my-self capable of ; and though I found
little of that which is called sensible deuotion , yet I found that with a little industry , I was able to vse it with much
profit , and that it did make any thing very tollerable which happened to me. Yea,
and it made me capable of vnderstanding
any thing that was necessary for me in a
spiritual life , and discouereth daily to me
that which is an impediment between
God , and my soul as far as is necessary :
and makes me abhor to do any thing in the
world for any other intention then out of
the regard of *God ,* and becaus *God* would
haue me so do. And I find by, and in the
exercise of prayer *God* doth find such means
to humble we that al the creatures in the
world could neuer haue found them out
for me , and also sends me such internal
crosses , and shews me yet so plainly what
I shal do in them (if I wil aduance my
soul by them as *he* desireth) that it were

but to obscure my soul to aske questions about them, and wil, or nil I, I must beare them. And thus I see that God doth so temper euery thing *he* layeth vpon me, that it is so much and no more then I am able to beare, & is conuenient for me. And me thinks I see that any thing I ouercome is so wholy to be attributed to God that I cannot presume to be able to endure the least cros in the world, and should think it an extreame presumption to expose my-self to hazard, by wilfully putting my-self of mine own accord to the suffering of any thing but what Obedience, and ne-cessity prouideth for me, which I find to be enough.

Thus vpon occasion I haue foolishly strayed from my purpose, and now I return to me matter of applying blindly the pra-ctise of Saints to our imperfect case : for God wil prosper vs by those exercises that *he* thinketh good, and not by those of our own inuentions. If the soul simply regard God in the best maner she can, it wil be as easy for her to see what *he* would haue her to do, or omit. (I mean in things that are not sin) when to ask, when to hold her peace ; when to pray ; and how to pray. &c) as it is easy to discerne her right hand from the left, or the Sun from the Moon, but this wil be if she go the

way of abnegation, and not els; and if she
rest in God aboue al creatures, and haue relation to him as wel as she can according to
her imperfect state in al things whatsoeuer,
either in a general, or particular maner as
the case requireth: for we canno: prosper
any other way in a spiritual course, or by
any other means then the *diuine conduct*:
And this not prospering any other way,
or by any other means then God pleaseth,
may be very wel applyed in some sort to
the case where the director out of his own
head, and out of his own customs would
haue the soul pray in that maner he hath
good by: And if God lead her by another
way then he hath gone, she is wrong howsoeuer it be indeed. And if the soul be ful
of perceptible imperfections in her out-
ward carriadge, and if in occasions she
be apt to ouershoot her-self sometimes in
ieast, sometimes in earnest, then he wil determin she is not fit for internal exercises
vnles they be very grose and sensible ones.
And if she wil not beleeue him in this so
far as presently to relinquish her former
directions, she goes astray. Iuto which directions notwithstanding she hath been
put by the aduise of her chief Superior,
and found by prosecuting what she had
begun that her soul was reformed by little and little, and that she was willing,

and enabled by *Gods grace* to amend any
particular defects that the Confeſſor found
in her, and reprehended her for/ : only
when he miſliked her courſe and would
not tel her why nor wherefor, but in a
confuſed maner ſhe ſtood vpon her gard,
and held her peace, hauing before endeauoured by al informations ſhe could, and
as vvel as ſhe could to expres her-ſelf, that
ſhe might do things vvith his good leaue,
and liking. I ſay ſhe held her peace, and
vvas confident that her cours vvas neuer
the vvors for his fearing, and meant not
by the *grace of God* to alter it : til Superiors by diligent examination of her (which
ſhe moſt willingly wil accept, and giue
them al the informations ſhe can, as ſhe
hath done *him*) ſhould iudge thereof to
whoſe determination ſhe finally meant to
ſtand. For my part I ſay, I ſhal foliow her
example the beſt I can. But if befids her
imperfections, he by ſome invvard dif-
courſe perceiued by her (when ſhe was in
ſome darknes, and much obſcured for that
time vvith the paſſion of feare) that ſhe
had ſome ſcruples of her former life which
troubled her ; though indeed ſhe had been
aduiſed by tvvo vvho knevv her conſcience as vvel as ſhe could make them, and
vvho vvere men of as much reſpect a any
in the Congregation, and one of them her

cheif Superior, and the other her director
for many years : Notvvithstanding I say
she had both their vvarrants for vvhat she
did vnder their hands, and indeed finds
her-self checked in conscience by God
him-self in an extraordinary maner, vvhen
she doth in this point yeld to follovv her
ovvn sense, desire, and feare rather then
vvhat they haue aduised her. Yet I say if
this Ghostly Father of hers should think it
not only fit, but altogether necessary to
bring her into al feare he could, pretending that the liuelines of her nature, and the
great couradg she had could not be abat-
ed vvith any thing els then vvith letting
her, and aduising her to diue into her conscience, and case as much as she vvould;
and that she could neuer come to profit but
by laying a good foundation by this means
which he pretended was so necessary for
some things which he discouered in her
that it was hard (if possible) for her to
be saued vnles she did proceed in this maner : vvhat would you aduise the poor
soul to do ? I wil tel you what I do, and
vpon what reasons I do it, as wel as I
can.

1. First, for the il ground which he said
I laid, he grounded it vpon, these reasons:
first was vpon the vnsetlednes he thought
was in my conscience : which indeed was

as

as it is at fometimes in which humour he once lighted vpon me. And as to this I comforted my-felf that I needed not to feare : feeing I had done what I had been aduifed to by the faid two vpon whom I relyed in it ; Nay alfo when he was better able to iudge in my cafe , he aduifed me the very fame him-felf. As alfo when I am in prayer , and moft cleer, I fee I cannot pleafe *God* by any other means then by ftanding to the aduife that hath been giuen me by the faid two in this kind.

2. Secondly , he grounded himfelf vppon a conceit, that I held fo conftantly to the cours I had been put into before he came out of Pollicy , becaus I would not be taxed with inconftancy , and alfo becaufe I might loofe the intereft in thofe who had the fame inftructions , and that partly becaufe they were many of them, the moft eminent perfons in the howfe for natural talents . But to this I anfwered my-felf that as for Policy , I did not wel vnderftand it , and fo far as I did vnderftand it , I did abhorre it euen out of this refpect that thofe who practifed it (in the nature I vnderftood him he meant) lead miferable liues, and muft oblige themfelues more to the humors of many to bring their ends about ; (then the loue

c

of liberty would haue permitted me if I
had had no better intention ,·) and yet
for the moſt part mis of their ends in that
which they moſt deſired , and perhaps
vndergoe great diſgraces in hauing their
plots diſcouered : this I ſay if I had had no o-
ther intētion would haue made me abhor it.
But I alſo comforted my-ſelſ with this : that
ſince I firſt entred into this cours , I neuer
deſired the friēnſhip or fauour of any creature liuing , nor ſo much as durſt wish
deliberatly that any thing ſhould happen
otherwiſe then it did. And when I thought
it for the honour of *God* , and good of the
Conuent , I did not feare any diſgrace , or
difficnlty that could happen vnto me in
that I thought fit to be done. And what
I did in it out of other intention or natural inclination , I deſired that *God* ſhould
purge me for it by any contrary ſucces in
the buſines as *he* pleaſed.

3. A third reaſon , he had (as the afore
mentioned writing of his giues me to think,
as I vnderſtood it) was out of this reſpect,
that I was cheerful, merry , and free, notwithſtanding he had iudged my caſe to be
ſo bad , and perillous , whereby he might
think that I ſleighted his admonishments,
and was inſenſible of my own miſerable
caſe. As to his I had theſe reaſons to comfort and helpe me. One was that refle-

&ing vpon my owne conscience between
God, and my soul, I saw no caus but that
I might hope that matters went wel between *him*, and me; and that I was neuer the wors for his fear of me, and
some things he charged me with I found
my-self innocent of, and some others
I found my-self guilty of I endeauoured
the best I could to amend. Also for my
shewing my-self cheerful, it was partly to
beare vp my-self; and partly because I
thought that was the way to make him
the sooner to let me alone, as indeed it
happened. And another reason was because I am naturally sad; and had more
then ordinary exerc se at that time which
made me more subiect to it. And also I
find it necessary to be as cheereful as I
can, becaus nothing obscures my soul, and
hindreth my *Prayer, and transcendance* so
much as yeelding to sadnes.

I also perceiued both by his writings
words, and sermons that he in al things
almost misvnderstood my case, that though
he were very spiritual as for his own particular, and in a course that he seemeth to
me to prosper very wel in, and which
was apt to be much applauded by the
admirers of sensible things; yet he was
far short of being able to direct a soul
to Contemplation who was in nature, and

c ij

by grace apt for thofe inftructions that
tend to it. And I perceiued alfo that although he could fauour almoft no books
but thofe of Contemplatiue Authors, yet
he ftil mif-vnderftood them fo in his application of their writings to others that
al his proceedings turned rather to the
breeding of a dangerous multiplicity in
the foul, then to the *riddance* which is fo
abfolutly neceffary : that without the director help the foul in that, in vain is al
he can do to her, as to her comming to
Contemplation.

I alfo perceiued that he mifliked the
happy inftructions we had receiued, (and
which caufed in me fo much peace, and
comfort : after fo much perplexity, and
affliction) becaufe fome had mif-vnderftood, and mif-practifed, and mif-apply-
ed them. This I fay made me much to
fufpect his fufficiency, as for rightly vnderftanding Contemplatiue inftructions in
which, and by which (as I had experienced for fiue, or fix years before) I
could only profper, and liue contented in
my ftate. This I fay I wondered, at becaufe it did plainly appear that thofe who
were weary of thofe inftructions, in which
other profpered fo wel, were for fome
notable reafons wholy vncapable of bene-
fitting them-felues by fuch inftructions at

leaft in thefe days when true *Spirituality*
hath fo many oppofitions, and aduerfa-
ries, and fo few that helpe, and beare vp
a foul in them, and I fay vpon thefe
tearmes fuch fouls can neuer hold to them.
And therefor it were fit (aud he as fit as
any) they fhould feek to be put into a
more fenfible cours, which might be
taught by man from time to time as they
ftood in need of. VVhereas others who
are truly capable of fpiritual contemplatiue
inftructions, after the foul is once wel inftructed, her director hath little to do but to
rid her in al things as much as he can lawfully, and to refer her to *God*, *who* can only
teach perfect *Prayer*, and bring the foul
to true *Perfection*. But thofe men who
think them-felues able to bring a fool to
perfection of Prayer by impofing their de-
uifes vpon her, and wil limit *God* by their
pretending that fhe is bound to obey them,
and can profper by no other exercifes then
fuch as they feeme to haue found good
by. From fuch men I fay *God* bliffe al capable fouls, leaft they put them-felues into their hands: for if they vnder any pretence follow their inuentions, and leaue
the way that *God* hath placed them in,
and would profper them by; the miferable effect wil fhew how little part *God* had
in this their doing: for as *his* workes

haue moſt happy ſucces, ſo ours haue moſt woful; and if we lay it vpon *Obedience* we do God infinit wrong. Becauſe the effect of *Obedience* if it be true. Obedience, is very profitable to a ſoul, and neuer preiudicial: *but it is when we giue that to Caſar, that is Gods,* that it ſucceeds il with vs by obeyng: for by this pretended Obedience we darken, and obſcure our ſoul contrary to *Gods* meaning, and intention. And it is always ſeen that when a ſoul ſuffereth her-ſelf to be put out of her way by a director, or Superior, that when ſhe thinks ſhe hath done al ſhe can, as to the doing their wil, yet ſhe is further from it then ſhe was before, and both the Superior, and ſhe mis of their deſire. She becauſe ſhe hath loſt her *peace* which made her capable of giuing her Superior his due without preiudice to her ſoul, and of doing it, as it was *Gods* wil ſhe ſhould ; the which now ſhe finds clean contrary by reaſon of her pernerting *the ſweet order of Iuſtice* , ſhe being now ſo obſcured that ſhe knows not *what to giue God, and what Caſar.* And by this means the Superior alſo miſſeth of what he intended, becauſe now the ſoul giueth him leſſe then ſhe did before.

VVe haue infinit examples of the happy ſucces of Saints though their Superiors were not always ſuch as ſeconded them in

al particulars, fometimes they being fuch
as did not vnderftood them, and God permitting it for their greater good. And a
foul shal always find contradiction from
fome Superior, or other : And yet if the
foul liue in her *interior* as she should, it wil
be no impediment to her progres, no more
then it was to *S. Terefa*, *Ioannes de Cruce*,
Balthazar Aluares of the Society of I E S V S
who was perfecuted by his order, and his
writtings fuppreft (as I haue heard euen
to this day. And *Ioannes de Cruce* befides
other cotradictions eight months put in pri-
fon by his Superior. And thefe fouls though
they might feeme to others to haue varied
from true *Obedience*; yet the effect shewed
they were far from fuch matter. And thefe
days there is in contemplatiue fouls a more
feeming difobedience then heertofore becaufe there are fewer Superiors then euer
there were that wil concur, or approue
of their proceeding. But doth this exempt
Religious from the right Obedience more
then heertofore ? No certainly; for their
is no way but by *Obedience* to come to *God*,
and no vertue without *Obedience* is pleafing to *God*. But it is an *Obedience* that regardeth *God*, and that doth what *he* would:
And not a foolish pretended *Obedience*
which is in the letter, and not in the *fpirit*.
None can truely fee how to obey but out

of an *internal light* giuen and imparted to
the soul by *God*, who is the true teacher of
Obedience, and al other solid vertues. And
in these dayes where true *Obedience* is so
little knowne, and where Obedience is
counted to be practised in perfection, when
the subiect is punctual out of a simpathy of
nature with his Superior, and can by reason of a quiet nature magnify him, and
think that they must haue no other relation to God in his world then by their Superior, whom to please, and whose good
wil, and good word to enioy is the perfection of what they came for, without
further acqnaintance with *God* in their
soul. This I say being now tearmed Obedience, it is no wounder the world is so
scarse of *Saints*. *God* I beseech him teach vs
that *Obedience* which is souud; for the other
vanisheth away as smoak as to any solid
effect in the soul.

It is an easy matter to talk, and exhort
souls to conforme themselues in their interior to others where there is no obligation, or any profit to come of it, & though
it be against the streame of a true *spirit, and
eal*; and though he that thus aduiseth vs is
heer to day; and gone to morrow; yet the
perplexity that comes by such proceedings,
if it be contrary to what *God* requires of vs,
may sticke by vs while we liue to our great

harme and grief. But were they that thus
vrge vs (out of a certain custom) euer put
to it themselues? No surely: for if they had
they would haue more feeling of others being put out of their way. I speak not of a
direct putting of a soul out; for that is to
palpable of being il, but of an indirect
which pretendeth many things in excuse,
and in particular more perfection, &c.
But the poor soul if she be by these pre-
tences put out of her way, wil find her-self
both void of comfort, quiet, and perfection. For God neuer prospers indiscreet, and
inconsiderate proceedings; though we in
them, and for them be applauded by al the
world. Al that draws to multiplicity, and
estranging from God, in our *interior* let vs
blis our selues from as the poison of our
soul, and any thing, or creature that would
interpose it-self between *God*, and our soul,
is an impediment to contemplation. Wo be
to those souls, if they haue a capacity for an
internal life that are studying how to write
and speake to creatures to the powring out
of their affections. For by this means their
affection wil be taken vp by the way, and
the creatures wil be more regarded then
the *Creator*, though the subiect of their
writings be of, and for God. Much vanity
I haue known in this kind, the Ghostly Father admiring the wit, deuotion, and humi-

lity of his penitent. And the penitent by
hauing her proceedings in that kind admired, published, & applauded by her Ghostly
Father, was in great danger to vanish away
in her own cogitations. These sensible proceedings often draw the soul (do what she
can) *more to men then God.*

There are two things now a days by which
we take vpon vs to measure other mens perfection. The one is by the quietnes of their
nature. And the other is if we be Superiors
we iudg, by the simpathy that is between
them, and vs ; tearming them most humble,
obedient, &c. that are most stutable to our
spirit, and sense, those specially do so whose
exercise is in sense, and who put much perfection in sensible deuotion. But certainly
true Humility is so subtile a thing that none
can iudg who is most perfect *therein*, but
God ; and those to whom *he* reuealeth it.
And this is the reason why it is said ; *That
the iudgments of God are far different from,
those of men.*

*Powre was giuen by God, for edification
and not for distruction.* The which edification principally consisteth in the Superior-
accommodating him-self to the *interior diuine cal* of his subiect ; and with that intention are al Religious professions made, and
to be intended by the Professors, and Acce-
prers of the Profession , and especially ac-

cording to the intention of our holy Mother
the Church, by whose warrant those Professions receiue their validity. And therefor
a Superior that neglects to proceed with
his subiects according to such their *diuine
cal* accommodated to the rule strayeth from
the scope, and intention of Religious Profession. And for the auoiding of these mis-
chiefs, as also for the difficulty that the Superiors find, & haue in the true discouery of
internal cals that are of meer spiritual things,
I may say was the caus, wherefor the Holy
Ghost (*who is the proper maister of true spirituality*) hath inspired the pens of the tor-
rent of his Doctors of the holy Church, to
declare, and teach that souls as wel in Religion as out of it, *Are free for their meere
interior* whereby they may be able to follow
such teaching from the Holy *Ghost him-self*,
as man cannot afford them : though man
may hurt, or destroy such teachings easily
where *God* permitteth it : and themselues
yeld to it to their own great los, and harme.
And the *interior* is of that great, and infinit
worth, and moment, that so that that may
be wel, it is no matter what commeth of
al other things. Yea then al other things wil
be wel, if *that* be in good case by harken-
ing to, and following *the diuine interior cal
which is al in al*, to a capable soul. O wo, wo,
yea a thousand times *wo* to a soul that is

frighted by any threats, ouercome by any
temptations, or caſt down by yelding to
feares into that perplexity which maketh
her vnfit to heare, and follow what *God*
ſpeaketh to her ſoul, and diſ-inableth her
from following prayer, which Seraphinus
Firmanus tearmeth for the Nobility, and
worth of it; *Omnipotent!* O you ſouls who
are capable of prayer, be greatful to our
Lord, for it is the greateſt happines that can
be poſſeſſed in this life. For by *it*, it is eaſy
paſſing through al things how hard, and
painful ſoeuer. By *it* we come to be familiar with *God him-ſelf*, and to conuers in
Heauen; By *it* al impediments wil be remoued between *God*, and our ſouls; By *it*
we ſhal receiue *light* for al that *God* would
do by vs; By *it* we ſhal come to regard
God in al, and wholy neglect our-ſelues:
By *it* we ſhal know how to conuerſe on
earth without preiudice to our ſouls. And
in fine by *it*, we ſhal prays *God*, and become ſo vnited to him, that nothing ſhal be
able to ſeparate vs for time or eternity from
his ſweet *Goodnes*. O let him be *al* in *al* to vs
who can only ſatisfy our ſouls. *He is his own*
Prays in which, and by which we are infinitly happy though of our-ſelues we are
able to prays, and *loue* him, but in a very
poor maner. Who can ſay (that deſires nothing but to *loue*, and prays *him*) that they

are poors feeing, *bc altho* is more theirs then they are there own, is fo rich, and ro *whom* nothing is wanting that should make *him* an infinit happines. In this let vs ioy, in this let vs glory without intermiffion. VVhen we are not able actually to attend to *him,* and prays *him,* let vs commend our hart, and foul to the faints in Heauen who with-out ceafing prais our *Lord.* Let vs by them do that w th we are not able to do by ourfelues. Yea let vs defir *him (who* is *his* own prays, *who* is only able to do as *he* deferueth) to fupply what he defirs we should wish *him.*

Let vs reft in him alone, and not in any thing that is, or can be created. Let vs not feek the guift but the *giuer.* Let vs feek no o-ther cofort, but to be able with out al com-fort to be true to *him.* O how little is al the loue we can giue him in coparifon of that *he* deferueth from vs. VVhere therefor is their roome in our fouls, for any created thing? Let vs wish, and defire, and as far as it lies in vs procure that al *loue* be giuen to *him.* Let *him* haue al Glory al Honour, & prays. Let vs defire the fauour of none but *him* alone, to *whofe* free difpofition let vs ftand for time, and eternity as abfolutly by our wil, as if we had neuer had beeing. No-thing we do or fuffer let vs efteeme great, for our fins deferue we should endure much more. Let our whole care rend to the ma-

gnifying of him; Let *his* Honour be ours, *his*
Glory ours & let vs seek nothing but to be
wholy *his:* who is most worthy to be that
*He is. It is his delight to be with the children
of men?* VVhat should comfort vs, but to
prays, and *loue him.* Those that seek *him* shal
find *him* if they seeke him withal their hart.
O who would seek any thing instead of *him,*
or any thing besids *him,* being *he* is not more
willing to giue vs any thing then *him-self,*
heere by *Grace,* and in Heauen by *Glory!*
Let vs adore him in Spirit and Truth, al we
can giue him is nothing vnles we entirely
giue *him* our selues; and that also cannot
adde to *his Greatnes,* and Glory; yet if we
do this, so much doth *his diuine Maiesty,*
esteeme of this guift, it being al we can giue
him; that for it, and in requital of it, *he*
wil giue vs *him-self.* Al *his* guifts, and graces are as means to the preparing vs for this
end, if we vse them rightly with *humility,* &
according to the iust wil of *Almighty God.*
Let vs extend our wil to serue, *loue,* prays,
please, and magnify our *Lord* to the vttermost we are able: yea without al limits, or
bounds, let vs desire his Honour, til such
time as we may be swallowed vp in the
bottomles ocean of al *loue,* & prais *God* in
him-self in *whom,* and by *whom* only we
can prays *him,* as we ought. Let vs *loue him*
here as far as we are possibly able without

To the Reader. **XII**

regard of our felues either,|for time' or eter-
nity. This is the *humble loue* that feeleth
no burden. This is the *true loue* that knoweth not how to attribute any thing it doth,
or fuffereth to it-felf. It choofeth not wherin *God* should make vfe of her, but accom-
modateth its-felf to *his* pleafure in al things.
If it were *his will* to haue it fo, she would
rather for euer be picking of chips, or ftraws
then out of her own election be doing that
which is moft admired, or might feeme to
her to procure her the greateft reward. O
you fouls on whom *God* beftoweth this *loue*
think it not much to beare the burden not
only of your-felues but of al you liue with:
for *God* beareth you vp in al, more then you
can conceiue or imagin! Beware aboue al
things of pride; for that caft euen Angels
out of Heauen. A foul of prayer as long as
she keeps *humility* is in little, or no peril of
going out of her way.

  Giue to Cæfar that is Cæfars, and that to *Matt.*
God, that is Gods. If there be not fome- **12.21.**
thing due to *God* which cannot be giuen to
men; or if it were fo confufed that there
were no certainty what were due to the *one*,
to wit *God*: and what were due for *God*
to the other, to wit, man: a foul would be
fo confufed as to teaching, and leading the
way of Perfection, that she would neuer
know where to begin, and where to end;

or when she did wel , or il. For certainly when the soul doth that by men , which ought to be done by God , and can be done by none but *him*; It goeth not wel with her, as for walking in a true cōtemplatiue cours. She also doth not wel when she would haue God do that by *himself*, which *he* would do by means of Superiors , or directors. And certainly if a soul be a capable soul of con-templatiue instructions, and be wel ground-ed in them by help of one experienced , and walk the way of *entire abnegation* seeking God , and not *his* guifts , and be diligent in obseruing what God wil do by himself in her soul , and wherin *he* referreth her to others , and walk with that *indifferency* that it is al one to her which way, or by whom God wil manifest *his wil* to her : She shal as easily see what, and how to do in al things to please God best , as she may discerne the Sun from the Moon. And this is *to giue that to God that is Gods, and that to Cæsar that is Cæsars.*

FINIS.

Deuout *spiritual* Reader.

I Desire none other should cast their eye on this *true interne spiritual Booke*; And I doubt not but your patience wil beare with the many faults escaped by a strangers presse; And your Charity correct them by taking your pen in your hand, and adding what is wanting a whole word, a letter, or letters, and taking away what is superfluous. One great one I wil particularly aduise you of, to wit page the 19. l. 22. in the preface there wants a *not*. So that you must read, *wanting not those*, in steed of *wanting those*. For so it is in the original in her own hand. The others the sense wil direct you how to correct. *Adieu*.

The Approbation.

HAuing read ouer this smal Treatise en-
tituled, *The Spiritual Exercises of the
most Religious and vertuous Dame Gertrude
More, &c.* with much comfort, and edification seeing the feruent expressions of
diuine loue in her pious soul. And finding
nothing in it iarring with the vniuersal
Belief, or Christian Morality of our Ca-
tholike Church, I haue willingly approued
it as such ; and set my hand heervnto, at
Paris the 26. of March.1658.

Hen. HOLDEN.

The Approbation.

THese Confeſſions or Soliloques writen by the late deceaſed Dame Gertrude More Religious of the English Conuent of Cambray of the holy Order of S. Bennet, *pious fspring* of that Noble and Glorious *Martyr ſir Thomas More*, Chancellor of England, contayning nothing but a true practiſe of that diuine Booke of the Imitation of Chriſt (reſtored of late to the true Author Iohn Gerſon Venerable Abbot of the ſame Order) approoued by al for the mirrour of Chriſtian and Religious perfection, needs no Approbation but a ſerious recommendation to al ſuch as deſire a true pattern to attain to the perfect *loue* of God by affectiue prayer and practiſe thereof. *Sic cenſeo ego.* Pariſiis. 1. Aprilis 1658.

Fr. VVALGRAVIVS Doct. Theol. Monachus & Prior Benedictinus.

CONFESSIONES
AMANTIS.

THE CONFESSIONS OF A
louing, & pious soule to allmighty God.

THE FIRST CONFESSION.

*M*Y *Lord;* we ofteñ read in our office (of the Breuiary) *that those that forsake all for thy sake, shall receaue a hundred folde in this life, and life euerlasting in the next.* This we read, and heare; this was spoken by *thy* owne mouth, and therefor of the *truth* thereof we cannot doubt, nor in the hope thereof can we be deceiued; presupposing we on our part be not wanting of that which is necessary to the performance of that which *thou* exactest.

Math 19.30.

A

But tell me, I beſeech *thee*, my *God*,
tell me I ſay for *thy* owne ſake, what is
it, that *thou* exacteſt of them who ſhall
obtaine this *thy* promiſe? for I ſee many leaue their parents, friends, acquaintance, their fortunes, their rich
poſſeſſions, contrey, and all, and yet
is it plaine that they finde not this *hundred folde* in this life; that is the forerun-
ner of the euerlaſting in the next. For
I ſee their ſtate is a burthen to them,
and the obligations of Obedience and
religious obſeruance is eſteemed by
them a great ſeruitude, and burthen.
What is the meaning of this my *Lord*?
Shall I doubt that thoſe who reſolutly,
and willingly forſake all the world for
for *thee* would ſticke at forſaking themſelues alſo, ſeeing that by forſaking,
and denying themſelues, they ſhould
find *thee* in a moſt particular maner in
their ſoules? Is ſuch forſaking of our
ſelues to be accounted a looſing of
our ſelues? O no! but it is a moſt ſweet,
and happy exchange, to leaue our
owne wills for to performe *thine*; to be
ſubiect for *thee* to euery liuing creatu-

re., is not a burthen, but the greatest
liberty in this world. But (alas) my
God, the reason why we finde *thy* yoke
a burthen, is, becaufe we beare it not
with *thee*, by which only it is to be made an eafy yoke. If foules who haue
actually forfaken the world, and in
defire themfelues alfo (which moft
comming into Religio are defirous to
do) were but putt into fome courfe
between *thee*, and their foules by thófe
who had the care of them, or authority ouer them, they would not, as th y
doe, fly backe from their firft intention, but would euery day more, and
more by conuerfing with *thee*, get
more *light* to know *thy* will, & ftrength
to performe it ; But being ignorant
how to conuerfe with *thee*, and how in
all things to haue relation to *thee*, *thy*
yoke becomes more, and more bur-
thenfome to them, and euery day
they fall into new difficulties, and in-
conueniencies, and are in danger at
laft to fall into open rebellion againft
their lawfull Superiors, and fome of
them into ftrange friendfhips; a thing

which is worthy to be bewailed with
blouddy teares, that harts capable of
thy loue, and by profeſſion conſecrated
therevnto, should so miſerably looſe
themſelues in powring out themſelues, where, and from whom no true
comfort can be found, or had. O *Lord*,
remoue theſe impediments from thoſe who are *thine* by ſo many titles; lett
them know *thee*, and of *thee*, that they
may *loue* nothing but *thee*; and lett
them *loue thee* that they may know
themſelues, and their owne weaknes;
and alſo *thy* power and *Maieſty*. O my
Lord, how infinitly is my ſoule bound
to praiſe, and *loue thee*, ſince by meanes
of a faithfull *ſeruant* of *thine*, I haue
been inſtructed in *thy* law, and taught
how to haue in all things relation to
thee, my only beloued, by which means
all Croſſes, miſeries, paines, diſgraces, temptations, are moſt tolerable
to me, I hauing *thee* ſo preſent to *whom*
I may ſpeake, or write, and by *whom*
(though I am contemptible in the
eyes, as I iuſtly deſerue to be, of all
the world) I am not yet deſpiſed, or

V. Fa.
Baker

neglected; for which infinite mercy,
all praife and honour be giuen to *the* .
O when shall I be gratefull to *thee* ? Or
what sha'l I render for all *thou* befto-
weft on me? I haue nothing, but a hart
defirous to *loue*, and praife *thee*; but
for ability to do either, alas, my *God*
it is wanting to me. O that all *loues*
might be wholy conuerred to *thee* ! At
leaft lett thofe who haue dedicated
themfelues to *thee*, ceafe to defire any
thing out of *thee*; Send them meanes
to know how fweet it is to haue no
friend but *thee*, and to be neglected by
all but *thy* fweet mercy.

O can that foule that loues *her* God
    For very shame complaine
To any other then himfelfe
    Of what she doth fuftaine !
No way to her was euer found,
    Nor euer shall there be ,
But taking vp thy Croffe my Lord,
    Thereby to follow thee.
This is the Way, *the* Truth, *the* Life,
    Which leadeth vnto heauen,
None is fecure, but only this,
                    A iij

Though seeming nere ſo euen.
Thoſe that do walke this happy path,
    IESVS doth company;
But thoſe who go another way,
    Will erre moſt miſerably.
And in this way do not think much,
    That thou doſt much endure;
No, though it be from holy men;
    For God doth this procure,
That thou maiſt ſeeke himſelfe alone,
    And putt thy truſt in him,
And not in any creatures liuing,
    How good ſo ere they ſeeme.
For ſuffring by the meanes of th'ill
    Will little thee aduance;
But to be ſenſur'd by the good,
    Goes neere to thee perchance.
Alas we ſhew but little loue,
    If we muſt chooſe which way,
Our Lord muſt try our Loue to him,
    And not in all obey.
We muſt ſubmitt our ſelues to him,
    And be of cheerefull hart;
For he expecteth much of them
    Who be of Maries part.
For ſhe muſt beare a cenſure hard
    From all without exception;

But thou, o Lord, wilt her excuse,
  Who art her soules election.
If she will patiently sustaine,
  And be to thee attent,
Thou fauourably willt iudge of her,
  Who know'st her harts intent.
For all but thou, as well she sees,
  May erre concerning her;
They only iudge as they conceiue,
  But thou canst neuer erre.
Complaine not therefor, louing soule,
  If thou willt be of those,
Who loue their God more then themselus,
  and Maries part haue chose.
If all thou dost be taken ill
  By those of high perfection;
And further if thou be accus'd
  To be of some great faction,
Our Lord will answere all for thee,
  If thou willt hold thy peace,
And from contentions, and complaints
  Willt patiently surcease,
Leauing all, care vnto thy God,
  And only him intend;
Yet what is ill, reforme in thee,
  And this will all amend.
As farre as he doth thinke it good,

Who is most iust, and wise,
He *will thee by afflictions purge,*
    From what displease his eyes.
Willt *thou of all that loue thy* God,
    From suffring be exempt?
O no, but blisse, as others do
    thy God, *and liue content!*
Amidst the various accidents,
    That do to thee befall,
Committ *thy selfe, and all to* God
    Who seekes our good in all.
Thy selfe art blind, and cannot iudge
    What is the best for thee;
But *he doth pearce into all things,*
    How hidd so ere they be.
My hart shall only this desire,
    That thou my Lord *dispose,*
Euen as thou *pleasest in all things,*
    Till these myne eys thou *close*
By *death, which I so much desire,*
    Because it will procure
Me to enioy my God, *my all.*
    Where I shall be secure
That none from me can take my Lord;
    But for eternity,
I shall enioy my only good,
    And to him *euer be*

Vnited by a knott *of* Loue,
  Which nothing shall vnity,
But will remayne, as permanent
    As his Diuinity.
O happy houre, when willt thou come,
  And set my Spirit *free,*
That I may loue *and prayse my* God
    For perpetuity,
Contemplating his *glorious face*
  With all that him *adore,*
Singing with them his sweetest prayse,
  For euer, *and* euer *more!*

In this is such and so great comfort,
and *peace,* that well may the soule be
tearmed to receaue a *hundred folde* in
this life, who despiseth it-selfe, and all
other things that it may finde *thee,* O
how free is such a soule to fly with the
wings of *Loue* to the throne of thy Diuine *Maiesty;* Neuer was there, or can
be imagined such a *Loue;* as is betweene an humble soule, and *thee.* Who can
expresse what passeth between such a
soule, and thee? Verily neither man,
nor Angell is able to do it sufficiently;
and the more such a soule knowes of

thee, the more found becometh her
humility, the which *thy selfe* only can
teach one perfectly; and it is impoſſible to gett it in *verity*, and perfection,
but by conuerſing with *thee*. O my God
beſtow this heauenly *gift* on me, which
only findeth fauour before *thee*. Thoſe
that poſſeſſe it are able in, and by *thee*
to be are all things, to *vnderſtand* all
things as farre as it is neceſſary for
them. For one learneth more in *Prayer*
of *thee* in one hower, then all creatures
in the world could teach one in fifty
yeares; for that which *thou* teacheſt is
found, ſolid, and ſecure; becauſe it
tends to nothing but to *loue thee*, & neglect it ſelfe. *Thy words* bring force &
ſtrength in themſelues; *thy* words are
words of *peace* to the ſoule; *thy* words
are not like the words of men, which
paſſe, as a ſound through the ayr; but
thyne pearſe the very bottome of our
ſoules; Lett me hearken therefor to
thee, who ſpeaketh *lowe* and moſt certaine *truth*; The wiſedome of the world
is fooliſhnes before *thee*; But *thy* wiſedome is much to be deſired, and for *it*

willingly ought we to giue all our sub-
ftance; to *it* we ought to be efpowfed;
and by *it* if we will be happy, all our
actions ought to be gouerned. Allthough *thou* didft fay, *that vnleffe we become as litle children we could not enter into
the kingdome of heauen*, yet withall *thou*
haft faid, *that we ought to be wife as fer-
pents, and fimple as doues*; where *thou* put-
teft that we should be *wife* before we
be *fimple*, and not *fimplicity* before *wifedome*; whereof I afke *thee* the reafon,
O my *Lord*, with all the *humility* I am
poffibly able. For it feems to me, that
therein, as in all *thy* words, there is
a hidden Myftery; tell me, I fay, my
God (of *whom* in all cafes, and doubts I
afke folution, and many times by it
thou doft make many things manifeft
to my *fimplicity*;) tell me (I fay) what
was the reafon? Verily it feemeth to
me, that *thou* biddeft vs be *wife* before
we become *fimple*, becaus that is only
true *Simplicity*, which followeth true
Wifedome. For we cannot become truly
fimplified in our foule, but by thy heauenly gift of *true wifdome*. For there

is a simplicity which is without wisedome, and *discretion*, which litle auay-
leth to perfection. This vertue of
Simplicity becometh more, and more
perfect in the foule, as she increaseth
in *humility*, and *charity*; yet at the very
first of our conuersion this is in some
fort practised by vs, if we do as we
ought to do. As for example; to become pleasing to *thee*, it is absolutly necessary that a foule walke simply and
sincerly before *thy selfe* and all men;
and read, and heare, obey, and performe all in a *simple*, and *humble* maner;
not fearching into that which belon-
geth not vnto her; this (I say) *thou*
dost exact; for nothing is more odious
to *thee*, then the contrary practise; But
yet this doth not diminish our naturall reason; but maketh it more cleere,
and able to comprehend what is necessary for vs. This vertue also therefor bestow vpon me, who euen in
my nature (as thou well knowest) did
euer aboue all things hate dissem-
bling, and dissimulation. O *Lord*, poore
as I am, and most sinnefull, thus thou

feeſt how I preſume to ſpeake vnto *thee;* but eaſily ſhall I obtayn pardon of *thee*, becauſ *thou* ouerfloweſt with the aboundance of *thy* mercy; for which Glory, Prayſe, Adoration be to *thee*, *who* art my *Lord*, and my *God*, and only deſired by me. I haue no friend to ſpeake, or treat with but *thee*, and ſome of thy Saints, to whom *thou* haſt giuen charge of me, and to whom I fly when my ſinnes affright me; amongſt whom next after thy Deare Mother, the Queene of mercy, is my beloued *S. Auguſtine.*

O Glorious Saint *whoſe hart did burne,*
　　And flame with Loue Diuine,
Remember me moſt ſinnefull wretch,
　　Who hunger ſtaru'd doth pine.
For want of that which thou enioyeſt
　　In ſuch aboundant meaſure;
It is my God *that I doe meane,*
　　My ioy, *and all my* treaſure.
Thy words O Saint *are truly ſweet,*
　　Becauſ thou doſt addreſſe
Them vnto him who's only meet
　　Our mis'ries to redreſſe.

At whoſe interceſſion much haſt
thou done for me; Honour them, my
Lord for me who am ſo poore that I
haue nothing to preſent them, or
thee; only a deſire of being gratefull
to *thee*, *who* be by all eternally pray-
ſed. *Amen.* (It was S. Auguſtine the
, Doctor and amorous ſeruant of *God*,
, yᵗ she heere meant.)

THE SECOND CONFESSION.

Luk.
14.

Omnis ex vobis qui non renuntiat omnibus
quæ poſsidet, non poteſt meus eſſe diſcipu-
lus. Qui habet aures audiendi audiat. All
you who renounce not all you poſſeſſe, can-
not be my diſciple; who hath eares of hea-
ring let him heare.

TH E S E are thy words, my *Lord*
which though they ſeeme hard
at firſt, yet being explicated to our
ſoules by *thee*, they become moſt eaſy,
and ſweet to performe; Teach me therefor my *God*, I beſeech *thee* for *thy*
mercies ſake, teach me I ſay, how I

shall perform this to the glory of *thy*
holy name, *Thou* hast inflamed my
hart, as thou knoweft, with fuch a continuall defire, and longing after *thee*,
that it feemeth eafy to me to performe
whatfoeuer is exacted by *thee*. For
though I be fraile aboue all I can expreffe, or imagin, yet I am confident
in *thee*, by *whofe* helpe and power it is
poffible to giue me to do all that it
pleafeth *thee* to exact of me; *Teach me*
to do thy will, becaus thou art my God. Lett
me *Loue thee*, becaus to want thy *Loue*
is a moft grieuous affliction to me.
Farre as thou knoweft, it is from me to
haue willingly a deuided hart to *thee.*
Is it poffible that hauing but one foule,
& hart, I should beftow any of the affection they are capable of, on any
thing but *thee*? O farr be this from me;
Nothing that could happen to my
foule would fo afflict, and difcomfort
me, as to fee it adhered to any created
thing, or to it very-felfe, willingly, to
the impediment of my being wholy
poffeffed by *thee*. Make me that *thou*
wouldft haue me, that I may as *thou*

Pfal.
142.

exacteſt, prayſe *thee*. This ſhall be my ſtudy, my care, and all my endeauour, to ſing in my hart ſongs of *Loue* to *thee*, who art only deſired and ſought after by me; In *thy* prayſe I am only happy; in which my *ioy*, I will exullt with all that *loue thee*, For what can be a comfort to me, while I liue ſeperated from *thee*, but only to remember, that my *God*, who is more myne, then I am my owne, is abſolutly and infinitly happy? O lett this *thy Loue* wholy transforme me into it ſelfe, that I may become inſenſible to all created things whatſoeuer; Lett me be wholy poſſeſſed by *thee*, *who* by ſo many titles laieth claime to me. Can I ſay, or think that any thing is worthy of *loue* but *thee*? O, no; but if I had then thowſand harts, all were to little to beſtow vpon thee. ☞ Shall I any more be ſo miſerable, as by louing, hauing, adhering to, or deſiring any created thing, to become eſtranged from *thee*, in *whom* I haue placed all my hope, *loue*, and deſire? I haue indeed choſen *thee* for my only *loue*, light, hope, comfort, refuge, delight, and whatsoeuer ells can be desired, or imagined, but it was not of my selfe; but *thy* mercy and goodnes enforced me, euen whither I would or no, by sending me the meanes to know how to serue *thee*, and withall giuing me grace of loathing all which was not to be a helpe to me. O these *thy* mercies when I recount before *thee*, euen depriueth me of my very senses, to see *thee* to haue been so good, & mercifull to her, who as it is made plaine to me by *thee*, hath offended, and been more vngratefull to *thee* then any I did either see, or heare off. Shall not I therefor humble my soule before *thee*, and at the feet of all for the *loue* of *thee*, who hath been thus tender of her good, who of all *thine* is the last, and least, and most contemptible; the which being so apparent to me, I will yet more and more humble my self by desiring to be despised by all, for *thy* honour, and glory. Thus, my *Lord*, dust, and ashes presumeth to speake vnto *thee*; and sitting alone I read what I write of *thee*, and calling to minde

what thou haft done for me, I reioyce
in the multitude of *thy* mercy. For
nothing can heere be found in what I
heere write for my comfort, being
bannished from *him whom* till I may
enioy as *he* is in *himselfe* nothing will I
reft in; for nothing can fatiat me. Yet,
as I fay, it alaieth my grief for hauing
offended *thee*, and of being thus remo-
te from my beginning (to which moft
ardently I long to returne as pure, as I
was created by *thee*) This my fpeaking
in all my mifery to *Thee*. None therefor
can wonder at me. For as one who defireth the prefence of her beloued, and
expecteth when it fhall be, can take no
comfort till fhe fee whom fhe fo much
defireth; In the meane while fpending
her tyme, fometymes with thinking
that this ioy to her will fhortly be, and
fometymes being wearied with long
expectation, fhe employeth her felf
in fome thing which may a litle recreat
her hart, while thus with her it muft
be; and aboue all it is a pleafure to
her to heare of him, which fhe cannot

yet fee. Thus, O *Lord*, it paffeth euen
in that *loue*, which will, and deferueth
to paffe ; which none deferueth but
thou. And there is no comparifon able
to expreffe the *loue* which is between a
faithfull foule, and *thee*. For the more
we *loue thee*, the more pure and quiet
becometh the foule by this thy heauenly charity ; Whereas, alas! it fareth
farre otherwife with vs when we loue
any thing out of *thee*, & which, is an impediment to *thy Loue* ; which mifery
before *thee*, in the bitternes of my foule, I bemoane ; becaus *thou* hauing made our foule fo capable of thy diuine
Loue, and fo able to haue relation in
all to *thee*, it is an ingratitude able to
aftonifh me, that we should caft away
our *loue* vpon that which is fo litle able
to fatisfy our foule, and whereof there
is as litle certainty as there is of the
wind ; yea euen in a moment we loofe the fauour, and opinion of one, vpon
whom we haue beftowed much tyme
in winning it. O folly, which be henceforth farre from me ! Lett that infinit extent, and defirable freedom of

my will, powre it ſelfe out wholy vpon
thee, that at laſt I may become perfectly vnited to *thy* diuine *Maieſty*. O
how litle worth (when I am with *thee*)
is the deſiring of the prayſe, applauſe,
and commendation of men, who are
now of one mind, and now of another,
nothing being permanent vnder the
ſunn. Verily when in *thy light* I ſee
this *truth*, it ſeemeth to me to be an
intolerable burthen to be eſteemed,
and praiſed by men, whoſe fauour often maketh vs incurre *thy* diſpleaſure;
at leaſt my frailty cauſeth it ſo to me.
Helpe me therefor, and make me by
all to become truly humble, and pleaſing to *thee* who be adored three and
one for all eternity, to *thy* infinit
glory. *Amen.*

THE THIRD CONFESSION.

O *That I were able* to winne the
harts of the whole world to *thee!*
which ſeeing I am not able to doe, lett
me be no lett at leaſt to any ſoules of

louing thee. All *loue* and prayſe is due
vnto *thee*, and all paine, reproach,
confuſion, and ſhame vnto me, which
grant I may beare without offending
thee, and then a thouſande times well-
come be any of them, which may increaſe my *loue* to *thee*. O let me forſak
all for *thee*, which *thou* willeſt vs to do,
yᵗ we may find *thee*! What is this *thou*
ſaieſt (tell me *thy* poore ſeruant) *leaue
all*? Haue I any thing to leaue which is
not more burthenſome to keepe, then
it is paine to leaue. If I ſeeke my ſelfe,
what do I labour for, but my owne
paine? If I forſake my ſelfe for *thee*,
behold a moſt ſweet *peace* is found by
me. Thus therefor are *thy* Lawes; The
more perfectly we performe them, the
more delightfull is thy yoke. They were made by *thee* out of *thy loue* to vs; and
if we *loue*, they will be moſt eaſy, and
pleaſant to vs. For indeed where *thou*
biddeſt vs leaue and forſkae all, that
we may find *reſt* in our ſoules, thou
ſpeakeſt to vs, as being ſenſuall. For
when we leaue our freinds, riches, honours, pleaſures, yea and euen (which

is moſt of all) our very ſelues, what
haue we left, or forſaken? Some thing
indeed, as it ſeemes to vs, theſe things
are, when through blindnes, and ignorance, we eſteeme them as benefits
and comforts; but doing it vpon *thy*
word, we find we haue left nothing, to
find *thee who* art all things. We haue
left our friends, who are incident to
leaue vs, when we ſtand in moſt need
of them. We haue left honour, which
being had proueth nothing ells but a
meere burthen to vs. And ſo in fine
nothing is there to be left, which if we
did but *loue* our owne *peace* and *quiet*
without all further reſpect, we would
chooſe as the very beſt what *thou* doſt
exact. For vertue is amiable in it ſelf,
and thoſe that had but a very ſhew of
it, as to what it is indeed, euen among
the Heathés were honoured for Gods
Who therefor would not follow *thee*
my *God*, in *whom* alone is to be found
true good? *Thou* teacheſt the milde,
and humble, *thy* wayes, and *thou* reſteſt
willingly in a peacefull hart. What can
bring true *peace* to our ſoule, but *thy*

Loue? Giue this *Loue* therefor to me,
who wisheth and desireth only, that
in all I may be *true to thee.*

THE FOVRTH CONFESSION.

O My *Lord* and my *God*, to *whom*
I duft and ashes am not worthy
to fpeak! Yet heare me my *Lord* recounting heere before *thee thy* owne
words fpoaken by thy feruant in thy
name, *who* art *truth* it felfe. *Venite filij*
audite me, timorem Domini docebo vos. Pro-
hibe linguam tuam à malo, & labia tua ne
loquantur dolum. Diuerte à malo, & fac
bonum; inquire pacem, & perfequere eam.
Come ô *Sonns Heare mee i will teach you the*
feare of our Lord. Forbid thy tongue from euil,
& thy lips that they speake not guile, turne
from euil and do good, feeke peace, & pro-
fecute itt. Heere *thou* biddeft me as *thy*
child come to *thee,* and *thou* willt teach
me *thy* feare, as that *thou* art my *Lord.*
Heere *thou* biddeft me refrain my tongue from guile, and my lippes that
they fpeack not guile, and alfo hate

Pfal.
33. 12.

Pfal.
33. 14.

euill, and do good, inquire after
peace and follow *it*, these last words indeed comprehending all. But of whom
shall I inquire *peace* my *Lord*, & my *God*;
of whom I say, shall I inquire to learn
it? Truely of *thy selfe*, *who* in teaching
me the way of *peaoe*, canst giue me grace to follow *it*. Of *thee* therefor I desire to learn, *whose* words are works.
Speak to my hart; speak so that I may
heare, and follow *it*; Giue me the Humility which knoweth no guile; Giue
me the *Loue* that accompanieth it. *Lord*
thou knowest that there was neuer more necessity of begging in this kind *thy*
helpe; because humble *Loue* is now of
the world allmost vnknown, yea euen
of them who should teach *it* the rest;
the wisedome of *thy truth* is sett a side;
and that which is the wisedome of the
world beareth sway ouer all; out of
which it groweth, that euen Humility, Obedience, and Charity (the most
noble vertues that are, or can be) are
exacted and practised euen by way of
humaine policy, which maketh so litle
vnion in the world betweene them
　　　　　　　　　　　　　　　whose

whose whole study ought to be, how
they might *loue*, and draw most forci-
bly all the harts, and soules in the
world to the pure *loue* of *thee*. O *Lord*
how farr haue our sinns cast vs from
thee! Inlighten my soule, O *Lord*, I
humbly beseech *thee*, while heere, to
my greif, I do in the bitternes of my
soule, rehearse these things befor
thee, *whom* I (most contemptible, and
vnworthy) find in all so willing to
hear, and help me. If we would *loue*,
we should aboundantly partake of
thee. For nothing is held by *thee* too
deare for them, who alone aboue all
creatures, and comforts seek the pure
loue of *thee*. Out of this true *loue* between a soul and *thee*, there ariseth
such a knowledg in the soul, that it
loatheth all that is an impediment to
her further proceeding in the *Loue* of
thee. O *Loue*, *Loue*, euen by naming
thee, my soul looseth it self in
thee! Nothing can satiat my soul my
Lord, as it is well known to *thee*, but
to be swallowed vp in *thee* for all *eternity*. No knowledg which heer we

B

can haue of *thee*, can satisfy my soul
seeking, and longing without ceasing
after *thee*. By *faith* we are certain of
thee, and by *Loue* we in some sort experience in our soules *thy* greatnes,
and goodnes, *thy* beawty, and sweetnes, which more confirmeth vs in the
hope of *thee*. O what knowledg is to
be compared to that which is taught
the *humble* by *thee*, which tendeth yet
only to *thy* making her vnderstand
her owne *nothing*, and meer dependance of *thee*. *Thy* words, (as my
deare *S. Augustin* sayth, speaking in
his wonted maner to *thee*) do euen
smile vpon those y^t neither seek, or
desire any thing but *thee*. What canst
thou deny to such, as thus *loue thee*? Verily *thou* seemest so enamoured of
them, as if *thou* wert forgettfull of
the infinitnes of *thy* Maiesty. The
more they become *humble*, the
more they are regarded by *thee*, and
the more (in *thy* light) do they perceaue their vnworthines to be thus
aduanced to *loue thee*, which the more
short it is of that which in will they

defir by more, and more *humility* to
become before *thee*, the more they
endeauour to become gratefull to *thy*
infinit mercy. O who can expresse
the ioy that an humble soule takes in
being despised for *thee*! Verily nothing doth she esteeme so great a
burthen, as to be fauoured, honoured, esteemed, or applauded by men,
whose opinion she feareth may deceaue her through her great frailty!
O how little is the opinion of men
to be esteemed, seeing they are so
fickle, inconstant, and easily deceaued! but *thy* iudgments, my *Lord God*,
are true, and iustified in themselues;
be *thou* my witnes, and defender, who
canst not be deceaued; and then lett
all the world censure me as they please; a good conscience is better then
a thousand wittnesses; giue me this
then; and I shall easily passe through
all things! Speak, my *Lord*, *peace* to
my hart, that I may attend to *thee*
alone my only *beloued*. Shall I after
all *thy* benefits desir any thing beside *thee*? O no, my *God*, farr, farr,

farr be this misery from me, after my
☞ soul hath been thus vrged by *thee* to
sigh, long, and thirst without ceasing
after being vnited with *thee*.

THE FIFT CONFESSION.

TELL me, my *Lord*, I beseech
thee, what can my soul pretend
if it seek any thing with *thee*, which
is an impediment to my truly *louing*
thee? What can I, I say, pretend,
seeing no *peace*, or comfort can be
found, but only in *thee*? What do we
when wee desire comfort of *thee*, but
depriue our selues of a most happy liberty, which they enioy who desire
☞ nothing for tyme or eternity, but
(without a l regard of themselues)
to be perfectly conformable to *thee*.
If we would liue without all intention, or wish: but of enioying *thee* (which cannot be done, but by a truly
humble and faithfull soule) the diuell could not ouercome vs by any
wile. We should easily retain true

peace with our selues, with all the world, and aboue all with *thee*. For when we adhere to any created thing we become a flaue to our Paſſion, and are in eminent danger of ſinne. No way is plaine, ſecure, and eaſy, and without perill of all errour, but this, that the ſoul ſeek nothing but *thee* her Creator; This is the way, *in* which a foole cannot erre ; this is the way without queſtions, in which a ſoul without all impediment adhereth to *thee*, the fountain of all true *wiſedome who* willingly illuminateth our needy ſoules, if we will but giue *thee* our *hart*, and ſoul to *thyſelf; thou* conſidereſt not our former ſinnes, after *thou* haſt once blotted them out, but doſt vpon them (who haue had the maners of beaſtes in times paſt) moſt bountifully, and aboundantly beſtow and refreſh them with the ſweet dew of thy grace, which hauing taſted in their ſoul, it maketh them loath all that is leſſe then *Thee;* neither can they take any content, but in hearing *thy* name, ſpeaking to

Eſay. 35. 8.

thee, and *longing* after *thee*, after *thou*
haſt wounded their ſoul with *thy*
Diuine Charity. O lett me ſitt alone
ſilent to all the world, and it to me,
that I may learn the ſong of *Loue*, and
praiſe of *thee*, which is ſo infinitly due
to *thee* from me! This ſong none can
ſing but thoſe that truly *loue thee*, and
whoſe only conſolation is to be without all comfort as often, and as much
as it ſhall pleaſe *thee*. Nothing as *thou*
knowſt, do I putt any ioy, or comfort in, but in ſighing after *thee*, *who*
art not heer (as *thou* art) to be by vs
ſeen. O teach me thoſe vertues, which draw a ſoul ſo out of her ſelf into
thee, that ſhe becometh inſenſible to
all things but *thee*; theſe vertues are,
true *Humility* which knoweth not
how to exallt it ſelf, perfect *Subiection*
to *thee*, and *Diſcretion* which can only
be taught by *thy Maieſty*, and yet is
ſo neceſſary, that no vertue hath
more vertue in it, then partaketh of
true *Diſcretion*. For without that, we
inſteed of true vertue practiſe abſurd
follies! O my *Lord*. aboue all things

lett me feeke *thy* glorie, *who* be praifed by all creatures for all eternity!
Amen.

THE SIXT CONFESSION.

IS it any wonder, my *Lord God* that
in all my doubts, temptations,
paines, and in this continuall warr-
fare which I find vpon earth, and in
my greif of being feperated by finnes dayly vnwillingly committed,
and liuing in flesh and bloud from
thee my only *beloued* and my moft *infinit good*, I recurre to *thee* for fuccour,
& help? What shall I do, if I should
not in all things fpeak vnto *thee*, confult with *thee*, and haue relation to
thee? what would becom of me, whofe frailty, and weaknes is aboue all
that can be imagined, much leffe expreffed by me; but by recurring to
thee I find, and gett *light*, and a certain
fweet, and heauenly repaft towards
the fuftaining of all the miferies this
bannishment of ours is fubiect vnto.

Alas, thou knowſt I haue placed all
my *peace* and hope in *thee*; All I deſire is, that I may *loue thee*, and become
totally ſubiect to *thee*; Do with me
whatſoeuer *thou* pleaſeſt. For I deſire
no more power to chooſe any thing
any more, then if I had neuer been;
only *thy-ſelf* I long for and deſire to
poſſeſſe, and obtaine; yet in what
maner, & meaſure as *thou* didſt from
all eternity will, and ordaine. For in
this deſire, my ſoul, hart, and will
haue no limitts, nor can they ſuffi-
ciently extend themſelues to their
fill, ſaue only by *louing* and praiſing
thee by *thyſelf* (which is my refuge)
all power in my ſelf I feeling vtterly
to faile. Certainly only by *louing*,
knowing, and enioying *thee* can my
ſoul become *truly* happy: bring me
to this I beſeech *thee*, ſeeing that *thou*
vouchſafeſt ſuch a deſire to her who is
thy pooreſt, ſinnfulleſt and moſt contemptible creature : neither is there
any creature, nor can there be, of ſo
litle deſert, but that they deſerue

what *thou* doft to and for my foule
farr, farr, farr befor me ; All the
Glory therefor be giuen to *thee.* For
nothing but confufion is due vnto
me; which grant I may beare patiently when through *thy* iuft iudgment it
falleth vpon me.

THE VII. CONFESSION.

I Haue *inquired* of others about all
thofe things which I thought ap-
pertained, or might be a help to me
for the better feruice of *thee* ; But no
ftability could I find in any Inftructions till I was referred to *thee,* who
art that *one thing which is only neceffary.* Few are the Inftructions
which to a good *will* were neceffary,
if we were referred to *thee,* as our prin-
cipall, and only *Maifter,* and *Director,*
who can indeed neuer erre, and is
allways prefent, and both teaches
vs what Obedience, and *Humility* is,
and giueth *grace* allfo to perform
them, which none can do but *thy*

self. O how happy are they who truly
adore *thee* in *truth*, and *Spirit*! For these in *thy light* shall see light, and in
thy strength are able to passe through
all difficulties, how great soeuer.
These adhering faithfully to *thee*,
sustaine their Crosses so cheerfully,
as if in their suffering they beheld
thee for whom they suffer, with their
corporall eyes. And they desyring
no knowledg of *thee* but what they
haue by *faith* (which is only secure,
and void of all perill of errour) *Thou*
wonderfully confirmest them in the
light of that which is in it-selfe so secure. What comfort can a soul take
in any created thing, who hath placed her ioy in *thee* alone? No Angell
can satisfy her, or make her greife
the lesser, while she is bannished
from her *God*, who is her *Glory*, and
her *Crowne*. Yet one thing she hath
to be some comfort to her while thus
it stands with her, which none can
take from her; and that is the hauing
of relation vpon all occurrents to
thee immediatly in her soul, in such

a maner that nothing can interpofe it
felfe betweene *thee* , and her. She
indeed highly efteemeth all that *thou*
haft made; euery thing as it is deri-
ued by partaking of *thy* grace; More
in perfection of which degree, are
Angells and the Soules of men, and
she preferreth the latter (that are
yet in this world) before herfelf in all
things; but yet as in comparifon of
thee, they are to her, as if they were
meere *nothing*, as for refting or pla-
cing her felicity in them. For well
she knoweth that if there were no
foul yet created, nor euer to be,
but only her own foul, and that
were (as all foules are) capable of
thee, she should by poffeffing *thee*
alone, and without them be infinitly
happy; for thus it is; for nothing can
fatiat a reafonable foul, but only
thou; And hauing of *thee*, who art indeed *all*, *nothing* could be faid to be
wanting to her. Thus my *God* it
ftands with me; for which all glory
and praife be giuen to *thee* eternally.
For if it had not ftood thus with

our foules, that our happynes had only depended on *thee*, fome defect there would haue beene, that might haue been an impediment betweene a foul and *thee*. O that fome who liue wholy to *thee*, and experience the infinit defire *thou* haft to impart *thy felfe* to all reafonablefoules, wouldcome out of their folitud, & their liuing wholy for the good of themfelues, & declare the way of *Loue* to hungry, and euen ftarued foules! O how many would then be as tractable *Lambes*, who now rebell as ftiffe-necked foules! Verily *thou* knoweft that before I mett with fuch a *feruant* of *thine* my hart feemed to me and alfo to others, to be growne (liuing yet in Religion) more hard as to any good, then euer was a ftone; but hearing *thy* law made by him fo eafy, & plaine, it was great ioy to my foul, and little did it feeme to fuffer all the paine, and mifery in the world, fo I might pleafe and ferue *thee* my only *beloued*. I had indeed inquired about *thee* of many before, and thofe fuch

v. Fa. Baker.

as were moſt likely to haue known; they all agreed in points neceſſary to ſaluation, neither should I haue erred as I did, if I had followed them; but what was the meane, and way to a perfect *Vnion* with *thee* in my ſoul, I could not at all hear, or learn. For they had (as ſome of them humbly profeſt) been for twenty yeares imployed in hearing Confeſſions; and in ſtudies, thereby endeauouring to *thy* great honour to work the ſaluation of ſtreying ſoules, which was a happy courſe for them, ſo yᵗ they had little experience in directing *Contemplatiue* ſoules; But as one of them profeſt, who was our cheife Superior, if we had not found one of our owne Order, who could in this haue giuen ſatisfaction to our ſoules, he would haue ſought ouer all the world moſt willingly to haue found, and procured one for vs; for which Humility, and Charity of his, I beſeech *thee* my *Lord God* to reward him as beſeemeth *thy* infinit *Goodnes* And grant that we, who haue, or shall find

V. R.
F. Ru-
deſind
Barloe

benefit by theſe moſt happy Inſtructions, may be as faithfull to *thee*, as
it is poſſible for ſoules loaden with
fleſh, and bloud; and lett our harts
ſtudy nothing ells, but how to *loue*
thee; and by perfect ſubiection lett
our ſoules liue quietly vnder whom-
ſoeuer is ſett ouer vs by *thee*. For in
vain do we pretend to obey *thee*, if
☞ we be not pliable to thoſe that are
ſet ouer vs by *thy* Diuine Maieſty.
For thoſe who truly endeauour to
pleaſe *thee* would obey a worm, if it
☞ could commaund in the name, and
power of *thee*. For ſo much is an
action pleaſing to *thee*, as it is done
in that maner it is exacted of vs by
thee; which good will, and pleaſure of
thine we cannot learn but by conuerſing with *thee*, which if we do, and
liue withall as well as our frailty will
permit, wholy to *thee*, and ſeek our
own abiection, it will eaſily appeare
to vs how, and which way in all things
we ſhall behaue our ſelues to become truly obedient to *thee*. For either by the Rule, cuſtome, or order

of the howse, or by the speciall ordinance of the Superior *God* sheweth vs what to do, they being infallible declarations of *his will*, and the most certain of all; Or ells for things for which they referre vs to *thee*, as for the maner of our Prayer, and such like things, *thou* teachest an humble soul what therein to do, and when to ask of others, and when to seek the solutions from *thee*; But indeed as I haue confessed to *thee* before, speaking ordinarily, few are the questions that occurre in the way yt is of humble Resignation; Only *thou* requirest, that how cleerly, or securely soeuer a soul walk, she be ready in all that is required of her by Superiors, to giue them a faithfull accompt, and to amend, and correct whatsoeuer they iudge amisse; This lesson they learn who in all haue relation to *thee*; and *thou* giuest them grace to obey in all for *thee*, if we dispose our soules to hear, and follow *thee*. For *thou* giuest one grace to one, and another to another, and some

may do that with profit, which would
to another be a mayn preiudice.
Thou giueſt wiſedom to all *thy* little
ones, but not to all in one maner,
but to a Superior in one kind, and to
a ſubieƈt in another. In all therefor
if we will truly obey, we ought to
obſerue ourſelues, what doth hinder, and what doth help towards the
obtaining of *thy* diuine *Loue*, for
which all things are and haue been
ordained by *thy* diuine *Goodnes*; and
yet to do this as we ought, paſſeth ſo
between *thee*, and vs : that none can
☞ diſcern it by vs, vnleſſe perhaps they
hold the *ſame courſe*. For this proceeding doth not make a ſoul ſingular in her aƈtions, and cariadge
(for ſingularity is a vice which *thou*
extreamly hateſt) but rather makes
one exceedingly *loue* the common
obediences, and externall exerciſes,
all of them putting ones ſoul in
mind of her duty towards *thee* in all
things ; and ſo haſt thou ordained,
and diſpoſed the orders of this howſe, that they are a ſufficient book

to teach vs our duty, and do shew vs
when to Praise *thee*, and when to cea
se from actually doing it; When to
speak, and when to be silent; and for
my part following them as well as I
can quietly, and out of Obedience
to *thee*. I find them all most necessary, and proper to aduance a soul in
the true *Loue of thee*; and particularly
the Diuine Office is such a heauenly
thing, that in it we find whatsoeuer
we can desire. For sometimes in it
we addresse vs to *thee* for help, and
pardon for our sinnes; and some-ti-
mes *thou* speakest to vs; so that it pearceth, and woundeth with desire of
thee, the very bottome of our soules,
and sometimes *thou* teachest a soul
to vnderstand more in it of the knowledg of *thee*, and of themselues, then
euer could haue been by all the teaching in the world, shewed to a soul
in fiue hundred yeares; and as I haue
often allready said *thy* words are
works; and therefor happy are the
humble, and peacefull of hart; for
these find such free accesse to *thee*,

that *thou* becommeſt indeed *all in all,
and aboue all* to them, while they ſeek
nothing but *thee*; and no perill is there to them in their way, as long as
they retain true *Humility* in their
ſoules. For who can hurt a ſoul, or
deceaue her, while ſhe adhereth
faithfully to *thee*? but if ſhe preſume
any thing of herſelf, what perills,
and danger ſhe is ſubiect vnto, and
ſhe apt to fall into, none can conceaue, much leſſe expreſſe. And to
this effect of ſhewing a ſoul how to
walk ſecurely, writeth thy great ſeruant the Author of the following of
Chriſt in his 21. Chapter of his third
book, whoſe words with great ioy I
read, and before *thee* ſpeaking too,
I will heere bring them in, beſeeching *thee* to inſtruct me in the true
practiſe of them. For they contayn
the way in which a foole cannot erre,
and without the practiſe of this, our
ſoules lye open to all the ſnares of
the Diuell: thine, and our enemy;
*No inſtruction did ſhe ſo much regard, ſo
frequently reflect on, or more volue, and*

,reuolue in her mind, nor more delighted in,
,then this that followeth, being meerly of
,her own finding, and obseruing in the said
,book; which she was familiar in; and no
,maruaile, considering the excellency, and
,necessity of it for the purpose which she hath
,mentioned, being the securing of one in a
,Spirituall course, thus therefor doth he say
,speaking to her soule.

- *Super omnia, & in omnibus requiesces
anima mea in Domino semper: quia ipse est
Sanctorum æterna requies. Da mihi dul-
cissime & amantissime Iesu, in Te super
omnem Salutem & Pulchritudinem, super
omnem Gloriam & honorem, super omnem
potentiam & Dignitatē, super omnem Sciē-
tiam & Subtilitatem, super omnes Diuitias
& Artes, super omnem Lætitiā & Exul-
tationem, super omnem famam & Laudem,
super omnem Suauitatem & Consolationē,
super omnem Spem & Promissionem, super
omne Meritum & Desiderium, super omnia dona & munera, quæ potes dare &
infundere, super omne Gaudium & iubi-
lationem, quam potest mens capere &
sentire: Denique super Angelos & Ar-
changelos: super omnem Exercitum Cœli,*

& super omnia visibilia, & inuisibilia, &
super omne quod Tu Deus meus non es.
Quia Tu Domine Deus meus, super omnia
optimus es, Tu solus Altissimus, Tu solus
Potentissimus, Tu solus Sufficientissimus
& Plenissimus, Tu solus Suauissimus &
Solatiosissimus, Tu solus Pulcherrimus &
Amantissimus: Tu solus Nobilissimus &
Gloriosissimus super omnia, in quo cuncta
bona simul perfecte sunt, & semper fue-
runt, & erunt. Atque ideo minus est &
insufficiens, quicquid præter Teipsum mihi
donas, aut de teipso reuelas vel promittis
Te non viso, nec plene adepto. Quoniam
quidem non potest cor meum veraciter re-
quiescere, nec totaliter contentari, nisi in
Te requiescat, & omnia dona, omnem-
que Creaturam transcendat.

Aboue all things, & in all things my
foule thou shalt euer rest in God, for hee is
the eternall rest of the Saints. Grante
Mee most sweet, and louing Iesus to Rest
in Thee aboue all Creatures; aboue all
Health, and Beauty, aboue all Glory, and
Honour; aboue all Powre, and Dignity;
aboue all Knowledge, and Subtility; aboue
all riches, and Arts; Aboue all ioy, and

gladneſſe; aboue all fame, and Praiſe; aboue all ſweetneſſe, and Comfort; aboue all Hope, and Promiſe, aboue all meritt, and Deſyre; aboue all Guifts, and preſents that Thou canſt giue, and impart; aboue all ioy, and Iubilee that the Mind can receiue, & feele: laſtly aboue Angells, and Archangells, aboue all the heauenly Hoſt, aboue all things viſible, and inuiſible; and aboue All that Thou art not my God.

For Thou my Lord God art good aboue all goods, Thou alone moſt high; Thou alone moſt powrefull; Thou alone moſt full, and ſufficient; Thou alone moſt ſweet, and comfortable; thou alone moſt beautifull, and louing, Thou alone moſt noble, and Glorious aboue all Things, in whom all goods together are moſt perfectly, haue beene, and euer ſhall be. And therefore it is too little, and not ſufficient whitſoeuer Thou beſtoweſt on Mee beſides thy ſelfe, or reuealeſt of thy ſelfe, or promiſeſt, whilſt Thou art not ſeene, nor fully obtayned. For ſurely my Hart cannot reſt, nor be fully contented vnleſſe itt reſt in Thee, and tranſcend all guifts, and Creatures whatſoeuer.

All things, desires, and loues are vaine,
　　But only that which tends
To God alone our cheifest good,
　　And all things ells transcends.
My soul therefor by this sweet Loue
　　shall day, and night aspire,
And rest in God *(all things aboue)*
　　My Loue, *and lifes desire.*
And while I liue , Ile neuer cease
　　To languish for his Loue *,*
Breathing, and sighing after him,
　　Till he *my life remoue.*
•For since I am not where I loue *,*
　　How can I comfort find ,
But only in the song of Loue
　　By Loue *to me assign'd ?*

　　　　　　　　　　　　loue
And　where so ere this　word is writt,
　　It yeilds a siluer sound ;
But if that word I misse in it
　　Me thinks I want my ground.
Nothing so simple can be penn'd
　　If it but treat of Loue,
But that it serueth in some sort
　　My sadnes to remoue.
And shall my soul by senselesse loue *,*
　　Which yet is neuer true,
Bestow more loue where it is lost ,

Then where't is only due ?
O no my God *, but rather lett*
    Such folly be to me
A meanes to vrge my sinnefull soul
    To Loue *more fernently !*
And henceforth lett me draw no breath,
    But to aspire by Loue
To thee my God *, and all my good*
    By whom I liue and moue.
No Stagge in chace so thirsty is,
    Or greedy of sweet Spring,
As is my soul of thee *my* God
    While I heere sighing sing.
My soul where is thy Loue *, and* Lord,
    Since him thou canst not find?
O cheere vp hart, be comforted,
    For he is in thy mind !
To him relation thou maist haue,
    As often as thou goes
Into the closett of thy hart,
    Thy griefs for to disclose.
As silly Lambes from rauening Wooluies
    For help to Sheapheards fly,
So shall my soul in euery case
    For help, and councell hye,
To thee my God *by humble* Prayer,
    In hope, and confidence,

That thou *my* Lord *willt succour me*,
    And be my soules defence.
And seeing that my God *is* rich
    How can I say, I'm poore ?
And hee *more myne, then* I *myne owne:*
    What can I wish for I more?
And in his Maiesty, *and* power,
    Much more I will reioice,
Then if of all in heauen, and earth
    I had commaund, and choice.
My God one *thing alone thou know'st*
    I feare and apprehend,
Which is my Lord *for to displease,*
    Whose mercies haue no end.
From all that doth displease thyne *eyes,*
    Be pleas'd to sett me free ,
For nothing ells in heauen, or earth,
    Do I d sire but thee.
And lett me rather death embrace,
    Then thee *my* God *offend,*
Or in my hart to giue thy *place*
    To any other freind.
Nothing would greiue my soul so much ,
    As in me to perceaue
Any affection in the world
    That thine *would me bereaue.*
I know thou *must possesse alone,*

Or els we are not thine,
In such good plight as we should be,
If light to vs did shine,
As thou desirest it should do
By grace our soules within;
For which are all the helps we haue
Intended, and haue been
Imparted, and bestowed by thee,
That we might liue alone
To thee who satiat'st pure soules
With ioyes that are vnknown.
And wo to them a thousand times,
Who interest haue in any,
Or haue deuided harts to thee,
After thy gifts so many.
For thou hast purchased our loue
At too too deare a rate,
To haue a partner in our hart,
Which iustly thou dost hate.
O this thy wrong makes Angells blush
O make it farre from me
Since that I am both body and soul
All conseerate to thee!
And I also n ill greiue with them,
To see thee haue such wrong
From soules selected by thy self
To sing with them the song

C

Of Loue, and praiſe to thee, O God,
  And euen in this place
To Contemplate thee, as we may,
  O ſweet and happy grace!
If we would dy vnto our ſelues
  And all things ells but thee,
It would be naturall to our ſoules
  For to aſcend, and be
Vnited to our Center deare,
  To which our ſoules would hy,
Being as proper then to vs,
  As fire to vpwards fly.
O lett vs therefor loue my God,
  For Loue pertaines to him,
And lett our ſoules ſeek nothing ells,
  But in this Loue to ſwimme,
Till we abſorpt by his ſweet Loue
  Return from whom we came,
Where we ſhall melt into that Loue,
  Which ioyeth me to name.
And neuer can I it too much ſpeak of, or
  it deſire,
Since that my God, who's Loue it ſelfe,
  Doth only Loue require.
Come therefor all, and lett vs loue
  And with a pure aſpect,
Regard our God in all we do,

And he will *vs protect.*

O that all things vpon the earth,
  Re-ecchoed with thy praise
My euerlasting glorious God,
  The Ancient *of dayes!*
And it I wish with all my soul
  Incessantly to sing;
But seeing this I cannot do,
  My sighes to heauen shall ring;
Yea if I writ out all the sea,
  Yet could I not expresse
The ioy, and comfort I do feele
  In what thou *dost possesse.*
No gifts, or grace, nor comforts heere
  How great so ere they be,
Can satiat my longing soul,
  While I possesse not thee.
For thou *art all my harts desire,*
  Yea all that I do craue,
In earth, or heauen now, and euer
  Thou *art all that I would haue.*
And I do wish with all my soul,
  That to thee *I could pray,*
With all my hart, and all my strength
  Ten thowsand times a day.
Lett peoples, tribes, and tongues confesse
  Vnto thy Maiesty;

And lett vs neuer cease to sing
      Sanctus, Sanctus *to thee.*

These are his words my *Lord God,*
which whosoeuer practiseth, shall
find a *Spirituall internall* life so easy,
sweet, secure, and void of all questions, that they will walk (euen in
this bannishment, where our life is
tearmed, and that most iustly, *a con-*
tinuall warrefare) with a heauenly *peace,*
and security. For to that soul who
proposeth nothing to herself but *thy*
selfe alone, aboue all gifts, and creatures, what can interpose it selfe for
to harm her, while she remaineth
thus confident, and humble between *thy Maiesty,* and her soul. Certainly so subiect doth such an one liue
to *thee,* and to all others in that maner, as shall be exacted by *thee,* that
there can nothing carry her away,
while thus it stands with her, to any
errour of vanity; and her *loue* is so
founded in true Charity, and practised with such *Humility,* and so in
her very soul, that nothing can in-

Iob. 7.
1.

terrupt her conuersation with *thee*;
Besides in a foul who walketh vpon
this secure ground of only seeking
thee, and only resting in *thee*, such a
diuine *light* doth shine, that she iudgeth according to the iustice of *thy
Diuine will*, and not accoiding to
sense, or custome, which in these
blind days takes place allmost in all
things of *true reason*; and this for want
of hauing recourse to *thee*, my *Lord*,
who art the only true *light*; and of this
defect it proceeds, that the diuine
ways of *Loue* are now held so perillous, and insecure, in which my *God*
thou hast an infinit wrong, seeing that
we were made only to *Loue*, and attend to the praise of *thee*, our *Lord*. It
is true, those who will pretend to
lead a Spirituall life, and yet seek not
in all to deny themselues, but desire
this gift, or this grace, this fauour, or
that comfort, lett them pretend for
their excuse in it whatsoeuer they
please, do often times miserably deceiue, not only themselues, but also
many others, and bring an internal

life wholy into a scorne, and contempt to the preiudice of their owne
soules, and also of many others.
But I wish that those that do this
simply by being for a Spirituall life
vnapt, might giue themselues to
that which by Superiors should be
☞ found most fitting for them, and not
be a cause that *thy* sweet mercy, and
goodnes should haue such wrong as
that other soules who were fit should
be hindred from hauing relation to
thee, by which their soules would be
turned wholy into *Loue*, by a vehement desire, and longing after *thee*,
that *one thing* that is only *necessary*; and
from this *house*.

(, To witt of the Benedictine Nunns at
, Cambray. The same she meanes for Paris
, issued thence, and where her natural Si-
, ster of the same Spirit Gouernes at present)
I beseech *thee* for thy own sake, keepe
this misery, which of all other is the
greatest that I can comprehend or
imagin.

THE EIGTH CONFESSION.

BLESSED *is that* Simplicity *(*faith my foremencioned Author in his fourth book of the Following of Chrift)that forfaketh the difficullt way of many queftions. Thofe are his words in his faid diuine Booke, where he proueth the way of *Loue* to be fo eafy, and fecure, as I haue before fignified. O how happy are they who follow *thee* in *Humility*, and *Simplicity* of *hart* ! for thefe haue few doubts which are the caufe of queftions. The more a foul is void of doubts, the more capable is fhe (fpeaking ordinarily) of thefe fecret wayes of the *Diuine Loue* For commonly her way muft be to refign herfelf to *thy* will. What roome is there left then for queftions ? Yet when it is *thy will,* that in a reall doubt fhe ask, *thou* teacheft her how to proceed in it, that it may be a help to her foul, and no hindrance, which fel-

dome happens when without *thy* leaue, and sending she presumeth to
endanger herself to be intangled by
falling out of one doubt, and que-
stion into fiue hundred others. Lett
it be with my soul, *O Lord*, as it is
said of Anna the Mother of *thy* Prophet Samuel, that she turned her
countenance no more towards *seuerall waies*. For hauing been taught,
and instructed by *thy* sweet mercy,
that *One thing* is to me only necessary, lett me not loose my selfe by following, or trying those seuerall waies
of which she speaketh. I haue as
thou knowst, my *God*, had sufficient
triall of them, to the great misery,
and difficulty of my poore soul for
that time; lett me now sing, and that
from the bottom of my soul, that it
is good for me *to adhere to my God*, *besides whom what is to me in heauen*, *or what
desire I on earth*? Only *thy selfe* my *Lord*
is desired by me, and only *thou* canst
comfort and satisfy me. It becometh
me to become wholy subiect to *thee*,
so that for time, and eternity, *thou*

Kings
1. 19.

Psal.
72. 28
Psal.
72. 25.

maist dispose of me as it pleases *thee*,
which with my whole soul I beseech
thee to do, and then I shall be as happy as I desire to be. *Thou* knowst
that since I was taught what it was to
loue thee, I neuer durst wish, or desire
any thing. For it appeareth plaine
to me, that my blindnes, and ignorance is so great, that euen in the
desire of that which in it self is good,
I may be extreamly deceiued. Only
thy selfe knoweth what is most to *thy*
honour, and best for me; and therefor whatsoeuer *thou* dost, shall be
best welcome to me. I desire no liberty to choose any thing besides
thee, because it suffiseth me if thou
wilt become *all in all*, and *aboue all*
to me; which desire I know is pleasing to *thee*, and therefor I beseech
thee inlardg my hart, and soul in
this longing, and sighing after *thee*
my only beloued. Lett my hart be
free to *thee*. For none deserues any
part therein besids *thee*. O how great
a greif would it be to me, if any created thing should be an impediment

to my being wholy *thine* ! Verily if I
should find, that my will were false
to *thee* by desiring any thing but *thee*,
nothing in heauen, or earth could
comfort me, while thus it stood between my hart, and *thee*. Giue me
therefor grace to be faithfull to *thee*,
who hath shewed such an infinit mercy towards me, as to lett me know of
the way of *Loue*, whereby all Crosses
become tolerable to me. Neuer
shall I be satisfied with blessing *thee*,
and thanking *thee* for this thy Mercy.
All, that loue *thee*, praise *thee* for me,
who am not worthy to name *thee*. Verily if I be now vngratfull to *thee*, it is
pitty *thy* earth should beare me. Yet
thou knowst my extreame frailty,
and therefor in all haue mercy on
me, and in the end saue me who putt
all my hope in *thee*. What shall I render for this *thy* infinit benefit bestowed on me ? Verily if I should be despised by all the world, as I iustly deserue to be, and should haue, and
feele the paines of all that euer haue
suffered for *thee*, and should be shutt

vp in a place which were only big
inough to containe me, and were
(as vnworthy of them, as indeed I
beleiue, and acknowledg my selfe to
be) debarred of the Sacraments, by
which such *grace* to soules, is so abou-
dantly imparted by *thee*, and were
held for a reprobate by all that are
most esteemed, and respected by me,
yet this were little to endure in requitall of this benefit which I haue
heere recounted before *thee*, and which I read with so much ioy, that it is
a solace to me in those difficulties
which are only known to *thee*, and
which would, if I were not exceedingly holpen by *thee*, quite ouerwhelme me for as it is well known to
thee, they do oftentimes make all my
strength decay so that I seem to be
left without so much as is sufficient
to go euen about the house; But
when I haue been thus dealt with by
thee, I haue been withall enabled
more feruently to praise *thee*; And
thy intention by it was apparant to
me. For by it *thou* didst so abate

pride that was moſt ſtrong in me, that all I could haue done, or deuiſed, or all other creatures with me, could not ſo much in many yeares haue humbled me, and haue bread ſuch a contempt in my ſoul of reſting, or taking delight in any thing which was leſſe then *thee*. Thus, my *God*, thou dealeſt with me, who, as I haue often ſaid, am not worthy to name *thy Maieſty*; and I ſee, if we will but giue our ſelues wholy to the ſeeking after *thee*, and diſpoſe our ſelues to ſuffer whatſoeuer it ſhall pleaſe *thee*, we ſhall not need to take care for any thing, but how to pleaſe, and ☞ praiſe *thee*. For *thou* wilt prouide Croſſes ſuch, and ſo much as will be ſufficient to make vs becom that, *thou* wouldſt haue vs to be; and in thoſe of *thy* ſending there is no danger, if we will endeauour to be faithfull to *thee*, and in them call often vpon *thee*. But when we place ſuch perfection in ſuffering, that we think we do nothing vnleſſe we be in matters of ſuf-fring; and are as it were loath to loo-

se time (as we think we do) by being
without occasion of suffering, we oftentimes faile in those Crosses which
we in such an *humor* do lay vpon our
selues or thrust our selues into without *thy* leaue, and disable vs from
vndergoing, and suffering those which then, or afterwards are by *thee*
thought to be fitter for vs; and we
seeing our selues to faile in these of
our own vndertaking, which we made our selues sure to be able to stand
vnto, grow to be deiected, yea sometimes euen so farr as to mistrust all
the course we had held before. For
we remembring we endured greater
matters before, (being of *Gods* sending, and through *his grace*) presu-
med now allso of that strength which
then we had, which was not, as we
conceiued, ours, but our *Lords*, who
rewardeth no works but *his* owne.
If we will therefor in all liue secure,
lett vs desire *nothing*, no not euen to
haue matter of suffering, saue so farr,
as it shall be *his* pleasure. For certain
ly to suffer for *him* is so great an ho-

nour, that one may iuftly efteem her-
felf vnworthy thereof; and yet it is a
thing fo neceffary to aduance vs in
the way of *Loue*, that we need not
doubt but *God* will prouide it when
he fees it fitt; and when he doth fend
it, come it which way it will, it will
be no impediment to a faithfull foule; but her only way, in this as well as
all other things, for to liue fecure, is,
☞ to be as a *little child* by humble Refi-
gnation, and lett *God* do with vs in
all what *he will*. For only by this
meanes we can liue in *Peace*, & auoid
the fnares of felfe-loue, and the diuell. For a foul that is apt to efteem
greatly of a little fuffering, and thinketh when she hath in it a flight occafion, that it layeth open the way to
great matters between *God*, and her
foul, *God* vfeth to lead her by another way, till she fee, and acknowledge her errour; and many times
she falleth into finn, and imperfection by her greedines to aduance
her foul by vntimely fuffering,
which at laft maketh her cry out to

thee; O Lord, how great is my blindnes, and frailty? help me therefor
my *God* in all these miseries, which
heere thy sinnefull seruant speaketh
of as a guilty person to *thee;* Great,
great is my folly, and frailty, and
therefor for help, and strength I fly
vnto *thee;* spare my soul sinning before *thee,* and lett me now begin to
loue only *thee;* help me in all, my *Lord*
for vaine is the help of man. I will therefor confide in *thee* my *God,* my mercy, *who* be Adored, Praised, and
Exalted, for tyme and eternity.
Amen.

Psal.
59. 13.

THE NINTH CONFESSION.

*L*EX *Domini immaculata conuertens*
animas; testimonium Domini fidele
sapientiam præstans paruulis; Iustitiæ Do-
mini rectæ lærificantes corda; præceptum
Domini lucidum illuminans oculos. The
Law of our Lord is immaculate, correcting
soules, the *Testimony of our Lord is faith-*
full, giuing *Wisedome to little Ones.* The

Psal.
18. 8.
9.

Iustices of our Lord be right , making harts ioyfull : the precept *of our Lord lightsome illuminating the eyes.* These my God are the words of thy Royall Prophet, which are (as it followeth in the same Psalme) *to be desired aboue gold, and rich pretious stones;* yea they *are more sweet* to a louing soul *then the honny, or the honny combe.* Lett this Law of *thine* conuert my soul, that it may become *one* of *thy little ones,* to whom the *grace* of *true Wisedome* is often promised by *thee.* Lett *thy Iustice* make my hart ioyfull. For in the performance thereof is true *Peace* only to be found They that liue according to this *thy Iustice,* do enioy such a *diuine* tranquillity, that it cannot be expressed by any pen whatsoeuer. None can walk in this path of *true Iustice (* in perfection) but the *humble.* Those find out in *thy light* what is *thy best will, and pleasure* in all things as farr as humane flesh will admitt , and perform *thy iust will,* as well as human frailty will reach. When we do perform any thing by this iust rule of *thy holy* *will*, we find an admirable effect thereof in our foul. This is that which by performing in all things we become truly fubiect to *thee*, and haue the merit of *Obedience*, which maketh all our actions fo noble before *thee*; and of which vertue of *Obedience* how much, or how little our actions partake, fo much, and no more do they deferue *reward*. Worthyly may *Obedience* be preferred before Sacrifice. For it is that which gouerneth heauen, and earth, and which only deferueth reward in *thy* fight. Happy are they who walk this way. For they haue a taft euen of the ioyes of heauen. For as they there obey *thy will*, fo thefe *thy* humble foules do alfo endeauour to do the fame. This *Obedience* to *thee* maketh the Angells as well content with their degree of Glory, as to be of the Seraphins, who are yet in a farr higher degree in *thy* Kingdome. This maketh the Saints content with theirs; this maketh foules on earth who afpire to *thee* with all their harts, to limit their

desires with *thy good will*, *and pleasure*;
and by this meanes they desire neither life, nor death; but in it conforme themselues to *thy* most iust
will; this maketh them desyre disgrace, nor Glory neither paine
nor health, neither Crosses, nor
comforts. This *Obedience* to *thee*, and
to Superiors for *thee*, made some soules pleasing to *thee* by liuing in the
wildernes, and others by liuing in a
Community, some by liuing to the
profit of their neighbour, and others
by liuing, and attending only to *thee*
in their soules, some by liuing in
high, and eminent degree, and hauing commaund ouer many others,
and some by being esteemed abiect,
and the very scumme of the world;
and these if they had of their own
choice, and election chosen the contrary state, would neuer haue arri-
ued to *true Sanctity*; Some also by
many paines, & Crosses come to *thee*,
& some only by an internall affectiō
to *thee*, hauing that in affection which others suffer in act, they also are
respected by *thee*; By which it appea-

res how great a subiection is exacted
by *thee* of thofe who defire to become vnited to *thee*, and neuer can we
profper in a *Spirituall life* vnleffe we
hearken to *thee*, and obferue euen in
the leaft things, what *thou* wouldft
haue vs do, and go that way *thou*
wouldft haue vs in all things whatfoeuer. For we may be fure *thou* willt
lead vs by the way of *Abnegation* which is the way of the *Croffe* which if we
will walk with *humility*, and *fimplicity*,
we shall with fecurity arriue at the
port of eternall Glory, and enioy *thee*
our only *beloued* in that degree *thou*
hadft ordained for vs from all eternity, liue we long, or dy we foone.
For only in *thee* can we be happy, and
by thy *meere grace* can we deferue to
enioy *thee*. What we ouercome is fo
done in *thy ftrength* that the glory is
wholy due to *thee* alone; and this I
find dayly, feeing that when I prefume of my own ftrength, though it
be in a thing which I haue often
ouercome, and many times farr
greater it feemes to me, yet I faile

in that, euen often to the offending
thee my *Lord* in an extraordinary maner. From this errour therefor my
God heerafter deliuer *thy* poore contemptible seruant, that I may praise
thee who art my *only strength*, and *hope*.
Lead me which way *thou* willt, so I
may blesse *thee* in all, and rest in *thee*
aboue all. From *thee* the strong receaue their strength, and in *thee* sinners that haue *nothing* of our owne
haue wherewith to supply all our
want; *thou* flyest vp with them who
by an ardent *loue* haue surmounted
all created things, and are firmely
vnited to *thee* in *Spirit*; and *thou* also
lendest *thy* sweet hand to *thy little*, and
imperfect ones who are of a good
will, to help them out of the mire,
and durt of passions, and inordinate
affections; In this mercy my soul
doth hope, and reioice, and I do in
my pouerty congratulate the perfections of others, beseeching *thee* to
make me partaker of their merits;
And aboue all out of the aboundance of *thy* owne store, giue me where-

with to retorn to *thee* for all the mercies *thou* haft shewed to my finnefull
foul. Lett me pleafe *thee*, and praife
thee, and defire no more but that *thou*
do with me whatfoeuer *thou* knowft
moft to *thy* honour. O that foules
would conuert their hart wholy to
thee the moft defirable beawty, to
whom if we compare all that is fair
which *thou* haft made, they will feeme
to be without all beawty, and light!
O if by *humility* foules would difpofe themfelues for the *Diuine Loue*,
what a reformation would there
quickly be in the whole world?
When I remember how many foules
feperate themfelues by finfull fin-
ning from *thee*, it pearceth my very
foul, feeing they forfak *him*, who is
an *infinit good* and a moft *amiable beawty.* Remember, O *Lord*, for *thy* own
fake our extreame frailty, and giue
grace that we may all conuert, and
return by *Loue* to *thy Diuine Maiesty*,
whofe mercies are aboue all thy works; for
which Glory be euer to *thee* by all for
time, and eternity. *Amen.*

Pfal.
144.9.

Pfal.
33.6.

THE X. CONFESSION.

*A*CCEDITE *ad Deum, & illumi-namini, & facies Veſtræ non con-fundentur. Come to Him, and be illumi-nated; and your faces ſhall not be confoun-ded.* Theſe words in our diuine Offi-ce are ſpoken not only by him, *who* by *thy* owne teſtimony was a man ac-cording to *thy* owne hart, but pro-ceeded from the *holy Ghoſt*, the *Spirit* of all *truth*, who ſpeaketh by the Prophets and Apoſtles for the com-fort, inſtruction, and illumination of ſuch as are true members of our holy Mother the Church, how weak, and contemptible ſoeuer they be; In the *beleif* of which *Church*, and in ho-pe of *thy* mercies, which I haue al-ways experienced to be great towards me thy poore ſeruant, I fly to *thee* in all my doubts, and obſcurities, wh-ich ſinne, ignorance, and imperfe-ction cauſe to my ſoul in her way towards *thee* her only deſired *Beloued*;

If he, by whom *thou* speak this, had excepted any, I should not haue dared to haue applyed it to my selfe; but as it is, I should do *thee* wrong, to fly from *thee*, when *thou* bidſt me *come, and be illuminated*; Though my ſinnes be great, yet *thy* mercies exceed all the ſinnes in the world; I will therefor come to *thee*, that *my face be not confounded*; I will approach to *thee* the only *true light*, that my ſoule may *Loue thee*, being guided by this *thy light*. In this *light* the glorious S. Auguſtin walked in an extraordinary maner, when he cried out with a moſt amorous hart; *Lord lett me know thee, and lett me know my-ſelfe*. Theſe two knowledges are inſeparable companions, and increaſe the one by the other. For who can know *thee* vnleſſe he know himſelf, vnleſſe he be taught by *thee*? Thoſe that would know ſome thing of *thee*, and would be fauoured by *thee*, for any end but to *loue thee*, and to learn to diſpiſe themſelues be in perill of a moſt dangerous ruine. For thoſe that walk

the *true way* of the *Croſſe*, deſire no
fauour but to be able without all
comfort to be faithfull to *thee* my
Lord God. Thoſe that haue done the
contrary (of which alas there haue
not been a few) are they which haue
brought a *Spirituall life* into ſuch a
contempt, that they ſhall haue in a
maner all the world about their eares
to cenſure them who enter into it;
one obiecting, it will put one out of
his wits, as they haue found by experience in many that ventured
vpon ſuch a courſe; Others ſay, Thoſe that affect ſingular waies of *Spirit*,
are in eminent perill of being delu-
ded by the diuell; Others pretend,
that thoſe (poore ſoules) pretend
ſuch perfection, that they ſlight, and
contemne the courſes of others, though their Superiors, and betters,
which is an euident ſigne, that they
are for all their pretence in a great
errour. Others obiect that they ab-
ſtract their affections from all the
world, and indeed would ſeeme to
be dead to all creatures, but that this
to be.

they do, that they may the better
loue themfelues;and while they feek
themfelues in a *Spirituall* maner in
the gifts, and graces of *God*, they fay
they are in more danger then thofe
that liue in finne, and wickednes.
Others alleadg, that the quietnes
they feeme to enioy in occurring accidents of difficulty, is either natural, or els becaus they pretending
to lead forfooth a *Spirituall life* are
bound in honour to endure them patiently, leaft otherwife they be proo-
ued to their difgrace to be but in an
imaginary courfe, which a *Spiritual
life* in thefe dayes is generally held
to be. Thus, and in infinit other
maners, as it is known to *thee*, I
haue in fome fort experienced
euen from them, whom I could
haue expected by the place they
bear, to haue been hartned in my
defyre of tending to *thee* to the vt-
termoft ability of my foul; but well
might they do it, feeing they were
alfo in place, where they were
bound to reform in me what was,

D

and is amis in my life, which I muſt
confeſſe is very much, but yet I confide in *thy* help. But in fine the obiections againſt an internall life are ſo
many, that much help is neceſſary
for a ſoul that ſhall be able to hold,
and go through with all obiections,
and difficulties in that kind. For one
ſaies; for want of this circumſtance,
all their life is in perill; and another
ſaith, that theſaid circumſtance may
ſtand with a true *Spirituall life;* but
yet that there is another matter, or
circumſtance which were neceſſary
to be reformed in their courſe; and
thus in their exceptions there be
ſo many mindes, as men ; and
yet none of them can ſay , there
is any ſinne in that which they alleadg for ſuch a mayn impediment,
the fault being indeed only that it is
not ſutable to their apprehenſion,
and experience in ſpiritual matters.
Thus therefor it ſtands with ſoules
that in theſe days would lead a *Spiri-*
tuall life; But thoſe who place all their
hope in *thee* my *God* , ſhall remain

stable as a rock, and in *thee* who art
their strength, and refuge they liue
peaceable, and content, hauing the
testimony of their conscience to be
their comfort amidst all oppositions,
and contradictions. But aboue all
obiections which I haue heard, that
goes neerest my hart, is when I read,
or hear, that it is perillous to walk
the way of *Loue*, and that (as some
would seeme to proue) no soul in
any other course, or state is in such
perill, as is a soul who giueth herself
to this study; But lett them affirm
that who will. For my part I will shutt
my eares from harkning to such men;
becaus nothing is more plaine, more easy, more secure, more pleasant
then the *way of Loue*. For that *way* of
Loue it cannot be called, if the soul
seek in it any thing but *thee* alone,
which these men would make it allmost impossible for one to do. But
thou knowst (my *God*) that in this *thou*
hast wrong. For it being *thy* own desire that soules should *loue thee*, and
thou hauing made them only for that

end that they might wholy attend,
euen in this life, to the *Loue*, and
Praise of *thee* alone; how can this way
be dangerous, where the only endeauour of the soul is that *thy* will be in
al fullfilled? who can doubt of *thy*
assistance, and help therein, though
we be able to do *nothing* of our selues?
Verily it cannot be doubted any more then it can be feared, that *thou*
willt cease to be *good* to *thy* creatures
which *thou* hast redeemed with *thy*
pretious bloud. Lett not soules therefor I beseech *thee* by any such
frights be brought into fear of walking this *noble*, and *amiable way*; but
lett vs sing in hope; *Dominus illumina-*
tio mea, & salus mea, quem timebo? Si
Deus pro nobis, quis contra nos. My Lord
is my light, and my Saluation whom shall
I feare? If God be with vs, what matter
is it who is against vs. Lett vs proceed
humbly, till we be admitted to enioy
thee the *God of Gods in Sion*, where *thy*
praise shall be perfected in vs. These
things therefor remembring, and recounting before *thee*, do strengthen

Psal.
26. 1.

my foul, that it fall not from the
ftedfaftnes, which is grounded, and
founded vpon *thee*; To harten, and
inconradg my foul by fpeaking, and
writing thus to *thee*, was the caus
why thefe things haue been written
by me, which I read, when I cannot
(for fome indifpofition in body or
mind) otherwife think vpon *thee*;
and when I am ouerwhelmed in any
mifery, it becometh moft tolerable
by hauing thus conference with *thee*,
who neuer difdaineft me; for which
all *Glory* be giuen to *thee*, *who art my*
Lord, and my God bleffed for all eternity.
Amen Alleluia.

THE XI. CONFESSION.

O My Lord, to *whom* I wil fpeak,
and before *whom* my hart shall
not be filent, while thus it ftands with
me, leaft the heauy weight of finnes
and my difordered paffions do op-
preffe my foul, and feperate it from
thee, the only *defire*, and *beloued* of my

hart. It behooueth me indeed to be silent, and that all created things be likwise silent to me, to the end I may hear the sweet whispering of *thy* voice, and attend in most quiet *repose* of soul to *thy Diuine Maiesty*, speaking to my hart. But this must be when my soul is drawn, and sweetly attracted by *thee* to attend to what it shall please *thee* to work in me. But now in these my sinnes which passions, and inordinat affections caus in me; My soul doth cry out in the bottom thereof, and call vpon *thee* who art my refuge, helper, and deliuerer in all these my afflictions, and miseries; and this my prayer is not reiected by *thee*, becaus *thou* art a bottomeless Sea of mercy. O when shall my soul see all impediments remoued, that it may be vnited to *thee*, and retorn to *thee*, from *whom* it had her being, to this end, that it might by pure *Loue* become capable of enioying *thee* for all eternity! What are all things to me without *thee*? Verily *nothing* but a shadow, neither can any

of them, no nor all of them together
satisfy, or comfort me. By *Louing,*
Pleasing, and Praising *thee,* as *thou*
wouldst haue me, shall I become
truly content, and happy, and by no
gifts, or graces, or fauours besids,
how great soeuer they be. Return,
retnrn my soul to *him* y^t only can satiat *thee*, and without *whom* all
things, as thou seest, are most bitter
and vnpleasing to *thee.* Only by *Hu-*
mility, and *Obedience*, can this be accomplished in *thee.* Humble, despise, and subiect thy self in all without exceptions, that *he* may take pitty on *thee.* Indeed, my *Lord*, I desire
thus to become for *thee*, For I may
truly say; *I was brought to nothing, and*
I knew it not; and I am as a beast before
thee; and yet allso I may say, y^t *I am*
allways with thee, and *thou* with me by
thy preuenting *mercy.* It is a poore
way to think to become honourable
by standing vpon our points; and yet
this is that which now is most in practise in these dayes. O how far is
this from the practise of *thy* Saints,

Psal.
72.23.
Psal.
72.

and seruants, who thought it their
greatest honour to be despised, neglected, reuiled, and contemned by
all this world, to the end they might
become honourable in *thy* eyes, my
Math. Lord, who hath said, that *blessed are*
5. 11. *we, when we are spoken ill of by men, and*
persecuted by them. Giue me this *true*
humility, I beseech *thee*, which maketh soules capable of receauing
this *thy* blessing promised to the *hum-*
ble, and those which serue *thee* for
Loue, whose ioy *thou thy self* art, and
who follow *thee* by the way of the
Crosse, which seemeth indeed contemptible in their eyes who do not
discern, nor discouer the hidden
treasure that lyeth in the *confusion* receaued, and embraced with the armes of *Loue* by a faithfull soul, who
seeketh *nothing* but to imitate her beloued, who died the ignominious
death of the *Crosse* to purchace her
loue, and to make her of an enemy,
to become an intimate, and inward
friend of this our heauenly Bride-
groome. This pouerty, and contempt

I fay, which *thy* little ones do vndergo in this life, (my *Lord God*) feemeth to the louers of this world, to
be an intolerable burthen; but thofe
that truly walk this way of *Humility*,
do find that in it lyeth the greateft
comfort, and fweetnes that can be
found, and enioyed in this world.
For *thou* beareft *thy-felf* the burthen
of the *humble*, and what toucheth
them toucheth the apple of *thyne* eye.
Nothing doft *thou* think to deare for
them, feeing all *thy* gifts, graces, fauours, and comforts, which *thy*
goodnes imparteth to them, they
vfe only to *thy* praife, and to the aba-
fing of themfelues vnder the feet of
all *thy* creatures, as moft vnworthy
of this *thy* mercy, of all of them. O
what power hath an *humble* foul with
thee, while she becometh totally fubiect to *thee*, euen as if no power of
willing, or choofing were giuen her
by *thee*, which while she doth, well
it goes with her before *thee*, and great
is the *liberty* of fuch an one, while she
only defireth, and feeketh *thee*. For

D v

in doing ſo, we do become capable
in an extraordinary maner of enioying *thee*, who though *thou* art not to
be ſeene in this life as *thou* art, yet an
humble ſoul is not ignorant of *thee*. For
her *faith* is wonderfully cleered, and
great is the knowledg of a ſoul, which
by *loue* obtaineth the heauenly *wiſe-*
Math. *dome* of *thee*, which *thou haſt hidden*
11. 2. *from the wiſe, and prudent of the world,*
and reuealed it to thy little ones, who
ſigh, and long without ceaſing to become vnited to *thy Diuine Maieſty*,
that *thy* Praiſe may be perfected in
them to *thy* eternall Glory. O how
frequently, and confidently do theſe
ſe ſoules fly vnto *thee*; and how often
are they euen amazed to ſee *thy* infinit ſweetnes, and moſt amiable beawty; Nothing is ſo preſent to them,
as is this their *Lord God*; yea my *God*,
ſuch a knowledg of *thee* doth *Loue*
caus in an humble ſoul, that it maketh her for a tyme neither to ſee,
feele, yea nor to think of any thing
beſides *thee*; but this in this vale of
teares is not of long continuance,

and hath many interruptions by reason of the strife between our *spir it* and our three enemies, the world, the flesh, and the diuel; but yet thy *grace* is in all occasions neere to our soul, and nothing shall blemish the purity thereof, if we humbly adhere vnto *thee*; and wholy mistrust our own forces (as we well may) and be confident in *thee*, who art so mercifull, and pittifull to those who presume not to haue any strength but *thee*. This *humble loue* is able to go through all difficulties, and to bear all burthens, and to sustain all paines and disgraces; becaus it seeketh only *thee* for her wittnes, *who* art her glory, her honour, and her crown, most neer, and deare to her, yea euen more present then she is to herself, and more hers then she is her own; and consequently being wholy forgetfull of herself, she only seeketh, and intendeth *thy* praise and glory, my *Lord God*, the *peace* of her hart, and the comfort of her soul. It seemeth to a soul at first that by deny-

ing, forſaking, neglecting, and deſ-
piſing herſelf she shall vndergo a
moſt grieuous Martyrdom; but by
approaching to *thee* my God, and
conuerſing with *thee* in a moſt *louing*,
and tender maner, and beſeeching
thy aſſiſtance in all her ſtreightneſſes,
and neceſſities, she findeth this way
☞ of *Abnegation* ſweet aboue all the
delights of the world. For by recti-
fying our will, and conforming it
in all to thyne, we walk an eaſy
way, and find a taſt of the ioy,
which they feele who are in heauen vnited to *thee* for all eternity,
with whom lett vs praiſe *thee* for euer
and euer. *Amen, Amen,* I beſeech
thee.

THE XII. CONFESSION.

Cant.
8. 7. SI dederit homo omnem ſubſtantiam
domus ſuæ pro Dilectione, quaſi nihil
deſpiciet eam. *If any Man shall giue all
the ſubſtance of his howſ for Loue, as if it
were nothing He shall diſpiſe it.* O my

Lord, and my *God*, to *whom* only all
Loue is due. Behold I defire with all
my hart to giue all for this *thy Loue*.
But alas what hath thy poore feruant
to giue *thee*? Verily nothing that may
deferue this *thy Loue*, as a requitall, it
being aboue all I am, or can fuffer,
or do. What can I giue *thee*, feeing
I haue nothing but what I haue receaued of *thee*? If I giue *thee* my body, and foul, what is that in comparifon of what I owe vnto *thee*? them
indeed I haue confecrated to *thee*,
but as due to *thee* by right, not as before appertaining to me, vnleffe I
would vfurp that which I was to re-
ftore to *thee*. What then shall I giue
thee for this *thy loue* fo much defired,
and fighed after by me? If I reflect
vpon my felfe, I haue nothing togiue
to *thee*; But shall I in this my extream
pouerty, and *nothing*, defpair of gaining, and obtaining this moft defirable *Loue* of *thee*, which reioyceth
my foul euen to name, and fpeak of
to *thee*? No, No, I will not feare to
obtain it of *thee*. For if that which I

haue, and am, be (as indeed it is)
short of deseruing this fauour from
thee (which is of being indeed one of
those who seek, desire, and *loue* only
thyselfe, and all others meerly for
thee) yet I will giue *thy-self* to *thee*,
who art all my ioy, and the only desire, and treasure of my hart; By *thy-
self* I will praise *thee*, and in *thee* I will
hope to be transformed into that
loue which shall be swallowed vp in
thee for all eternity. Only to *loue thee*
was my soul created, and only by
being turned wholy into *loue* can my
soul be truly happy. What can my
soul desire out of *thee*, seeing *thou* art
only *Good*, and the most incompre-
hensible *beawty, which* the Angells are
neuer satisfyed with beholding,
being infinitly delighted while they
are wholy turned into the pure *loue*,
and Praise of *thee*. We heer in this
vale of teares do sigh with teares in
our eyes; longing to enioy *thee*, and
to be freed from the occasions of offending *thy* sweet Mercy. We (I say)
sigh, and make our moane to *thee*

while it is dayly said to our soul, *where is thy God?* Yea, euen I say so, speaking to *thee*; where art thou my *Lord*, and when shall I without all mean be vnited to *thee*, that my loue may be intierly bestowed vpon *thee*, and nothing but *thy selfe* liue, and raign in me, that without ceasing I might Praise, and Adore *thee*, the most glorious, and *amiable Maiesty*, to *whom* all knees ought to bow; and prostrat: we ought to acknowledg our meere dependance of *thee*. O how plaine dost *thou* sometimes shew it me, that I am *nothing*, and lesse then *nothing*, while I stand before *thee*, neither can any thing be by iustice due to me, otherwais then by *thy* meere mercy ifI should neuer, so faithfully serue, and praise *thee*! For what can they challenge of *thee*, who were not able so much as to moue, or be without *thee*, much lesse do any good, or suffer any thing purely for the *loue* of *thee*. Giue me therefor, that I may haue to giue vnto *thee*, seeing by my selfe I am not able according to my deſire to *loue*, and praiſe *thee*; by *thy-self* without ceaſing I will praiſe, and *loue thee*, and in *thy* mercy, and grace ſhall my ſoul hope to become truly pleaſing to *thee*; heere I wil by *faith* adhere to *thee*, and by *loue* my ſoul ſhall both day, and night aſpire vnto *thee*, till at laſt by the merits of thy death, & Paſſion, *death ſhall be ſwallowed vp in victory.* In the meane time lett the *loue* of true *Charity* inſtruct me, which is more ſtrong then *death*, that I may faithfully ſerue *thee*, though it be not yet admitted me to enioy *thee*. Lett me reſt in *nothing* but *thee*, and lett *thy* name be my defence, and comfort, which to hear, and behold, doth aboue all earthly things delight, and refresh me amidſt the ſtormes of temptations which daily aſſault me. O my *God*; indeed *thou* art that vnchangeable *light*, which I euer come to conſult with in all my afflictions, and neceſſities; and behold (to my vnſpeakeable comfort, and ſtrength) I heare *thee* giuing anſwers, by *ſaying this*, and *commanding*

1. *Cor.* 15.55.

that, and this I do by resorting to *thee* often! This is that which delighteth me, and I fly as speedily to this pleasure as I iustly may from all the actions which are imposed vpon me euen by necessity it self, and it exceedingly reioiceth me to sitt down and sigh after *thee*, and by speaking, and writing to, and of *thee*, to become at least for that short time forgettful of all things besids *thee*. This is that which maketh the grieuous burthen of flesh, and bloud tolerable to me: in which liuing my soul by sin cometh often (to my grief aboue all other miseries) wounded to *thee*, crauing and beseeching, for *thy* own sake that I may neuer faile to beg, and find mercy of *thee*, *whom* to offend is the only misery that can in this life befal me, and no pain, or difficulty is feared by me, saue so farr as it may (considering my extreame frailty) be a meanes to make me offend *thee*. O *Lord* do not reiect me, though I haue neuer done any good, and am so farr from truly louing *thee* ! I will now take the aduise giuen me, to ¹ *fly*, be *silent*, and *quiet;* and I will howerly come to learn the *ſong* of *Loue*, and Praiſe of *thee*; teach me to know my ſelf., and to know *thee*. I deſir that *wiſdome* which deſpiſeth all for *loue* of *thee*, and only yᵗ *knowledg* do I wiſh for, that ſecurely guideth a ſoul towards *thee*, and into *thee*. Thoſe that *loue thee*, and ſeek only to pleaſe *thee*, are thoſe which haue a ſight in part, of what in heauen we ſhall enioy cleerely for all eternity. O what *knowledge* doth a truly *louing* ſoul obtain of *thee*, and how much is her *faith* confirmed in the greatnes, beawty, and infinitnes of *thy Maieſty* ! but alas they are drawn down by the weight of their corruptible fleſh, and ſometimes euen forgett what they haue with the eyes of their ſoul ſeen, and learnt of *thee*; and ſometimes fooliſhly think they are ſomething, till they feele the effect of this their miſery, and offend *thee* through their pride, and forgettfullnes of their own *nothing*, and of the greatnes of *thy Maiefty*, which pride aboue all things deliuer me from, I befeech *thee*, becaus it makes foules fo odious before *thy felf* and all that *loue thee*. Lett me giue all Glory to *thee*, *who* without any defert of myne, haft thus fweetly with *Grace* preuented me, for which be *thou* euer by all Praifed, and Adored. *Amen.*

THE XIII. CONFESSION.

O *Lord, whofe Power, Maiefty,* *and Wifedome* haue no end, haue mercy on me finner, and giue me leaue to fpeak vnto *thee* my *God,* and aske *thee*, whither men are pleafing to *thee*, becaus they abound with human knowledg. And behold *thou* affirmeft; *no*; but vnhappy are they who can pearce into all things, if they be ignorant of *thee*. Lett me therefor *loue*, and then I shall not be ignorant of that *knowledg* which maketh foules fo pleafing in *thyne* eyes, to wit, *knowledge* of *thee*, and my ſelf. O *Loue* which inlightneſt ſoules, and inflameſt harts w th chaſt *loue*, flow into my ſoul ! This *loue* is honourable *wiſedome*, and though the enioyers thereof be accounted fooles by the wiſe of this world, yet thou haſt another opinion of them; and their humble ſoules find much fauour in *thy* pure eyes, my *God* ! With this *Loue* did thoſe abound, of whom S. Paul ſpeaketh,

Hebr. 11. y t they *went vp, and down in goats skinnes, needy, deſpiſed, hidden in dennes, and caues, of whom the world was not worthy*; yet ſome of *thy* Saints became very honourable, and glorious euen in the eyes of the world, the which was forced to acknowledge *thee* great in, and by them; and there was no reſiſting of *thy wiſedome* ſpeaking by them, amongſt which of theſe thy ſeruants was the great S. *Auguſtin* Doctor, and *light* of *thy* Church, a moſt ardent *louer* of *thee* my *God.* Hee in thoſe books o c his that I hau ſeene, turneth his ſpeaches ſo to *thy*

Maiesty, that his words thereby become sweeter then ordinary; and while he declareth his own misery, he giueth to vnderstand to vs *thy* most abundant *mercy*, that all that desire to *loue thee* my *God* may (being inuited by him) praise *thee* with him, and for the fauour shewed by *thee* to him. O that all to whom *thou* offrest the fauour of bestowing on them *thy* diuine *Loue*, (if they would after sinning by true Humility dispose themselues for it) would become (by *his* example) gratefull to *thee*, and *loue thee* as *thou* wouldst by them be *beloued!* O how soon dost *thou* by *thy* Grace wipe out the sinnes of such, who now detesting their former il liues do striue by humble *loue* to become gratefull to *thee* for *thy* preuenting Mercy? O *Lord*, my *God*, though *thou* hast forgiuen me much, yet I am farr from *louing thee* much; Those who now enioy *thee*, y^t haue heertofor beene sinners as I, be they Intercessors to *thee* for me, and be *thou* euer praised for *thy* infinit mercy by all

thy *Maieſties* creatures for euer and
euer; *Amen.*

THE XIV. CONFESSION.

O Lord *my God*, who ſweetly diſ-
poſeſt all things, giue *thy* poore contemptible creature leaue to
ſpeake vnto *thee*, *who* art the only deſire of my ſoul, and my hope from
my youth, and entierly *beloued* of my
hart; To *thee* I will ſpeak, and write,
not as to one a far of; but to ſtirr vp
my ſoul to *Loue thee* alone, and to
draw occaſions out of all things to
praiſe, and exalt *thee*, whoſe mercies
are aboue all *thy* works. To whom
ſhould I make my moane in all my
miſeries, but to *thy ſelf who* art my
God, and All, and *who* art neerer to
me, then I am to my ſelf? To whom
ſhould I go to be inſtructed but to
the fountain of all *wiſedome*? Behold
men change their mindes, and almoſt euery man differeth in opinion
from another, in matters that are in-

different, and so great is my ignorance, and blindnes naturally, that vnlesse *thou* instruct me, I shall allwaies wauer, and neuer come to any true *perfection of knowledg.* They stand at too great a hazard, who confide in themselues, and cast not their hope wholy vpon *thee.* All creatures are vnstable, and those that seeke not *thee* aboue all creatures, but putt their trust more in men then in *thee,* will find no true *peace* in their soules. O that I did truly *Loue!* for by *Loue* only my soul shall becom capable of vnderstanding *truth.* *Loue* is humble, peaceable, subiect to *thee* in all things. The soul that *loueth thee* is more conuersant in heauen then on earth; and what heere she of necessity must admit of, serues to her rather as a cessation then any consolation. The soul that *Loues,* findeth occasion in all, and by all things to praise *thee* my *God,* and to humble it self. Such are willingly subiect for *thee,* and do see how odious it is to *thee,* to see that subiects should contemn, contradict, or withstand *thy* power in Superiors, and make their imperfection a colour for our sinnes. If it be right between our soules, and *thee*, we shall gladly obey *thee*, speake *thou* or ordain *thou* by whom *thou* pleasest. Teach me therefor to obey; for *thou* only canst instruct me what true *humble Obedience* is. If *thou* do not teach me, I may perhaps giue to Cæsar what is *thyne*, and deny to giue Cæsar what is due to him by *thy* will. Let me obey therefor for *thee*, and in order to *thy will*, and with an internall regard of *thee*, *whose* due is all the *subiection*, and *loue* that can be giuen by my poor soul. Open the eyes of my soul that I may see what *thou* exactest in all things. Instruct me by whom, and in what maner *thou* pleasest; So I may but know what *thy* will, and pleasure is, it suffizeth *thy* poore seruant. Giue me grace to obey *thee* my *God*, with all that *Loue thee*; for euer, *Amen*.

THE

THE XV. CONFESSION.

O *Lord my God*, what soul that truly *loues thee*, can complain what difficulties soeuer she endures, or how great a desolation soeuer obscures her soul, or how great paines soeuer she sustaines, seeing *thou*, *whom* she *loueth* more then her life, and self, art always the same, beholding with an amorous, and *louing* eye, the *louing* soul, afflicted by *thee*, or by *thy* permission, rather to try her fidelity, then to oppresse her with such a burthen that might separate her from her only *beloued*; for seeing nothing is dreaded by her but to be seperated from her *God*, she holding *humility*, and confidence, *thou*, O *Lord*, wilt neuer permit her to be ouercome. For *thou* makest the quarrel *thyne* own thus fought by vs, and the *victory* ours, though indeed gained by *thee*, not by our own selues. O how happy am I in *thy Power*, and

Glory? Verily, though I were to return to my own *nothing*, yet I could not account my self void of an infinit happines, seeing my *God*, *who* is more mine then I am my own, would remain, and be the same in all *Wisedome*, and *Maiesty*; This is the repose of my labour, and the crown of my glory, in which I will exult in my greatest calamities, and miseries. O *Loue* lett me liue in, and to *thee*, and dy to all created things whatsoeuer! O *Loue*, *Loue*, liue, raign, and wholy possesse my soul! Consider not, O my *God* so much what I am, and haue beene, as what I desire to be. O *Lord*, my *God*, and all my *Good*.

THE XVI. CONFESSION.

O Lord my *God*; Father of the poor, and true comforter of all afflicted soules; be mercifull to my desolate hart, and stirre it vp to perfect *loue* of *thee*, that I may simply seek *thee*, and sigh after *thee* my beloued abfent, and not for the forrow I feele at the prefent. Lett me long to embrace *thee* with the armes of my foul, and think it litle to endure any mifery in body, or foul, to be at laft admitted into the boofom of my *Loue*, *faireft*, *and choiceft of thoufands.* Lett all fall down, and adore my *God*, the glory o^f my hart. Lett the found of his Praife be heard to found, and refound ouer all the earth.

O when shall my foul, hauing tranfcended it felf, and all created things, be firmely vnited to *thee*, the *beloued* of my hart, refting in *thee*, not in *thy* gifts or graces, and neither defiring, nor taking any fatisfaction in any work, or exercife whatfoeuer, but in all paines, temptations, contempts, defolations, pouerties, and miferies either of body, or mind, conforming my felf to *thy* fweet *will* for time and eternity, *who* as iuftly as euer *thou* didft any thing, mayft condemne my foul eternally to hell, from which nothing but *thy* meere mercy were able to saue, and deliuer me; and dayly I should incurr this sentence, if *thou* didft not out of *thy* goodnes euer help, and protect me, *thy* sinfull seruant!

This only I desir, this only I ask, that I may in all things praise *thee*, and that I may desire no comfort, but to be able without all comfort, human, or diuine, to be true to *thee*, and not offend *thy Haiesty*.

THE XVII. CONFESSION.

TO *whom but to thee*, my *Lord* should I fly in all temptations, and Crosses, whose armes are open to embrace, all repentant sinners, and whose hands are lifted vp to giue a *sweet benediction* to all in misery; If I either had, or desired to haue any *friend*, or comforter but *thee*, I could not with confidence fly into *thy bosome* for succour in this which is now faln on me. If euer *thou* hadft re-

ieƈed any that hoped iu *thee*, I might
feare; but as it is, I will fing in my
affliƈion with teares in myne eyes to
thee, and neuer leaue to hope in *thine*
aboundant mercy.

Is it much that I serue *thee*, whom
all creatures are bound to serue? and
we are so happy in being subieƈ to
thee; that no *liberty* is to be compared
to the *happines* of depending of *thee*.

THE XVIII. CONFESSION.

WHEN thou art present, O my
God, then my hart reioiceth, and
in *peaee* singeth *thy* praises; but when
thou hideft *thy* beawtifull *face*, my
foul becometh exceedingly obfcured, and troubled; yea euen ouerwhelmed in darknes, and mifery, in
which cafe long remaining (which
is moft iuftly permitted by *thee* for
my humiliation) what shall I do to
liftvp my foul to *thee*, but as one fick
with *loue* of her abfent beloued? to
fpeak with him it is impoffible, the
E iij

diftance of place is fo great; but yet
she may hear others who fpeak of
him, which a little mitigateth her
mifery, though while *he* is abfent al
is irkfome to her, becaus the delay
afflicteth her hart; But yet, is she
without all comfort? No; for she
may write to, and of him; and if none
will carry it to her *deare beloued*, it
shall remain by her, that *he* may fee
at his return, how she languished for
loue, and could take comfort in nothing that all creatures could offer,
or propofe to her foul, while she poffeffed not what she only *defired*; her
life by *loue* being more with her *beloued*, then where she liued; for which
caus, she heareth, and yet mindeth
not what is faid, vnles perhaps they
treat, feelingly of her abfent loue,
and fpeak in his praife; She feeth,
and yet cannot take comfort in what
she beholdeth; She fleepeth, but
her hart waketh; and in fine while
she cannot enioy her *beloued*, nothing can fatisfy her *vnquiet* hart.
Thus my *God* euen fenfual, and vn-

reafonable loue tranfporteth a reafonable foul; But if naturall loue be
of that force, what doth that foul
feel, whom *thou* haft wounded with
thy pure Loue? And of what power is
that *loue* that is feconded by *thee*, *who*
art the fountain of all *true Loue*, and
fweetnes? What shall I fay of a foul
y^t hath *tafted how fweet our Lord is*? Verily she yet liuing, dieth a thoufand
deaths, becaus she feeth herfelf fo
far from poffeffing *thee* my *God*,
whom none can fee, and liue; nor
none enioy as *thou* art in *thy felf*, till
thou free her of the heauy, and finful burthen of flesh, and bloud;
And allthough *thou* doft admitt her
longing, and fighing after *thee* alone,
to, I know not what, nor can I expres, the vnfpeakable ioy, and delights, which I fay *thou* fome times
admitteft her to; (therein not like to
the louers in this world, who oftimes
reiect where they are moft beloued)
yet out of *thy* care of her, *thou* fud-
dainly turneft away *thy* face, at which
till she *loue thee* for *thy felf*, she will

become troubled, and too too impatient in the delay which *thou* makest of returning to her again; the which if she bear with a resigned mind, making *thy will* her law, aboue all the desires of her hart; and sitt solitary like the turtle doue, *thou* willt in good time assuredly return., and being absent wilt be present to hear her prayers, and see her teares shed for the sorrow she conceiueth to offend *thee* her desired *beloued*, *whom* she would *loue* withall her hart, with all her soul, and all her strength, and praise *thee* day, and night without ceasing, as it beseemes a soul languishing with *thy loue.*

THE XIX. CONFESSION.

REMEMBER, *O my God*, that *thou* madst me for to *loue thee.* Why therefor dost *thou* permit me to offend so sweet a Goodnes? Although none do find *thee* in an extraordinary maner in the bottome of

their soules, but thofe that ferue *thee*
my *God* for *Loue*, and walk by the
way of the *Croffe*, yet I do confidently affirm, that *thy* yoke, and burthen,
thy Law, and *thy Croffe*, are not by
far fo heauy, greeuous, and burthen
fome, as be the painful wayes of
fin, which feeme to be fweetned
with fome delights, but in the hart it
proueth more bitter then gall; whereas *thy* yoke being born by a truly
louing foul, is many times heauy when
thou leaueft her, thereby to shew her,
how little she can do, or fuffer of her
felf, and that she may glory in *thee*,
and not in her own power, and humble herfelf, and not preferre herfelf
before others; when I fay *thou* plea-
feft to leaue her thus as it were for-
lorne, she feeleth indeed a great
burthen, and nothing can comfort
her, till *thou* her defired, and only
beloued return. For she hauing forfaken all for *thee*, and hauing tafted of
thy fweetnes, faieth with the Pro-
phet; *Turn away myne eyes that they fee* Pfal.
not vanity; leaft like a dog she re- 1.8.37

turn to her vomit; and after hauing
had a glimering of *thy light* , she , becaus she feared she should not be
able to ſuſtain *thy* chaſtiſements, and
should forgett, and looſe herſelf by
theſe tribulations, and deſirous that
she might be happily enabled to enter the more fully into *thee* , and fearing (I ſay) her own frailty , she thus
againe crieth out to *thee* by theſe
other words of the Pſalmiſt, ſaying;

Pſ.
187.2.
*Domine Deus ſalutis meæ ; in die clamaui
& nocte coram te.* O Lord God of my ſal-
uation , *day* , *and night haue I cryed after
Thee.* For who but *thy ſelf* can comfort a ſoul that indeed neither ſeekes
nor deſires any thing but *thee* my
God? O when shall I ſpend all my
ſtrength, and forces in ſinging *thy*
Praiſes! Who would ſett their harts
vpon any thing but *thee* , ſeeing *thou*
haſt made all other things ſo hard to
be obtained, that we might ſeeke
only *thee* , for whom we were made,
and whoſe *Loue* we may more eaſily
obtaine then any thing els whatſoeuer? O lett me *Loue thee* , who only

for that end didſt create me! We
would haue that which is worth nothing, and many times greiue for
the loſſe of that which would but
cauſe vs perplexity, and trouble to
haue; In the meane time neglecting
that which *thou* ſo infinitly deſireſt to
beſtow vpon vs, to wit, *thy loue*, then
which nothing is ſo good, or ſweet,
or that bringeth ſuch *true peace* to the
foul.

THE XX. CONFESSION.

WITHOVT *paine*, it is impoſſible (O my moſt *Amiable God*) to
liue in *loue*. But if the difficulties which *thy* true friends, and ſeruants feele, were weighed with the miſeries
of thoſe, who rather ſeek to pleaſe
themſelues, and others then *thee*—
there would be found an infinit diſ-
parity. For *thy yoke is ſweet, and thy
burthen light* to the *ſimple*, and *humble*,
and to thoſe who ſerue *thee* for *loue*,
and whoſe ioy *thou thy ſelf art*, and

who nothing els but *thee*, my *God*, do
seek for, in *time*, or *eternity*, These
I say, are despised, contemned, afflicted, pained, tempted, troubled,
and many times sit sorrowfull with
a heauy hart, and sad countenance;
But *thy will* being their law, and *thy*
disposition their consolation, I may
boldly affirme, that in all this they
suffer nothing, in comparison of the
fond louers of this world; becaus
thou being euermore present to them
then they to themselues, dost when
thou seest *thy* time refresh their souls
with the *light*, and comfort of *thy*
grace; yea seeming to be euen pro-
digall of *thy* sweetnes, to such as abide faithfull to *thee* in their tribulations, and hope, confide, and glory
in *thee*, and not in themselues, and
who take occasion in all they see,
heare, suffer, ouercome, to humble
themselues vnder *thy* mighty hand,
and blesse, and praise *thy* Iustice, and
Mercy in all things whatsoeuer;
Amongst which number admit me
poor, and contemptible sinner, to

thy greater glory (for this *thy* Mercy)
from all creatures, for euer and euer
Amen.

THE XXI. CONFESSION.

O My *Lord*, and *my God*, remoue al impediments between
thy Goodnes, and my poor foul,
that I may *loue thee*, *who* only defer-
uest all *loue*, and honour. Giue me
an humble, and *peacefull* hart, that
thou maift inhabit therein, as *thou*
defireft Suppres in me by *thy* fweet
Grace the fin of pride which maketh me as yet fo odious to *thy Diuine*
Maiefty. O if we did but by true *Hu-*
mility abafe our felues, what beames
of *true light* would fhine in the bottome of our fouls! O what *amity* is
there between *thy Diuine Maiefty*,
aud an humble foul! Nothing but
Humility could haue drawn *thee* down
to the earth; and only *Humility* can
make vs capable of being drawn by
thee vp to heauen. The truly *humble*

conuers familiarly with *thee*, and *thy* Saints; They preſuming nothing of themſelues can do all things in *thee* who ſtrengthneſt them. And *thou* art ſo chary, and tender of the humble, that what concerneth them, *thou* eſteemeſt to concern *thy owne ſelf*, and euen *thy* own hart; And they thinking they do *nothing*, do by *thee* do all things. Many vnknown to the world, and of no eſteem wirh it, ſhall before *thee* haue the honour, and merit in the next world, of that which now other men boaſt of, and attribute to themſelues. For the *humble* liuing ſtil in their own *nothing*, giue all glory to *thee*, by *whom* only all good is performed, in the mean while *thou* enriching them of *thy* meere Mercy with *thy* Merits. O happy exchange, *thine* for ours, durt for the moſt pure gold What is all we can do? Verily nothing. Enrich me therefor poor begger with ſome-what of *thyne*; At thy feet I lay whatſoeuer *thou* giueſt, or haſt giuen me: Giue, or take away as *thou* pleaſeſt, ſo *thou* do not blot mē

out of the book of *life*. Open to me
knocking at the door of *thy* Mercy.
I haue been fiue and twenty yeares
,(this fignifieth her age at the, writing
,heerof, as that she was then fiue and
,twenty years olde) in my infirmity
of moft loathfome finnes ; behold
my mifery, and take pitty vpon me.
Sonne of Dauid ! I defiled that foul
that was made to *thy* owne Image,
and liknes; haue compaffion on her,
who hath no other *friend*, or comforter, but *thy felf* the only defired of
my hart. For *thy* owne fake be pro-
pitious to my fin for it is much. Nothing that I haue done can I alleadg
to *thee*, which hath deferued any reward in thine eyes ; Onely defires,
of which manie burn in hell, they
being little without good works.
Giue her to drink who withers away
for want of *thee* the fountain of al
fweetnes. I will powre out my foul
before *thee*, that at leaft I may comfort my felf with relating to *thee*
my finnes, and miferies. Behold all
my ennemies triumph ouer me, of

whom moſt eaſily in all temptations
they get the victory. Fight for me;
or els I know not what will become
of me ; giue me *true Humility* by
which all things are eaſily ouercome , and all *thou* exacteſt , moſt
perfectly accomplished by vs *thy
Maieſties* poor creatures. Giue *thy
ſelf* to me , who hath *nothing* of her
own to offer *thee* ; and if *thou* giue
me *thy ſelf*, I am as rich as I deſire
to be ; and if *thou* shouldſt beſtow
vpon me all *thou* haſt, or can create,
it would be little to me , vnles I
poſſeſſed *thee*. By *thy ſelf* I Praiſe
thee, *whoſe* name doth not be-ſeeme
the mouth of a ſinner. O let me
Loue, or not liue ! I giue my ſelf
to *thee*, *whome* alone I wish for, and
deſire with all the forces of my hart,
and ſoul. O my *God* , how neere
thou art to vs , ready to heare and
receaue our prayers and petitions?
Behold *thy ſweet prouidence* sheweth
it ſelf in all things ! O how long
shall my *God* be thus forgotten by
creatures ! When wilt *thou* by *Loue*

be by all sought after, as *thou* ought-
est to be by vs?

THE XXII. CONFESSION.

O My Lord , let all things praise
thee ! Let *thy iust will* be our
law. Let subiects humbly obey in,
and for *thee*. For inferiors contend-
ing, and withstanding their Superiors
in that *thou* wouldst haue them obey
in, is most odious in *thine* eyes, and
nothing they can do will pleafe
thee, vnles they will heare *thy* voice
as well by others, as from *thy self*. For
it is not so much the greatnes of the
action that *thou* regardest, as the being don by vs in that maner *thou*
wouldst haue it don by vs , and in
nothing can wee obey *thee* as wee
ought to do, vnles wee first regard,
and intend *thee* in that which by
vs is accomplished ; and a Superior
reflecting on his owne authority,
rather then on what in *thy* behalf
he ought to exact ; in that case or

cafes , and rather on what by his power he can command , then on what according to *thy* pleafure were beft to be done, rather gouerneth in his owne power then in *thine*, and the effect (vnles it be very ftreight and right betweene his fubiects harts , and *thee*) will confequently be more human then *diuine* ; and the Superiors while fenfible of their honour abufing the power giuen by *thee* , doe yet loofe what they would haue. For their fubiects often looking vpon rather what is defectiue in the Superior, then vpon their owne duty , both of them faile in their duties to *thy* dishonour, *who* fo fweetly haft difpofed of all things, if we did not peruert *thine* order , with feeking , not *thee* , and *thine* honour, but our own , and our felues , from which mifery bleffe vs, I befeech *thee* for *thine* own fake, that *thou* maift be glorified both in the *Commaunders,* and the *Obeyers.*

THE XXIII. CONFESSION.

O *How happy* are thofe *thou* in-
ftructeft in *thy Law*, and in
whom it goeth ftreight between
their foules and *thee*. For their only
care is to pleafe and praife *thee* in all
things. Thefe *humbly* obey for *thee*,
and fee how dangerous it is to refift
thy will in any thing how little foeuer.
But very much muft we ftriue to
humble our felues, if we defire to
know, and ftand vnto the things
that are exacted of vs by *thee*. For
nothing is able to inlighten our
blindnes, but *thy* Grace shining in
an *humble* foul. If we knew neuer
fo much and could do wonders, if
we had neuer fo great guifs of nature and grace, yet could we not
thereby become pleafing to *thee*,
vnles withall we were diligent in
the exercife of *true Humility*. O giue
me this *Guift*! For none of himfef
is able to attain to it. My *God*, make

me truly *humble* that I may be wholy *thine*. Let me by *Loue* adhere to *thee*, that all impediments may be remoued between my foul, and *thee*. Let all created things be to me as if they were not, as to their becoming any impediment between my poor foul, and *thy Godnes*, that fo I may not be hindred by any thing from being vnited to *thee*. For this *thou* maidft our fouls, that by *thy Grace* we might return to *thee*, *whom* by finne we had ftraied from, and that *humbly* feeking to *Loue thee*, and vfing all things created only to this end, that we may at laft find, and poffeffe *thee*, who only art able to fatiate vs; and therefor miferable are we, when we feek any things befide *thee*, from which doing I befeech *thee* defend vs. *Amen.*

THE XXIV. CONFESSION.

Non in solo pane viuit homo , sed in *Math.* omni verbo quod procedit de ore Dei. 4. 4. These are *thine own* wordes, my *Lord,* which I rehears before *thee* (to *whom* I powre out my hart and my soul) with vnspeakable ioy , hoping that *thy* word shall be a *light* vnto my feete , *that* I may auoid the ginnes and snares , which the world , the flesh , and the diuell doe lay to catch and intrap my sinful , and weak soul. *Thy* words indeed are sweet becaufe *thou* speakest *Peace* to the hart , and giuest by them strength to the soul. It is well known to *thee* why I do thus dilate my self in speaking and writing to *thee* , my *Lord* and my *God* , rehearsing to *thee*, to *whom* all things are manifest , the desires , intentions , and afflictions, or comforts of my hart. For as *thou* well knowst , if I should not when I enioy some more *interior light* set

down in writing some thiugs which
I may peruse at other times that
are of obsurity, I should be apt to
forget to praise *thee*, yea and euen
wither away with the grief and
anguish which by *thy* sweet permission ouerwhelmeth my soul; be *thou*
blessed for all ; *who* take away. I
beseech *thee*, or giue, as it best pleaseth *thee*, from thy poore seruant,
only depriue me not of *thy Grace*.
So I may *Loue thee*, I care not what
happeneth to me. Let *thy will* be
done for time, and eternity. Root
out of my soul that pride which
maketh me so far from being that
thou wouldst haue mee to be. My
desire is great to Praise, *loue*, honour,
and *truly* serue *thee*; but my power is
so little, that none hath been lesse
faithfull to *thee*, then I ; But where
doth the liberality of *thy infinite mercy*
extend it self more willingly, then
where there is greatest pouerty and
misery ? Though I be poor yet my
Lord is rich; though I be in al blind-
nesse , as to the discerning of *truth*,

yet my *Lord* is *light* it felfe. To *him* therefore I will approach, that in his *light* I may fee *light.* I will begge of *thee,* that I may become capable of gloriyng in *thy* riches, and then nothing shall be wanting to me, feeing my *Lord* poffeffeth in *himfelfe* all good things. Be *thou* my *Lord* what *thou* art, and I a miferable finner cafting mine eyes vpon the earth doe cry to *thee* to bee mercifull to my finnes. I fitting heere in the shadowe of death, morne, and lament, that I haue made no more haft to conclude an euerlafting league and *peace* with my *Lord God,* to *whom* now my foul doth afpire day and night without ceafing. o my *Lord* when I remember what *thou* haft done for me, I faint and faile to fee how vngratefull for it I haue been and am to *thee* ! What didft *thou* meane to helpe me, and recall me from my finnes, when I leaft thought of *thee*? And not content with that, *thou* didft alfo by means of *a faithfull feruant* of thine, R.F.
Baker

make my ſtate which was ſo heauy a
burthen to me through my fault,
and ignorance, to become ſo delightfull to me, that I may and do
truly acknowledg, that *thy yoke* of
Religion is ſweet aboue all the delights, and pleaſures of the world,
and *thy burthen* ſo light, that croſſes,
paines, afflictions internal, and external born, as *thy burthen* are moſt
light and eaſie, and cauſe more *true
peace* to my hart, then I can expres,
which be it ſaid to *thy* honour: and
grant me to humble my ſelf in al,
that I may grow ſtil more and more
pleaſing to *thee*, *who* art the only deſire of my hart, and comfort of my
ſoul. Let his inſtructions of whom
I ſpeak to *thee*, according to his deſire ſtill more and more inflame my
loue vnto *thee*. Be *thou all in all*, and
aboue all, vnto me. If *thou* teach not
my ſoul to *loue*, in vain is the
endeauour of man ſpeaking and
preaching to me. Let me heare
thee by him, and let me not ſo
harken to him without; that I grow
                                    deaf

deaf to *thee who art within.* *Thy* words
are works. Either fpeak by others
for our good, or by *thy* felf in the
moft *interior* of our foul. O happines, that there fhould be fuch a
capacity in vs of hauing relation to
thee in all things ! Al things created may faile vs; but *thou who* only
canft fatiat our harts, canft neuer
change or alter, but art ftil the
fame, and *thy* yeares fhall not faile.
Thou teacheft a foul true Humility
and folid vertue. In *thee* nothing is
negle&ed; *thou* art the *Maiefter* of
Perfection. *Thou* teacheft the fimple,
humble, and *louing* foul *thy* wayes
and giueft her hidden *Manna*, in
the ftrength of which fhe may walk
euen to the hous of her *God* where
fhe fhall praife *him* for euer and
euer. *Qui ambulat fimpliciter*, *ambulat*
confidenter; *who walketh fimply, walketh*
confidently; if we *loue thee*, all will co
operat to good, which graunt to *thy*
own Praife. Amen.

THE XXV. CONFESSION.

Io.8.2

Omnis populus venit ad Iesum, & sedens docebat eos. All the people came Iesus, and hee sitting taught them. Can I heare' and consider these words written by *thy* best beloued Disciple, and not euen melt into tears of *ioy*? If indeed any had been by *thee* my *Lord* reiected, I might haue feared, and that most iustly, remembring my past, and present sinnes. But to put me out of feare, and doubt, thy holy Euangelist saith, *Omnis all.* To *thee* therefor I will fly, and of *thee* I will learn, how I may Please, Praise, and *loue thee*, and how by *true Humility*, I may dye to my self and all created things: Hereby wholy to liue to *thee* my *all*, and onely *good*. *Thou* knowst that my soul without ceasing doth long after *thee*, and to see it-self free from all that which is a hindrance to my perfectly *louing thee*. O *Loue* of my *Lord God*, how

forcible art *thou* in a pure soul? O
who will giue *thee* to me, that my hart
may be purged, and purified, thereby to becom a pleasing habitation
for my *God*? O *Lord*, who art *Goodnes it self*; can there be found any
ioy, comfort, or true content in any
thing but *thee*? Can there I say?
for as for me; far hath it been from
thee to permit any thing but *thy*
self to be sweet to mee. O all ye
that think it a burthen to be obliged by your Profession to tend to
great Perfection, and fear the punishment of our doing the contrary, raise vp your harts, and remember what it is that our *Lord* exacteth
of you by this your *Profession!* and
this as it may seeme at first a seuere
exaction, so remember wel, and consider (I say) what it is, and your
harts will rejoyce, that feare our
Lord. It is, O it is, to *loue*, without
bounds or measure; It is to leaue
your self, that you may find *God*;
It is to fly from the world that you
may hear our *Lord* speaking *peace* to

your soul ; It is to submit, and subiect your self wholy to *him whose will*
none can resist, but as they are permitted by *him*; It is to be subiect to
euery liuing creature for *him* , *who*
submitted *himsef* to the *death* of the
Cross, that we might become capable
of enioying *him* ! This is that *he* exacteth of vs , who haue dedicated
our souls wholy to *him* ; This is
that he requireth , which though
at first it seeme a burthen to perform , yet that which seemeth so,
is indeed quite otherwise, as we shal
find in effect , if we performthatout
of *loue*, which out of *his loue* to vs, *he*
exacteth of vs. For what is sweeter
then to *loue* ? Yea and to *loue him*,
whom the more we *loue* the more it
becometh delightful to vs to *loue*;
the more strict our obligation is to
him the lighter is our burthen we
haue to beare; For *he* doing all that
he hath done for vs to bring vs into
this state to oblige vs to *loue* , doth
also , if we be not the hindrance,
oblige *himself* to giue vs this *Diuine*

loue of *his*, which is able to vnite a poor contemptible creature to *his Diuine Maiesty*, *whom* we are not worthy to name. O sweet and most desirable *yoke!* well maist thou be said to be sweet, thou bringing *true* and perfect *liberty*. For *loue* maketh light all burthens, and sweetneth al labours; and to them that *loue*, it is easy to suffer any aduersities for their loueds sake! O let me being obliged by *thee* to *loue*, let me, I say, through *thy* mercy obtain this *loue* of *thee*, wch maketh a soul in all things grateful, and faithful *to thee!* Let me not offend *thee* in my miseries, and then come as many as pleases *thee* ; for I account that only a misery, to wit, to offend *thee*. Let all things praise *thee*, and let me in all praise *thy Diuine Maiesty*, with them that *loue thee*. Behold, Fire, Sea, Snow, Thunder, Lightning, Hail, and rhe Spirits of storms do *thy will;* and yet I in all contradict it, who am capable of *thy loue*, and am inuited to *loue* so many ways by *thee* my

God. O let this thy *loue* wholy poſ-
ſeſ my ſoul , that all that is within
me may bleſſe *thy* holy *Name!* I renounce into *thy* hands all that is in
me contrary to this *thy loue* ; Let it
wholy conſume me that I may be-
wholy turned into *loue* , and that
nothing els may be deſired by me.
Let me be drowned, and ſwallowed
vp in that of *Diuine loue* , in which
my ſoul may ſwim for all *eternity,*
neuer more by ſin to be ſeparated
from *thee.* O when wil this day come,
that I may return to *thee* my beginning! When will *thy Glory* appeare ?
When ſhal death be ſwalowed vp in
victory, that I may without ceaſing
Praiſe *thee* my *God,whoſe name* I write
with no ſmal comfort, though otherwiſe I be ſo drie, that I can ſcarce
think vpon *thee.* To heare *thee* named, or to write to, or of *thee,* refreſh-
eth my ſoul in al her miſery , and
to it I flye from the thoughts, feares, and cares which as *thou* knowſt
often oppres me for my humiliation, who for my pride deſerue iuſt-

ly to be reiected for euer by *thee*;
But in such case I hope both liuing
and dying, that thou my *Lord* art
my *God*, my Mercy; and what is
wanting to me, I shal aboundantly
posses, if I confide only in *thee*,
which grant that I may not faile to
do, *who* only art to be Adored for
all *eternity. Amen.*

THE XXVI. CONFESSION.

Luk 15.1.

ERant appropinquantes ad Iefum Pu-
blicani, & peccatores, vt audirent
illum? *There were finners and Publicans
approaching to Iefus that they might hear
him.* This is writ in the Gofpel of
this day *my Lord*, which doth much
comfort my finfull foul, flying to
thee for help, and fuccour in the
neceffities wherein I daily languish.
For none didft *thou* euer reiect, neither fick, as witnes the Leapers,
and diuers others which were ab-
horred by men for their loathfom
difeafes, nor the deformed, nor the

E iiij

blind, nor the lame, nor the poor
and contemptible, no nor the sinners
whose loathsome sinnes made their
souls much more deformed in *thy*
pure eyes, then any disease could
make a body in the eyes of the be-
holders. But why do I presume to
speak to my *God* in this simple maner? verily my *Lord*, only presuming
of the most aboundant fountain of
thy mercies, do I thus refresh my soul
with recounting these things before
thee becaus these places in the Ghos-
pel which treat so particularly of
thy receauing, and forgiuing sinners
doth particularly appartain to me,
who hauing among them found *grace*
in this kind before *thee*, I do likwise
in these things I read, find that which
putteth me in hope of the continuance of *thy Mercy*. Behold I desire
now to conuert my hart wholy to
thee, and to becom totally in all
things subiect to *thy Diuine Maiesty*.
Let *thy Grace* affist me. For it is not
any thing I can do, can saue me. The
Angel that hath care of me, praise *thee*

for me, and assist me with his intercession for me. *Thy Mother* hath been
indeed a *Mother* to me (for which
be she honoured for all *eternity*, as it
beseemeth so great an *humility* to
be.) she vouchsafing to take pitty on
me poor miserable sinner, for all
which Praise be to *thee* my *God* and
All, for all *eternity*. *Amen*.

THE XXVII. CONFESSION.

P*Atientia pauperum non peribit in fi-*   Pf. 9.
nem. The patience of the poor shal   19.
not perish in the end. O *Lord*, my *God*,
seeing the way of the *Cross* is the
way that al in this life must walk,
of what state, or dignity soeuer they
be; none exempted from suffering,
some in body by paines, and sicknes;
some by pouerty, and want of ne-
cessaries; some by loss of friends;
some by the disloialty of such whom
they confided in; some by loss of
their goods by fire, wars, and the
like, and some by their own indis-

cretion , vnwarines , and want of
foresight falling into disgrace; some
by setting their affection where it is
reiected , grow desperate mad; and
some therby liuing in perpetual
discomfort become woful murthe-
rers of themselues ; some fortune
frowning vpon them, haue al things
go contrary to their desire ; and in
fine, no place , no person , nor any
condition can be free from suffering
in this miserable life. But shal we
think this was ordained to be thus
by *thee* , by chance , or becaus thou
dost not *loue* what *thou* hast made?
No , *God* forbid we should euer
think so ; but that which made *thee*
ordain it so, was only to the end that
we being proued or tried, as gold in
the furnace, should thereby become
capable of *thy* pure *loue*; the which
if we could obtain , easy would it
be to suffer any thing which *thou*
permittedst to happen vnto vs. For
as for some of the *Crosses*, which happen in this life , we are the caus of
them our selues ; and by them we

not only suffer paine , but also detriment in our souls ; becaus they proceed from our yeilding to sin, and giuing way to our passions, and inordinat affections , therby becoming a slaue to sensuality ; ouer which we should be absolute maisters, if we did, as we ought , concur with *thy grace.* And verily, my *God ,* to *whom* I speak and write with much content to my soul , *thou* by this meanes *inlightning* me with that *diuine truth* which leadeth in some sort to *thy self,* and much inflameth my hart with a most ardent desire of *thee* the only desire of my soul , to *whom* I aspire day and night , without ceasing, in my simple maner : Verily I say that I am ignorant how it is possible to proceed with any confidence, or comfort in any thing , if our foundatiõ be not founded in *thee* by a sincere intention. For til I resolued, what difficulties soeuer ther by I endured , to make *thy wil mine owne* and *thy* Disposition, my consolation, I found no stability in any thing, or ☞

F v)

exercise whatsoeuer; and since that time I haue found certeinty and *quiet* in all the vncerteinty of contrary occurrence. For if *thou* be intended in al our actions, what should we fear? For we only intending and desiring *thy* honour in all things, how can we doubt but that this by *thee* in al things wil be accomplished, seeing that which *thou* dost desire and *wil* we should seek, and intend (to wit *they* honour) which is only aimed at by vs? Can we imagin *thou* wilt faile on *thy* part, we desiring to do what lyeth in vs? No, No, but confidently we may hope, that nothing shal be wanting to vs; and *thou* kwnowst, my *Lord God*, that when any thing happeneth, which seemeth so to derogate from *thy diuine honour*, that it greiueth my hart, *thou* presently quietest me with these words saying to my soul. *Vacate & videte quoniam ego sum Deus, exaltabor in gentibus, & exaltabor in terra.* Be quiet, and see that I am God: I shall be exalted among the Gentils, and shall be exalted in the earth.

Psal. 45. 11.

With thefe words, I fay, *thou* com-
fortest my foul, For though I haue
defired to make an exchange with
thee, that I may take only care to
feeke *thy* honour in al things', committing the care of my welfare to
thee, yet in thofe things, which happen as I think contrary to *thy* honour, I ought to conforme my wil
to *thy* fweet difpofition, or permiffi-
on, and not difquiet my foul vnder
any pretence whatfoeuer. For the
quiet and humble hart is the place
where *thou* delighteft to dwell. *Thou*
who art the *God* of *Peace*, giue me that
true *loue of thee*, which only bringeth
true Peace, and bleffe this *thy* little
flock, and efpecially thofe in it
who are by their patience and difcretion helpers and furthers to *true*
peace and concord in this poor Conuent of *thine*; My moft deare Lady
thy Mother, and mine by *thy* fweet
Mercy, pray to *thee* for this hous
of hers, as alfo our good Angels,
who haue care of vs. Saint Michael
who was fo zealous of *his* honour,

Saint Raphael who guides vs in the way of *thy* Law, Sanit Gabriel, who brought vs the happy tidings of *thy* coming into this world, to reconcile vs sinners to *thy* heauenly Father, Our most holy Father S. Benedict, our Mother S. Scholastica, as also S. Ioseph, S. Iohn, S. Thomas, and S. Gertrude, in whose hart *thou* didst delight to dwell; and also my beloued Father S. *Augustin*, whom *thou* hast giuen me in a particular maner, to be a help to me in doubts and feares, and an incouradgement by his books to hope for pardon for my innumerable sins, and as a *fire* are al his words to inflame me to seek after and aspire to *thy diuine loue*, and to wish only, that that may wholy posses my soul, which grant for his sake, as also *thine owne*, who art Blessed for euer. *Amen.*

THE XXVIII. CONFESSION.

IN CINA cor meum Deus in te- Pfal.
stimonia tua ; Ecce concupui man- 118.
data tua ; in æquitate tua viuifica me.
Incline, my God, my hart to thy testimo-
nies , and in thy truth quicken my soul.
For behold my soul doth exceedingly couet to performe *thy law.* For
thy law is *truth*, and the effect thereof is Iustice, and *Peace*, and Ioy in
the holy *Ghost.* When I remember
how I haue strayed from *thee* by sin,
I become ashamed before *thee.* But
when I consider *thy* Mercy I hope
stil (notwithstanding what is past) to
become through *thy grace*, which so
sweetly preuented me , pleasing to
thy Diuine Maiesty. O *Lord*, inlighten
my soul obscured by sin and ill
customes ; inlighten it that I may
walk the way of Iustice, and *Truth*,
which is the way wherof *thou* speakest by Esaie the Prophet, in *which a* Esaio
foole cannot err, as he affirmeth. O let 35. 8.

me by *true Humility* become a *fool*
according to his meaning , let me
become as a *bittle child* , that I may
be capable of entring into the Kingdom of Heauen! Certeinly we ought
to liue so subiect to *thee*, that we haue
no election of any thing, as pretending our selues , for time , or eternity ;
And also we ought to haue in our
soul such a relation to *thee* , that in
thy light , in *thy truth* , and wholy according to *thy will* , we perform all
we do , and out of that respect omit
what we omit. O my *God* , let me,
I say , walk this way of *Loue* which
knoweth not how to seek it-self in
any thing whatsoeuer ! Let this *Loue*
wholy posses my soul , and hart ;
which I beseech *thee* may liue , and
moue only in, and out of a pure,
and sincere *loue* to *thee* , *who* aboue
all ought to be *loued* and desired.
Let this *fire*, which *thou* camst into
this world to send , and willedst it
should burn , consume me wholy
into it self , that forgetful of my
self, and al created things, I may be

mindfull of *thee*, my *Lord*, and my *God*. It is *thy* promise, that where sin hath abounded, *grace* shall super-abound, that the riches of *thy* Mercy may appear and shew it-felf to the Glory of *thy holy Name* ; which Mercy, I beseech *thee*, extend it self to me, that I may praise *thee* for euer and euer. O that *thy* pure *loue* were so grounded and established in my hart, that I might sigh, and pant without ceasing, after *thee*, and be able in the strength of *this thy Loue*, to live without al comfort and consolation, human, or diuine, therby to become the more conformable to *thee*, the *beloued* of my soul ! O how happy are they that truly *loue thee* ? Certainly, whatsoeuer they suffer, it is very tolerable to them, beeaus *he* for *whose loue* they suffer, is their helper; Indeed, my *Lord*, *thou* art a hidden *God*; but yet not so hidden from our soul, but that in some sort we haue therin according to our poor capacities, not only a *taft*, but also a *fight* of *thee* ; for as euen *thou thy* self haſt ſaid; *Bleſſed are the cleane of hart, for they shall ſee God.* O ſight to be wished, deſired, and longed for! becaus once to haue ſeen *thee* is to haue learnt al things. Nothing can bring vs to this ſight, but *loue.* But what *loue* muſt it be ? Not a ſenſible loue only, a childish loue, a loue which ſeeketh it-ſelf, more then the *beloued.* No, but it muſt bc an ardent *loue,* a pure *loue,* a couradgious *loue,* a *loue* of *Charity,* an humble *loue,* and a conſtant *loue,* not worn out with labours, nor daunted with any difficulties. *O Lord,* giue this *loue* vnto my ſoul, that I may neuer more liue, nor breath but out of a moſt *pure loue* of *thee,* my All, and only *Good!* let me *loue thee* for *thy ſelf,* and nothing els, but in and for *thee.* Let me *loue* nothing in ſteed of thee. For to giue al for *loue* is a moſt ſweet bargain; for *Loue is as ſtrong as death.* O that this *thy loue* might flow in ſuch aboundance into the harts of al capable therof, that the ſong of thy *loue,* and Praiſe might conti-

Mat. 5. 8.

Cant. 1. 8.

nually be heard through out al the earth! O what do we do louing vanity, and feeking a lye? What do we abufing the moft noble capacity of our fouls by defiring that which paffeth away like fmoak? What do we louing that which is more changeable then the Moon? Can any thing fatiate our harts but our *God*? Can we find true repofe out of *him*? Is any thing worthy of our *loue*, but that Goodnes which is *loue it-felf*, and *whom* the more we *loue*, the more we are able to *loue*; becaus for *loue*, *he* made vs capable of *loue*? But alas, my God, my foul was in honour, and I knew not it; I was compared to beafts, and by fin became like to them, or worfe then they. Is this my requital for al *thy loue*? Is this excufable that my foul made by *thee* to be delighted with the food of Angels (which is *loue*) fhould delight it-felf with the bread of fwine? O is my hart able to rehears this before *thee* and not through exceffiue grief break in funder? Could I in my

nature not abide to be disloyall to
one whom I found to be a faithful
friend to me ? and can I endure to
remember my disloyalty to my *God*?
Could I with ioy vndergo for my
friend, disgrace, and difficulty, and
can I endure nothing for my *God*?
Was the abfence of a deare friend
intolerable to me, and can I abide
to fee my felf ceafe at any time to
figh and long after my *God*? O no
my *God*, let that be far from me, I
heere renounce before heauen and
earth al inordinate affections to creatures. Place with *thy* own hands *thy*
loue in their room, that it expelling
thence al rhat now is therein difpleafing to *thine* eyes, *thou* maift
thy felf wholy poffes me giuing,
and diftributing my affections, and
difpofing the paffions of my hart
according to *thy* fweet *will*, which
only is iuft, only holy and true in
it-felf. O how finceare then are our
affections, when we loue our neighbour only in, and for *thee* ? Then
we pitty not one, and are hard-

harted to another according to the
inclination of our peruerfe nature,
but behold *thee* in al , and confequently willingly ferue and affift al
for *thy loue;* then we do not shew our
feues meek only to our friends ;
but alfo to thofe by whom we fuffer
moft contradiction, and gladly vpon
all occafions extend our charity. For
there is no *true friendship* but that
which is founded vpon *thee* , and
which is maintained without impediment to *thy loue.* This is only the
loue of *Charity* : which *Charity* knoweth not how to repine, to be angry,
to be exceptious , to be inconftant,
to be troublefom, to be fufpicious,
or iealous ; for it regardeth *thee* in
al , and defireth *thee* aboue al ; It
taketh al in good part; it wondreth
not to fee men exceed in words,
finding it-felf, fo often to offend in
deeds; it beareth al things , it hopeth al things , and it confideth in
thee aboue al things; *it* wisheth only that *thy n ill* may be performed in
al and by al creatures ; by which

meanes it retaineth true *peace* in al
that happeneth. O giue me this *thy
loue* which worketh such wonderful
effects in an *humble* soul! Giue it to
me, and I wil aske *thee* no more. Let
it posses my soul, that nothing but
thy self may be *loued*, or desired by
me. Can *thy Goodnes* find in *thy* hart to
see me thus languishing for want of
thy loue, seeking my self in al things,
and not being able out of *true loue*
to suffer any thing? It is true *thou*
hast made my soul to loath all created things, and hast shewed me most
plainly that all is vanity and affliction of *spirit*, saue to *loue thee*, and
that nothing is permanent vnder the
Sun, and that vain and inconstant
is euery creature liuing, so that I
cannot, me thinks if I would (so am
I held by *thee*) desire the friendship, or fauour of any creature; but
this is not sufficient for me; and
therefor take pitty on me begging
and beseeching *grace*, and mercy of
thee; It suffiseth not me that my soul
refuseth to be comforted, but I must

also remember my *God*, that with *his loue* my soul may be inflamed. Art *thou* ignorant that my soul hauing had through *thy* sweet *Mercy*, a *tast* of *thee*, cannot find comfort in any thing but in inioying of *thee*? O no, this is as al other things are, most manifest to *thee*; and if *thou* wouldst not haue had me thus for *loue* to importune *thee*, *thou* wouldst not haue made me incapable of being satisfied without *thee*; This which I say, I do not speak of presumption, but out of the vrgent desir of my hart, which hath resolued to conuert it self wholy to *thee*; *thou who* didst bid me to aske, hast promised I shall receaue; *thou who* didst bid me knock, hast promised it shall in time conuenient be opened to me; which howre, O my Lord, when shall it be, that without ceasing I may praise *thee*, and neuer any more offend *thee*? Til which be granted me, I wil sigh after *thee*, and in my hart in the bitternes of my soul, I will cal vpon *thee*; and somtimes I wil also being

enabled, and inuited thereunto by
~thee~, sing ~loue~ songs to my *well-beloued*,
~who~ is euer within the hearing of me.
For ~thou~ art not like the louers of
this world (vpon whom that loue
yet which is only due to *thee* is often bestowed) heere to day and a
far off to morrow: No, no, thus it
is not between *thee* and *thy louers*. For
though *thou* triest them, that their
loue may become more pure, yet
~thou~, seeing them begin to faile vnder their burthen, dost quickly cast
~thine~ eyes vpon them, and with the
sweet dew of *thy Grace* refreshest
them, that by these changes their
loue may grow more strong, and be
firmely established in *thee*, *who* art
that *only thing* which is only necessary for me, and which only I require of *thee*. Let this *thy loue* work
in and by me, becaus *thou* rewardest
no works but *thine* own, and let me
loue thee, as *thou* wouldst be *beloued*
by me, I cannot tell how much *loue*
I would haue of *thee*, becaus I would
loue thee beyond all that can be imagined

gined, or defired by me; be *thou* in
this as in al other things, my choo-
fer for me, *who* art my only choice, *Paſ.*
moſt deare to me; *Glorious things are* *86.3.*
ſaid of thee my Lord and *God*, the
moſt abſolute, and amiable beawty;
the more I shall *loue thee*, the more
wil my foul defire *thee*, and to ſuffer for *thee*. Let me *loue thee* for *thy*
ſelf, and not any thing inſteed of
thee; and let my whole ſubſtance by
thy loue, and Praiſe be conſumed in
me, that I may return pure vnto
thee, *who* be by al in Heauen, and
Earth bleſſed and *loued* fer euer and
euer. *Amen.*

THE XXIX. CONFESSION.

O My God, my only *beloued*; me
thinks I heare *thee* ſweetly
checking my foul with theſe words;
(when vnder what pretence ſoeuer)
I pretend by my care, or vnreaſona-
ble ſolicitude, that more then *One*
thing is neceſſary to my foul, therby

G

falling into that multiplicity which
is fo apt to dimme, and obfcure our
foul, and fo contrary to a pure tending to *Thee* our only *good,* and to a
remouing of al impediments between our fouls and *thee* by tranfcending al created things whatfoeuer) thefe words (I fay) *thou* often fpeakeft to my hart; *Quem quæris*
mulier , *Viuentem cum mortuis ?* Whom
doft thou feek woman, one liuing amongst
the dead? But *Lord* I anfwer *thee* now
in al defir, and *humility* of hart, that
I feek nothing but *thy felf*, no guift,
no comfort, or fweetnes; no friends
but *thy felf*, and *thy* heauenly Citte-
zens; no power but of wishing that
thy wil may be my *law;* no honour but
thine? no confolation but that I may
in folitude, and filence al the dayes
of my life be able to liue without all
confolation *human*, or *diuine*, no re-
creation by conuerfation, or other
bufinefs, or imployments, but fo far
as it is neceffary to beare vp my *fpirit*
to attend vnto *thee* more ferioufly at
conuenient times , and rather let al

Luk
24..

necessary distraction, by help of *thy Grace* serue, as a meere cessation; then by the least affection to them, or comfort in them, they should become an impediment to my aspiring to *thee.* For this is a rule *thou* knowst hath been giuen me by a faithfull seruant of *thy diuine Maiesty,* who indeed gaue me most generall instructions, that we might not be tyed to him, or any other creature, but might being left more free to *thee,* fly the more freely with wings of Diuine *loue,* which carieth a soul euen in human flesh aboue all that is not *thy very self* ; of such force is *thy Grace* concurring with our will, which is by naiure capable of an infinite extent towards *thee*, when as it neither seeketh, intendeth, desireth, willeth, nor resteth in any thing, but *thee*; This (I say) was his generall rule that if we did not do things with affection, they would cause vs no hurtfull distraction, which grant may be so vnto me I beseech *thee, who* am not able with-

R.F. Baker

G ij

out much, and often diuerting my
mind to indifferent things, to attend
to *thee* in my foul at other fitting
times, and this by reafon of my great
weaknes of body and head. Let al
this imperfection in mee, humble
me and let it be no impediment to
my truly *louing*, feruing, praifing
thee, and adhering only to *thee*, which
is my only defire by al I do, or omit.
Let not my greeuous finnes paft, or
prefent too much deiect, or trouble
mee; but let them ferue to humble
my foul, and be a meanes totally to
fubect it to *thee* and al others, fo far as
it is *thy wil* it should be. Let me praife
thee in al, *whofe* prouidence, and
care hath been fo infinit great towards me *thy* moft contemptible creature, the which verily I may, and
muft confeffe, and acknowledge
to *thee* moft particularly in this,
that *thou* haft fo particularly, and
plainly as *thou* haft done for my humiliation, difcouered my finnes vnto me, wherby I might know and
confeffe my obligation to *thee*; and

with al compassion on the sinnes, and imperfections of others, which they also are permitted to fal into, that rising vp, their *loue* may be the greater, when they remember it before *thee*; And this I may add to *thy greater glory*, that *thou* didst reserue this knowledg of my sinful, and miserable state from me till by meanes *V. F Baker* of thy said seruant, I was put into the way of *loue*, and aspiring to *thee*; for els it would haue wholy deiected, and ouerwhelmed me be *thou* by al *glorified* and Praised for *thy Mercies* to me. *Amen.*

THE XXX. CONFESSION.

O My Lord God, to and before whom only, I desire to powre out my hart, and the desires, affections, and afflictions therof! For *thy owne sake* forsake not me who desireth to leaue al for *thee*. If *thou* wilt *thou* canst saue me. Though I haue neuer to my knowledg done any

thing that deferueth any *grace* , or
fauour before *thee* , yet meerly out
of *thine* owne goodnes forgiue me
my finnes, and haue mercy on me.
Let *thy Mercy* which withour any defert of mine preuented me , bring
me to *thee*. Let nothing for time, or
eternity but *thy felf* be defired by
me. Let not my foul loofe , it-felf
by refting in any thing but *thee*. Let
me take comfort in hearing of *thee;*
and let al inordinate loue to creatures be rooted out of my hart by
thee. *Thou* knowft for that which is
paft, I am hartily forry, and it often
draweth teares from mine eyes to
think that their loue should haue
been more ftrong and powerfull in
me, then that fweet *loue* of *thine* is
now, which challengeth fo ful, and
wholepoffeffion of my hart; and foul
by fo many titles which none can
deny to *thee*. Take it now therfore
wholy to *thy-felf*, and let me rather
ceafe to be , then to giue any part
to any , but as it shall be diftribu-
ted by *thine own fef; thy* friends on-

ly shall be mine, that in *fine* I may
haue only *thee* for my *friend* aboue
all friends ; take from me of them
thou giueſt me as it beſt pleaſes *thee*.
For ſo I ſhal come to *loue* al in *thee*,
and yet they wil be , as if they were
not , as to any impediment to my
being vnited to *thee*. Let me without ceaſing aſpire by loue vnto *thee*
that I may be lifted aboue my ſelf
and all created things, ſo to be pure,
and free vnto *thee*. *Amen*.

THE XXXI. CONFESSION.

O *My Lord* , when I remember
my innumerable ſinnes, it ſeemeth not much to me that I ſuſtain
theſe things both without and within. But yet my deare *God* I may
ſpeak to *thee* (in the bitternes of my
ſoul) *who* art my only refuge , and
comfort in affliction , and ſay , that
thou ſeemeſt to me to ſhut vp al
hope of meanes to help my ſelf, by
ſome things which I already do, and

more am like heerafter to suftain;
Of whom should I beg help but of
thee, or ftrength to beare this to
thy honour with conformity to *thy*
bleffed wil? Who can beftow this on
me but *thy-felf?* Thou knowft that
fince I gaue my-fef to a ferious tending to *thee*, I neuer defired the
friendſhip or fauour of any creature liuing. Nay, (to *thy* honour I
fpeak it) *thou* many times, and feueral ways shewed me fo plainly the
vncertainty, inftability, and chan-
geablenes of al created things, that
my foul euen loatheth the fauour
of any how good foeuer, neither
do I wonder to fee thofe whom to
day vpon occafion I am refolute I
may be confident in, to morrow
be in an humor of interpreting al I
haue done, or faid in another fenfe
then indeed I meant it. This indeed
thou permitteft to the end we may
truft in *thee* alone, adhere to *thee*
alone, and for to purge our fouls
of the intereſt, which nature getteth euen in the actions which we

do with beſt intention. *Thou* knowſt
I neither deſire nor pretend any
thing, but do wiſh with al my ſoul
that *thy* Wil be perfectly accom-
pliſhed, and take this anſwer from
thee (which I ſhal anone recite)
when I am too ſolicitous of my own
good, or too much troubled with
the preiudice, or affliction of thoſe
thy ſeruants with whom I (moſt vnworthy ſinner) liue, who are in *thee*
al without exception moſt dearly
beloued by me, with this anſwer
following of *thine*, I am (I ſay) put
in mind of my dury, where thou ſaieſt; *Quid ad te? tu me ſequere*; What
is that to thee, do thou follow me; And
I anſwer *thee* my Lord, that as for
me, it is good for me to adhere to
thee, who art that *One* thing, which
is only neceſſary. *Thou* alone ſuf-
fiſeſt me, and al things but *thy-ſelf*
ſhal be to me, as if they were not,
that I may find and enioy *thee*, after
whom my ſoul doth pant and ſigh
without ceaſing, longing after *thee*
with all my forces, who art my al

Io. 21.
22.

G v

and only *good*. No rhirſt in any
though neuer ſo weary and tired,
can be ſo great for want of that
which naturally quencheth our thirſt
when we pant, and are dry with heat
and thirſt, as is the thirſt which my
ſoul doth ſuſtain ſighing, and pan-
ting after *thee* the liuing ſcuntain,
which yet I cannot enioy, til my
ſoul be ſet free from this corruptible fleſh, but the more I ſigh, the
more I am delighted to ſigh after
thee, *whom* I would ſo fain enioy,
The more I *loue*, the more I am yet
able farther to *loue thee*; the more I
deny my-ſelf, the morc ſweet it becometh to me to ſuffer for *thee* the
only *beloued* of my ſoul. Wo is
me that euer I offended ſuch a *goodnes* as art *thou* my *God!* Certainly my
ſinns deſerue to be puniſhed in an
extraordinary maner, becaus I committed them more wilfully then ordinary. Such was the carefulnes of
thy ſeruant my natural father, who
was ſo careful that I ſhould be kept
out of al occaſions of ſin, that I

might (confidering the nature alfo
which *thou* gaueft me) haue liued
very innocently ; But what through
my greater fault , and negligen-
ce is due to me for my finns , be
,it fupplyed by the fuperaboun-
dance of *thy* Mercy , which I will
from henceforth with all my forces
extol ; and I befeech *thee* remember
thy true feruant my faid Father, who
through his care preuented my further euil; and alfo I offer to *Thee* him V.F.
whofe happy inftructions hath made Baker
thy yoke fo fweet , and thy burthen fo
light to me , *who* as thou knowft
found it fo greiuous and heauy before I took my inftructions from
him, that I was weary of the yoke,
and defpaired euer to beare *thy* burthen with any comfort or quiet,
whereas afterward being put into a
courfe of Praier and Mortificatiõ by
him, my greateft obligations feemed
to be moft moft defirable burthens,
for al *thy* benefits be *thou* by al praifed for euer. *Amen.*

THE XXXII. CONFESSION.

*M*Ay I aske thy *Maiesty* this que-
stion, being not worthy so
much as to name or think vpon
thee; May I (I say) aske *thee*, how
it is possible that *thou* canst find in
thy hart thus to heap benefits vpon
the most vnworthy, vngreatful, and
contemptible of al *thy* creatures? Is
there any sin that I haue not comitted, at least by my wil? Yea verily
so great, and numberles do my sins,
and imperfections appeare to me
that I neuer read, or heard of any,
whose sinnes (for one reason, or
other) could be compared to mine.
Shal not *therefor* my soul praise my
God? Can any wonder to see me
in al occasions fly to *thee*, and speak
to *thee*, who haft without any theleaft
desert on my part thus sweetly with
thy Grace preuented me, and not
only auerted my wil from al that
displeaseth *thee*, but also drawn me

fo forcible to defire only *thee*, that my foul euen loatheth al that may any way hinder it from truly adhering to *thee*; and fuch an inclination hath my wil continually towards *thee*, that it cannot endure to reft in any thing but *thee* alone; I would haue *thee* alone; I defir to *loue*; and feeke *thee*, efteeming al gifts, and graces fo much, and no more, as they may and do enable me to reft only in *thee* which grant I may euer do for *thy owne fake*, who art *Godnes* it felf, and *who* be euer bleffed; *Amen.*

THE XXXIII. CONFESSION.

O *Thou who* defpifeft not any in greif, and mifery flying to *thee*; hear and help me in that which is fuftained by me, to *whom* should I fly but to *thee*? If I had or defired to haue any friends befids *thee*, *thou* mightft bid me go vnto them, and fpeak to them to help me, But as it is, al hauing forfaken me, and I al

for *thee* ; behold I come vnto *thee,*
not as one , who thinketh herſelf
any way to deſerue to be beheld,
or heard of *thee* , but as one who
hath no other refuge beſids *thee.*
Thy mercy , which infinity ſurpaſſes
my ſinns , inuiteth me howrly to
come confidently to *thee* ; Theſe
therefor are *thy* words , with which
thou art moſt willing to be challeng-
ed by thy poor ſeruants , who by
reaſon of their great frailty and
weaknes may alleadg them in their
neceſſities and want of help in which
they are , to *thee* I ſay who ſpeakeſt
them for our help and comfort ; *Non*
vos relinquam orphanos ; Petite & acci-
pietis , vt gaudium veſtrum ſit plenum.
Paraclitus docebit vos omnia. Si quis di-
ligit me , ſermonem meum ſeruabit , &
Pater meus diliget eum , & ad eum ve-
niemus , & manſionem apud eum facie-
mus. I wil not leaue you orphans ; Ask
and you ſhal receiue, that your joy may be
ful. The Holy Ghoſt wil teach you al
things. If any loue me he wil keep my
word, and my Father wil loue him, and we

Io.14.
18.

wil come to him, and wil make our man-
sion with him : If *thou* wilt be our
Fathe rwhat cause haue we to complain though we be despised, and
forsaken, yea and traoden down by
the whole world ? But as for me I
shal neuer be weary of saying; *it
is good to adhere to my Lord God*; This
I wil ask; this I wil beg euen for
thy own sake, that *thou* wilt be my
helper, defender, and refuge in al
my necessities, and do not for euer
forsak her who is so poor, and frail
of her-sef, that she hath nothing of
her own doing, or suffering wherein
she can glory, or confide. If *thou* wilt
not forsake me, I shal be safe; If *thou*
leaue me to my-self, nothing can I
expect, but vtterly to perish. Let
me obserue al *thou* exacteth of me,
out of pure and sincere *loue* neither
desiring, no nor so much, as reflecting vpon other reward, then that I
may be so happy, as in al things to
be conformable to *thy holy wil.* It is a
sufficient comfort euen of it-self, to
be tyed, and bound to *thee* by the

obligation of vows, and to serue *thee*
for *loue*, and to endeauour in al to
be so subiect to *thee*, as if it were not
in our power to wil, or desire any
thing whatsoeuer. In this lyeth hidden a most sweet, and peaceable life,
euen amidst the various changes
and alterations which this our banishment daily experienceth, which
is truly tearmed a *warfare*; in which
sometimes we ouercome by *thy af-
sisting grace*, and sometimes we are
vanquished by our enemies the world,
the flesh, and the diuel, the which
giues vs occasion to acknowledg
iustly before *thee* daily our exceeding great frailty. But this in my
daily combats is my comfort, that
my *Lord* and *loue*, my only *beloued* and
most dearly desired *Lord* my *God*,
after *whom* I thirst, and languish,
seeth and beholdeth me, and is neer
to be called vpon in this my necessity. For as *he loueth* those that fight
with great couradg, and strength, so
he despiseth not *his* litle children,
to whom gnats and flyes seeme so

great enemies (for fo I may tearm
my litle fufferings if I compare them
to thofe of *his* ftrong and faihful
feruants , which without changing
their countenance they moft cou-
radgioufly endure, yea euen before
my face) that we weep and hide our
faces in *his* boofom , to auoid the
biting, and ftinging of fo fmal ad-
uerfities. This, my *God*, is my cafe;
help , and affift me that I may be
daily more ftrengthened, and confirmed in *thee*, that at laft I may be
that in al things *thou* wouldft haue
me to be. *Amen.*

THE XXXIV. CONFESSION.

BEatus homo quem tu erudieris Domine, & de lege tua docueris eum. Nifi Pfal.
quia Dominus adiuuit me , paulo minus 93 11.
habitaffet in inferno anima mea. Bleffed is 17.
the man , whom thou shalt teach O Lord,
and shalt inftruEt him in thy law? Vnles
God had helped me within very little my
foul had dwelt in hel. This is my folace in
forrows, and my refreshment in la-

bours to cal vpon my *God* and to write vnto *him*, so that when my soul
groweth more heauy, and dul, I may
in that case read in my own writings
as in a book, the mereies of my *Lord*
shewed vnto me, therby to raise vp
my soul to a sweeter remembrance
of *him*, *whom* my hart desire thin al,
and aboue al to *loue*, and enioy. Wel
may I confes being taught this my
lesson by *thee*, that if *thou* hadst not
most powerfully holpen and deliuered me my soul had dwelt in hel,
where it might most iustly haue now
been, if *thy* meere *Mercy* had not hetherto deliuered me, which continue
to do, my *Lord*, I most humbly beseech *thee*. For as it is said in the
Psalme, vnles *thou* O *Lord*, keep my
soul, in vain is my labour in defending it. Who therfor can blame me
flying vnto *thee*, or for hauing in al
things relation to my *God* my *mercy*,
so that if I at any time grow slack in
flying to *him*, or in calling vpon *him*
in my doubts and miseries, this which
I now write lying by me, and often

being looked vpon by me, may be a meanes to put me in mind of *his* former *mercy*, which hath been so great to me, that it cannot possibly be expressed; and whatsoeuer heer-after becometh of me, be the fault wholy attributed to me; for nothing hath my *Lord God* left vndon, which might win me wholy to *himself*, and make me despise my self and al cre-ated things for *his loue*. For when I sinned, he recalled me, and forsook me not in that my misery of offen-ding such an infinit *goodnes*, so sha-mefully, and that also after my en-try into Religion, the happines and worth whereof I did not yet know by which meanes I grew weary of bearing therein his *sweet yoke* and *light burthen*, the which is heauy only through our fault, and not of it-self. Through which default, and igno-rance of mine it grew so greiuous and intolerable to me, that I wished often it might haue been shaken of lawfully by me, pretending it was so incompatible with my good, that

I could scarfly work my faluation in this my ftate and Profeſſion. This, my *God thou* art witnes of is true, and fo it did continue with me aboue two years after I had in shew forſaken the world, and the world, indeed forſaken me, but did my *Lord* in theſe biter afflictions forſake me? No, no, but he prouided ſuch a help for me by meanes of a *faithful ſeruant* of *his* that quikly was my ſorrow turned into ioy, yea into ſuch an vnſpeakeable ioy, that it hath ſweetned al the ſorrows which ſince that time haue befaln me. For as ſoon as my foul was fet in a way of tending to my *God* by *Praier*, and *Abnegation*, I found al my miferies preſently diſperfe themſelues and come to nothing; yea euen in fiue weeks my foul became fo enamoured with the *yoke of this my deare Lord*, that if I muſt haue made not only foure, but foure thouſands vowes to haue become wholy dedicated to *him*, I should haue embraced this ſtate with more ioy, and content, then euer I did

find in obtaining that which euer I
moſt of al wished, or deſired ; yea
and as *thou* knowſt my *God* , by my
ſouls being put into a cours of *prayer* , I ſeemed to haue now found a
true means wherby I might *loue* without end, or meaſure , and that without any peril, or danger. For who
can *loue thee* , my *God* , too much ? O
let me melt wholy into *loue* , to record theſe thy moſt aboundant Mercies? Let me neuer be weary of ſinging *thy* Praiſe , *who* thus haſt inuited
and drawn me (euen whither I would
or no) to a perfect contempt of al
created things , that I may adhere to
thee aboue al gifts whatſoeuer. This
I do ſo particularly write down , becaus my frailty is ſo great , that I
may perhaps grow vnmindful of *thee*,
notwithſtanding al this that *thou* haſt
done for me , which I beſeech *thee*
for thine own ſake neuer permit me
to be, that I may *praiſe* and *loue thee*
without ceaſing. *who* art my *God* bleſſed for euer and euer. *Amen.*

THE XXXV. CONFESSION.

Io.3. 21.

Qvi facit veritatem venit ad lucem,
vt manifestentur opera eius quæ in
Deo sunt facta. O *Lord* what is more
amiable, and desirable then *Truth*.
That is it which powerfully preuail-
eth in all things, and no wonder,
seeing *thou* art *Truth*. Wel may *Truth*
be oppressed, *thou* permitting it, but
suppressed *it-self* can neuer be, becaus as *thou* saieft, heauen and earth
shal fail; but *thy* word shal not fail.
He that *loueth verity*, and doth desir
to liue to *thee* cometh to the light?
And what is this *light*? Is it not *thy-
felf my* God? Yes verily. For in *thy
light* only can we see *light*. By *faith*
we are made capable, or disposed
for this *light*. For as *thou* saieft; *My
iuft liueth by faith*. By this *light* we are
strengthned in hope, and inflamed
in charity, and by appr aching to
thee, who artour *true light* and life, we
obtain a *light* which teacheth vs to
do our works in *thee*, and for *thee*. In

Rom. 1.17.

this *light* we difcouer our own *nothing*,
and perceiue we are poor, and frail of
our-felues aboue al we can imagin,
or conceaue ; and by it we plainly
perceaue , that whatfoeuer is wel
done by vs , is as *truly* to be attributed to *thee* , as if it had been don
without any concurrence of ours
with *thee* ; and that it is as iuft our
will should in al things obey *thee*,
and that without any challenging
of reward for it of *thee* (but only fo
far as it is due by *thy* meere *promifed*
mercy) as it is certain , that without
thee we could neither liue , nor be.
Alfo in this *light* we fee in fome fort
(as it were in a looking glaffe) how
great, and good a *God* we haue, and
that he is more prefent to vs then
we are to our felues , which maketh
my foul exult and rejoice amidft
the troubles , tumults , and various
changes which the difficulty of paffions, and croffe actions , and the
inftability of human , and tranfi-
tory things daily and howrly caus
to my foul. For who can mourn for

want of a friend, who hath her only *friend* always present with her?
who can choose but hope seeing *he* is
her helper, for *whose loue*, she fighteth
against flesh and blond, yea and
against the power of darknes? But
how doth she fight? Not as one
confiding in her own strength, but
in *his* help, *whose loue* hath made her
proclaim warre with al that would
hinder her from being *true* to this
her only *beloued*. To those that *loue*
what can be wanting, seeing *loue* is
able to sweeten al labours, and
lighten al burthens? As for me therfor I wil sing without ceasing in my
hart; *It is good for me to adhere to my*
God, and to put my whole trust in
him, For vain is the help of man. After
him I will sigh; to *him* I wil sing. For
my offences I wil weepe, and humble my self at the feet ef al creatures, becaus nothing pleaseth *him*
so wel, as *humibity*; and I wil approach
to my *God*, and walk solicitous with
him; Of *him* I wil write, and I wil not
depart from *him*, least darknes, and
the

Psal.
72.

the shadow of death do apprehend
my sinfull soul. He shal be my *God,*
who am his vnworthiest creature, that
so no euil may haue power ouer me.
I wil long, my *Lord,* to be dissolued,
and that I may more fully, and perfectly enioy *thee,* and neuer any-
more offend *thee, who* art so worthy
of al *Praise, Glory, Honour,* and *Ado-*
ration for euer. *Amen.*

THE XXXVI. CONFESSION.

O *My Lord,* to *thee* I wil speak,
to *whom* yet the secrets of my
hart are otherwise most cleerly, manifest; To *thee* I wil speak, and vpon
thee I wil cal. If *thou* wilt my *Lord*
thou canst saue me. This day my
Lord God; it is read of *thee* in rhe holy Church, *that thou didst heale the man* *Mat.*
sick of the Palsey. Let me also find 9.3.
grace before *thee,* that my diseases
may by *thee* be cured, that so I may
become pleasing to *thee.* For the
diseases of the mind in which I lan-

H

guish are much more grieuous then
thofe of the body. For thefe make
vs but vngratful to men, but the
other make vs difpleafing in *thine
eyes*. But *thy goodnes* as it is feene in
this example together with the cure
of the one, did alfo vfe to grant
pardon for the other. For *thou* didft
fay to him; *Thy fins are forgiuen
thee*; by which he became cured in
body, and foul. This *thy mercy* I remember with great ioy, and comfort, and falling down at thy feet
my *Lord*, I beg of *thee*, that *thou* wilt
be merciful to me a finner for *thy
own fake*, and fay vnto my foul; *Thy
finnes are forgiuen thee*; and grant that
I may now begin to liue to *thee*, that
fo by *thy grace* al impediments may
be remoued, which hinder me from
louing thee, as *thou* wouldft *be loued* by
me, which is al I wish, or defire. To
this end, I fly to thee; to this end I
figh after *thee*, only wishing and
defiirng that in al things *thy holy
wil* may be perfectly accomplished in me for time, and eternity.

If I should not howrly approach to
thee, who art the only true *light*, darknes, and the shadow of death would
ouerwhelm me, and make me vncapable of this *thy light*, which leadeth
to the *true loue* of thee. O how happy
were I, if I could truly say; *Anima
mea in manibus meis semper*, *My soul
in my hands always*, that so my soul
might *truly* hear, and follow what
my *Lord* speaketh to my hart For *thy*
words ate works! O giue me a *true*
contempt of my sef, that I may dy
to al that the world esteemeth, or
desireth! For I find where I seek my
self, there I am caught as it were
in a snare, and where I forsake my
self, there I become more, and
more capable of that *true liberty*
of *spirit*, which carrieth the soul
aboue it self and al created things,
that it may more perfectly be vnited
to *thee*. For this is *thy wil*, that by true
Abnegation in al things both external, and internal, and by a total subiection to *thee*, both as concerning
our selues and al others in any thing

H ij

that can be wished by vs, we should
enioy a certain diuine heauenly
peace amidft the croffes, paffiôs, contradictions, and mutabilities which
are incident to our life in this warfare of ours. For the more found a
soul is in the practife of this doctrin
of *thine*, of denying herself in al,
and following *thee* by propofing no
other end to her self in any thing,
but *thy self* alone, the more she
getteth, as I may fay, her foul into
her hands, and the leffe she is moued
in al things that happen either without her, or within her. For she feeth,
and knoweth that fuch haue euer
been *thy* practife, and permiffions
about croffes, and difficulties falling
vpon fouls, which was and is, with
and for this intention of *thine*, that
they of neceffity muft fuffer, and
therby become difpofed and in fome
fort worthy for to enter into *thy Kingdom*; Neither doth the foul that at-
tendeth to *thee* wonder at croffe accidents nor at the wayes, or meanes
by which they fal vpon her, but in

al of them she confideth in *thee*, that
they shal al turn to her greatest good.
And as for the faults which she co-
mitteth, she humbleth herself, hoping stil more and more in *thy* merciful forgiuenes , and assistance. It is
not strange to her to see so many
and different opinions of al men
concerning the vse of matters and
things that of themselues are indifferent; but remembring that as S.
Paul saith ; *Euery man aboundeth in
his own sense,* she adhereth to *thee,* who
art stil the same , and hath relation
to *thee* in al she doth or omitteth; By
which meanes *thou* teachest her (seeking simply *thine* honour in al things)
where , when, in what maner , and of
whom she shal ask in doubtful
cases. For it is al one to her, O my
God (If *thou* require it) to be resolued by another, or by *thy self*; But indeed in the way of Abnegation
questions are rare , and to go forth
questioning without *thy* sending , is
but a meere immortification , and
doth intangle the soul, and bring her

*Rom.
14.5.*

H iij

into inconueniences incomprehen-
sible; and for such doing, when we
so do, we cannot passe without a
bitter check for it in our int.rior by
thy diuine Maiesty , as *thou* knowst,
my good *Lord* , my soul hath experienced. For those souls that *thou* lea-
dest by the way of *loue* of them I say,
thou exactest, that they should make
their moane, only to *thee*, *thou* hauing
as it were giuen them a pledge that
thou wilt become *al* in *al* , and aboue
al to them , if they wil but remain
faithful to *thee*. Also they so litle desire. or esteem any graces, comforts,
or fauours which can be granted, or
bestowed vpon them (but only so
far as they are meerly necessary to
maintain them in *grace*, and fauour
in *thee*, and only as they are thought
fit for them by *thee* (*whom* they desire to be gratful to for al thy benefits) that they neuer desire them,
but wish rather to adhere to *thee*
by *pure faith* , that they may become therby the more deare and
pleasing to *thee*. For a'as, my *Lord*

God , what is al *thou* canſt giue to a louing foul who ſigheth and panteth after *thee* alone , and eſteemeth al things as dung , that she may gain *thee* ? What is al , I ſay , whilſt *thou* giueſt not *thy-felf* , who art that *one* thing which is only *neceſſary* and which alone can ſatisfy our ſouls. Was it any comfort to Sᵗ Mary Magdalen , when she ſought *thet*, to find two Angels , which preſented themſelues inſteed of *thee* ? verily, I cannot think it was any ioy vnto her. For that foul that hath ſet her whole *loue* and deſire on *thee* , can neuer find any true ſatisfaction, but only in *thee.* Yea comforts granted by *thee* make the foul become affraid, leaſt that by them she should the leſs fa thfully ſerue *thee* ; and ſo far as it may ſtand with *thy* wil , conſidering my extraordinaty frailty , I had rather ſerue *thee* without con ſolation then to find, or feel that which may make me eſteeme any thing of my ſelf , or hinder me from reſting only in *thee*, who art my *God*, and al my desire for euer. *Amen.*

THE XXXVII. CONFESSION.

THis day , *my Lord* , it is read in the Gospel of our Office, that *thou* did!t send thy seruants into the lanes for the poor, lame, blind, and deformed, to cōpel them to en. ter and taft of *thy* fupper, the which *thy* Mercy did fo particularly extend it felf to me, that with great ioy and comfort I heare it read , and with exceeding defire of gratitude, I re-count it heer in the fight of *thy di-uine Maiefty*. For firft , who could be more deformed in body and foul then I ? and yet *thou* didft not def-pife me; and Secondly , who could haue lefs defir to enter into holy Religion , which is the place where we may moft aboundantly taft and fee , *how fweet our Lord is* , then my frozen and ftupid foul ? And yet *thy*

Goodnes compelled me to enter. O who wil giue me power, and ability sufficiently to extol *thy* mosta boundant Mercy, which in this and al other things *thy* sweet *Goodnes* hath shewed towards me! Blessed infinitly be my *Lord* by al his creatures. My only study shal be to praise *thee*, and my only desir that I may be faithful in al crosses, and miseries to *thee* my only beloued. Let *thy Grace* flow I beseech *thee* vpon *thy* seruant, who with so much care, paines, and solicitud, for *thy sake* endeauoured to win my hart wholy to *thee*. Remember him vnto good according to al he hath done for me; He hath truly made me to see *F. F.* and feel (though through my great *Baker* fault, and ignorāce) before thought otherwise) that *thy yoke is sweet and thy burthen light*, which now I shal also being conuinced by experience, acknowledge before heauen and earth to *thine honour* and my confusion, who durst presume to think otherwise. Pardon, I beseech *thee*

H v

therefor for *thine own fake* , this my
finne among the reft which are innumerable ; and let me heerafter be
a true feruant and child of *thine, who*
be bleffed by al , for euer, and euer.
Amen.

THE XXXVIII. CONFESSION

1 *Thef.*   S Emper *gaudete* , *fine intermiſsione*
5. 17.   orate. *Always reioyce, Pray without*
ceaſing. O my *Lord* and my *God ;* They
that truly *loue thee* , may indeed iuftly always rejoyce , and without intermiffion praife *thee* ! But I that
daily and howrly offend *thy diuino*
Maieſty ought to weep and lament
my fins bitterly , fitting folitary
and making my moane to *thee* my
God , *who* art only able to help and
comfort me in this mifery.

   O when fhal I become truly *hum-*
ble ! Teach me *Humility* , Obedience , and Patience , enlighten my
foul , obfcured by my pride , and o-
ther fins , that I may *loue thy Law,*

and *humbly* embrace *thy bleſſed wil* in al things. O let me be truly ſubiect to *thee*, as *thou* wouldſt haue me, and euen to al others alſo, as it is exacted by *thee* of me! Wo be to my ſoul, if daily it become not more and more obedient ro *thee*, and to others for *thee*. Giue me true *Diſcretion*. For no vertue hath more of vertue in it, then it partaketh of this diuine *vertue*. Giue me true *Wiſedom*, which maketh ſouls ſo pleaſing to *thee*, and which *thou* imparteſt to the *hnmble*, and thoſe that ſerue *thee* for *loue*, and that ſeek *thee* aboue al gifts and created things whatſoeuer. O *loue*, *loue*, flow into my ſoul, that I may ſigh and pant after my *God*, alone, and praiſe this my *beloued* for al eternity. *Amen.*

THE XXXIX. CONFESSION.

O *Deus meus, quis ſimilis tibi! O my God who is like to thee!* Who wil giue me that wirhout ceaſing I may

adhere to *thee* , and with an amourous afpect, regard *thee* in al things,
not feeking my-felf nor the pleafing
of any creature for it felf , in any
thing I, do or omit?

Ier. 12
11.
  Defolatione defolata eft omnis terra;
quia nullus eft qui recogitet corde. With
defolation al the land is made defolate;
Becaufe there is none who confidereth in
the hart. O my *God,* what wonder is
it that we liue in blindnes , ifwe
come not to *thee who* art the only
true light ? What do we with fouls,
and harts capable of *loue* , if we do
not by them afpire to *thee* , with al
our ftrength, and adhere to *thee*, the
only true and perfect *good?* What is
fweet, what is to be defired , but *thee,*
my *Lord* , who art beawty it felf?
What couldft *thou* do more then
make out fouls to thine own image
and liknes , and able to be fatisfied
with nothing but thy felf? O mifery, of al miferies the greateft, that
thou shouldft be offended , and forgotten by vs , and that any thing
should poffes our fou's befids *thy*

loue, which only can make vs happy, and pleaſing in thine eyes. Wo is me, who haue ſtraied from the fountain of liuing water , by which my ſoul is dryed vp , and euen withereth away in thirſt after tranſitory things. Change this my thirſt by *thy* ſweet *grace* and Mercy to a thirſting after *thee* my *God* , the glory of my hart, and the *peace* and comfort of my ſoul. O let me *loue* , or not liue ; and let me in al, by al , and aboue al praiſe *thee* , who art bleſſed for al eternity. *Amen.*

THE XL. CONFESSION.

MY *ſoul bleſſe thou our Lord , and al things within me his holy name.* Al ſpirits praiſe my *God* , for euer and euer magnify *him.*

   I wil declare to *thee* my *God* in al things, how it ſtands with me , that I may hope and be ſtrengthened in and by *thee.* I wil beg what is neceſſary for me to pleaſe and ſerue *thee.* For what canſt *thou* deny to them,

Pſal. 102.1.

who haue no hope or comfort , but
only in *thee*. He who giueth him-
self, giueth al; and when *thou* deni-
eſt what we ask, it is that *thou* mayſt
giue *thy* own ſelf more fully to vs
thy poor ſeruants, and that impediments may be the more truly remoued between our ſouls and *thee*.

Simplify my ſoul that it may return to *thee* ; adorn me with *thine*
own merits, that I may not appeare
naked of *good* befre *thee*, and ſupply
my defeƈt in praiſing and *louing thee*.
To *thee* my *God*, al my interior powers shal aſpire day , and night without ceaſing. Let me draw no breath
but therby to ſigh and pant after
thee the liuing fountain. Let al aƈtions which by Obedience , or neceſſity be impoſed on me, be vndertak-
en, and done by me with an *interior*
regard of *thee* , that I may truly in
them obey and ſeek *thee*, the moſt
amiable *beloued* of my hart and ſoul;
let them be as a ceſſation , or pauſ-
ing for the time , that I may afterward with the more force and ſa-

nour at times conuenient attend to *thee* in the bottom of my foul, and therein praife *thee. Amen.*

THE XLI. CONFESSION.

COme al ye that haue vowed your bodies, and fouls to our *Lord*, Come let vs *loue.* Let vs giue al, not only once, but euery moment to *him*, that made vs to beftow on vs *himfelf.* Let vs not only *loue*, but be wholy transformed into the *Diuine loue.* Let vs liue to *him lone*, leauing al others for his fake only. Let vs charitably interpret the words and deeds of thofe with whom we liue; and if any fail in that which he ought to perform, giue vs *grace*, my God, to remembet how weak human nature is for *good* and how great is our frailty as to a fin, and how foon we alfo (if *thou* didft not protect vs) might fail in a more shameful maner. O my God, *thou* haft commaunded vs to *loue* our neighbour as our felf, and behold we either , loue them inordinatly to our impediment of *louing thee* , or els we are short towards them of rrue *Charity*. From both thefe errours deliuer the foul of *thy* poor feruant , and grant me to *loue al* as *thou* wouldft haue me. Let no difficulties they caufe to me , make me in them the lefs to behold and confider *thee*. Verily , if there were no other reward to be giuen to thofe who for *thy* fake requite euil with good , then the *true peace* which they find in their fouls by it , it were moft worthy our labour. But *thou* , my *Lord* , referueft great reward in *the* next life for thofe , who for bitternes caufed to them by others , do return fweetnes vnto them ; yea nothing is more pleafing , and acceptable to *thee* , rhen that we by *humility* and patience do pacify thofe *who* are offended with vs. But alas my *God* , I wil fpeak , and wil not be filent in the eares of my *Lord*, and with teares in mine eyes wil bewail my fins, and offences. I know there is no more *true loue* in our fouls to our neighbours, then we are dead to our felues, and liue vnto *thee*. What therefor can I think of my poor foul, fo barrein of al true vertue? If I *loue thy very-felf* fo little, as indeed I do, where wilt *thou* find in me, that *Charity* which by *thy* law I owe for *thee* tow-ards them? Verily, when I confider how deftitute I am of al that might make, me pleafing in *thine* eyes, I cannot but tremble, and fear. Yet again taking hart, remembring *thy* Mercy towards me, I find I haue caufe of hope, *thou* being *goodnes it-felf*, *whofe* nature is to defir to impart it-felf; which if *thou* wilt be pleafed to do to my poor foul, I fhal notwith-ftanding al my fins become yet in *thee* and by *thee* moft happy; tow-ards which I befeech *thee* grant me *grace* to difpofe my-felf for thy on-ly honour, *who* be Bleffed for euer. *Amen.*

THE XLII. CONFESSION.

O Lord *my God*, what Mercy art *thou* pleafed to shew to my finful foul ? Is it poffible after fo many abominable offéces that *thou* shoudft thus particularly fauour me ? If it were euer poffible to be lawful for *thy* creatures to exclaim againft *thee* and taxe *thee* of iniuftice, it might be admitted them in this *thou* haft done and doeft for me , the moft finnful and moft contemptible of al *thy* Maiefties creatures. if I had euer done any good, they perhaps would not wonder at *the* ; but as it is, they cannot but at leaft admire *thy* infinit fweetnes and Mercy. For w at fin is there I haue not comitted at leaft by my wil. But the greater *thy* Mercy the more I hope the honour and praife wil be which *thy* feruan s wil yeild to *thee* for it ; and do *thou thy felf*, I befeech *thee*, fupply our defect in this and al other things, fo that perfect praife may be yeilded to *thee* in al and by al for euer and euer. *Amen.*

THE XLIII. CONFESSION.

Lord, *with great ioy* I defir to ce-lebrat this diuine Solemnity of *thy* Refurrection. Thou haft shewed *thy-felf* in al formes, fo that the weakeft capacities might in fome fort apprehend *thee who* art incom-prehenfible. *Thou* appearedft a child, that *thy* little ones might conceiue more eafily fome things that might moue them to *loue thee*, and being as it is were aftonished at *t y loue* towards vs, and at *thy* infinit humi-lity, we might thirft after *thy* example, and *loue* only *thee*. For al *thou* haft done, or faid, is for our comfort and inftruction. What haft *thou* left vndone, which might any way fur-ther our good, if we would but con-cur with *thy Grace* ; But we ftreying from *thee*, how can we choofe but be blind. For only in *thy light* can we see and discern that which only imporeteth vs to see and know, to wit, to know *thee*, therby to *loue thee*, and to know our selues, therby to humble vs in al things before *thy Diuine Maiesty*. For nothing but true *Humility* can make vs gracious in *thine* eyes. So much as we truly *humble* our selues, so much, and no more, do we encrease in our *loue to thee*. O how peaceful amidst al storms is the souls of the *humble*? how fauoured by *thee*, though they be difpifed by the whole world. They are indeed often neglected by men; but moft conuerfant with *thee* and thine Angels and Saints in heauen. Neuer was there euer fuch acquaintance, *loue*, and friendship, between any in this world, as there is between *thy Goodnes* and an humble foul, that feeketh *thee* aboue al graces and gifts whatfoeuer, and tranfcendeth al created things, that fhe may adhere to *thee* in the bottom of her foul. Verily it is fo ftrange, that it putteth the heauenly Court into admira-

tion, that we that haue dedicated
our souls wholy to *thee*, should *loue*,
seeke, or desir any thing besids *thee*.
But alas human frailty, as they wel
know, is very great, and therefor
they also cannot choos but pitty
and pray for vs ; and especially we
women , silly to all things that this
world admires , and therefor most
contemptible of al creatures, if we
do not labour for the *loue* of *thee*,
(the which to do , *thou* dost as willingly enable vs as *thou* dost the wife
of the world , if we hinder not *thy*
grace who despisest not any thing
thou hast made. How much are we
to be therefor blamed and condemned if we labour not , I say , for *thy*
loue? Yea to shew *thy* power *thou* hast
been pleased many times to bring
a silly woman , *louing thee* , to that
wisedom that no creature by wit or
industry could attain to the same.
But where my *Lord* haue these *thy*
Spouses in these dayes placed there
harts ? Where , I say , seeing they
seek, and desir so much the fauour

and praife of the world, to haue the
friendſhip of men , and by letters
and tokens to draw their harts from
thee vnto them , notwithſtanding (as
good reaſon) it profpereth not with
vs in ſuch doing ; for they by this
meanes ſeeing our defect in *louing*
thee , cannot confide in them , who are
not true to *thee*; but cōtrary compare
vs to thoſe , who profer *loue* to al, and
yet , as we ought for *thee* , loue none.
O *Lord* remoue theſe ſcandals from
thy Church ; Let vs , though we cannot ſerue *thee* , in great matters , yet
let vs , I ſay , haue no harts but to
loue thee , no tongues but to praiſe
thee , nor eyes but to behold *thy*
creatures , as things inuiting our
ſouls to *loue* , figh, pant , and euen
languiſh after *thee*; No eares but to
heare what is *thy will* ; and in fine
not to liue but in , and for *thee* , and
for *thy* loue to be ſubiect to euery
human creature, as far as it is exacted of vs by *thee*. Giue that *humility*
which by thy bleſſed Apoſtle Saint
Paul thou requireſt in vs , that I

may willingly fubmit my-felf to the
power of Superiors fet ouer me by
thee. It is true I fee and hear daily,
what fcandals, what difcorders, and
what confufions arife in Communities for want of due fubmiffion in
fubiects to their Superiors; but alas,
my *God*, certeinly a chief caufe therof is (at leaft in many who haue good
wils) becaus thy are not taught to
obey *thee interiorly* in their fouls,
out of which it would proue eafy to
them to obey exteriorly, w eras
now it femes a burthen intolerable;
and forfooth vnder pretence of
greater perfection we often fal in
to open rebellion. Surely this was
not the practife of Saints, who yet
found often great oppofition and
mortification by meanes of Superiors, which they bearing patiently
and obeying ftil out of an *internal*
regard of *thee* in their fouls, al turned to their greater aduancement in
thy loue; and their Superiors at laft
by *thy* help concurred to that which
they defired, fo far as it was *thy wil*,

who, haſt diſpoſed of al things in order and iuſtice, and nothing can be wel done but that we do out of an *internal light* from *thee* and out of obedience to *thee*, to *whom* obedience is due in al things whatſoeuer. *Thou* haſt ſet an order in al things, and euery thing as it is ordained by *thee*, wil concur to a moſt heauenly harmony; but corrupting *thy* meaning, al things are out of order, and *peace* on al ſides is diſturbed. O how happy are they, whoſe ſouls are in a right way to hear and follow *thy wil*, and *who* do nothing without conſulting with *thee* in their ſoul, giuing that to *God* which is only *Gods* own, and to Cæſar that which is due to Cæſar for *God*? for both theſe obediences are neceſſary to make a true ſpiritual life. For in vaine do we giue to *thee*, if we deny Obedience to them who are ſet ouer vs by *thee*; and alſo in vaine is it to pleaſe and haue the fauour of our Superiors, if we *internally* neglect to haue in al things relation to *thee*;

from

from both thefe errors deliuer me,
I befeech *thee*, that my foul may be
a *peaceful* habitation for *thee*. Let me
humbly behaue my-felf towards al;
and let me not meafure my cafe before *thee* by the opinion my Superiors and Sifters haue of me, for they
may applaud me, and yet it may
ftand il with me before *thee*; and they
may take al in another worfer fenfe
then *thou* knowft I meant it, and that
iuftly, and yet it may go wel between *thy goodnes* and me through *thy*
abound Mercy.

THE XLIV. CONFESSION.

O *How happy* are thofe fouls who
loue nothing but *thee*? Verily
there is fo little ftability in al things
but in *thee*, that it is a ftrange thing
that we should liue fo miferable liues *thou* offering vs a moft *peaceful*
and quiet life, if we would but feek
thee alone, *who* art more prefent to
vs, then we are to our felues; and
by *thee* our foul doth liue, more

I

then our body doth by our soul;
Those that posses *thee* haue al things,
and those who want *thee* , if they had
al the world can afford , do yet indeed posses nothing. If we desire to
loue where our *loue* may not be lost,
what shall we *loue* but *thee* , wh, hast
said; *Sicut dilexit me Pater , & ego di-*
lexi vos ; As my Father loued me , so
haue I loued you; Do we not therefor
wel deserue to liue in al perplexity
and misery, if we do not leaue to *loue*
al other things to set our whole *loues*
vpon *thee* , *who* hast made vs such
sweet promises ; yea let vs hear
what *thou* dost further add; *Qui ma-*
net in me , & ego in eo , hic fert fru-
ctum multum. Who *remaineth in me,*
and I in him, bringeth forth much fruict.
O let me be remain in *thee* , and
then let al the world be against me!
I desir not , my *God* , by any particular fauours in this life to be more
certain of *thee* ; But I do beg of *thee*,
that by true *Humility* , Obedience,
and Patience, I may be more confirmed in *thee* by true *loue* , only in

Io. 15.
9.

Io. 15.
5.

simple faith; in al defolations, crofles, pains, difgraces, miferies adhering to *thee* the only defire of my foul, and not refting in any gift or *grace* of *thine* whatfoeuer ,t hat I may at laft for *thy own fake* find fauour in *the* eyes of *thy Diuine Maiefty* , notwirhftanding my fins and ignorances, in which I haue hetherto liued; for whieh *thy mercy* of forgiuing them me , be *thou* for euer blefsed and praifed by al *thy* creatures. *Amen. Amen.*

THE XLV. CONFESSION.

O Lord, *my God*, to *whom* vpon al occafions, I (moft vnworthy) with *thy* leaue prefume to fpeak, and ask queftions in my fimple maner. Open the eyes of my foul, that I may know and vnderftand *thy Wil* and *Law*, and *Grace* to perform them to *thine* honour. *Thou* my *God*, *who* art more mine, then I am mine own, do not rcieĉt me fpeak-

ing and writing to *thee*. For what do
I defir, or wish but *thee* ? Or what are
al things to me without *thee* ? Surely,
nothing. For *thou* haft shewed me
through *thy* sweet mercy , and *grace*
without any defert of mine own,
that al things are vanity but to *loue*
and pleafe *thee*, which I befeech *thee*
that I may do with al the forces of
my hart , and foul . For truly there
is no true *peace* , or comfort out of
thee. Let me therefor know my-felf
and know *thee* , that in al I may
praife and pleafe *thee*. *Amen.*

THE XLVI. CONFESSION.

Io. 20. LORD it is read to day of *thee*
that Saint *Mary Magdalen* approaching to kis *thy* feet , it would
not be admitted her by *thee*. If it
may pleafe *thee* , I wil humbly aske
of *thee* the meaning of this. For I am
fomewhat amazed at it. For when
she came to thy feet loaden with
many and greiuous fins , *thou* admit-

tedft her moft eafily ; and when she
had a long time been trained vp in
thy happy school of Perfection , and
had accompanied *thee* in *thy Pafsion,*
and mourned for *thee* at *thy* tomb,
taking no reft til *thou* her *beloued* re-
turned to her again; and befids she
offered - to haue taken *thee* away
from al the world , if they would
haue but told her where they had
laid *thee* ; and yet doft *thou* now deny her to touch and kis thy blefsed
feet. What, shal we think she *loued*
thee lefs now then when she firft defired to loue *thee* ? Or shal we think,
that as her *loue* grew more, and more
to *thee* , *thine* grew lefs and lefs to
her ? No., *God* forbid I should euer
admit of fuch a thought ; But, O
my *Lord* , *thou* being a *ifedom it-felf,*
intendedft to bring this great and
ardent *louer* to a *loue* more fpiritual,
then that with which she *loued* thee
when *thou* conuerfedft with her before *thy* death and Pafsion. For it is
thy cuftom with great mildnes to receaue finners , and when they grow

I iij

more ftrong in *loue thou* feemeft to
treat them with more feuerity, that
they at firft may hope in *thee* , and
go forward in *thy loue* and feruice, and
that after being a litle ftrengthned
with *light* and comfort from *thee, thou*
mayft try them many ways , leaft
they should attribut that which they
haue done to their own forces , and
that fauour which they haue receaa-
ed , to their own labours , and deferts ; which *thou* knowft we are
very apt to do , if *thou* didft not
through permitting vs to fal into
temptation , fhew vs our own frailty. But this bleffed Saint (whofe in-
terceffion I moft humbly implore
for *thy fake* , *n hom* now none can depriue her of) did not think that by
denying her to touch *thy* feet fhe
receaued wrong. For her humble
foul thought it-felf too vnworthy
of fuch a fauour , when *thou* didft
put her in mind , that fhe was to
conuers with *thee* in a more fpiritual maner then before ; neither did
fhe refle&t on the labour , pain and

grief she had fuftained. For, as *thou* knowft , *loue* feeleth no labour, nor complaineth of any burthen. For only to haue feen *thee* aliue again, was fufficient to make her forget al former afflictions. For her fake, and for al their fakes that *loue thee* , be merciful to my fins , and bring me by true *loue* to be vnited to *thee* with them, where for euer without ceaf-ing I may praife *thee* my only *belou-ed. Amen.*

THE XLVII. CONFESSION.

O LORD, *my God;* I wil fpeak to *thee* again , and again I wil cal vpon *thee* the entierly *beloued* of my hart. I wil melt away in *thy* prai-fes, and I wil inuite al *thy* fpoufes to to feek *thee* alone aboue al *thy* gifts and aboue al creatures. For in *thee* alone is *true peaee,* and comfort to be found, and enjoyed. O how happy should I efteem my felf , if I were able to praife *thee* without ceafing, or be any cauſe that any should more and more languish with *thy loue*. What should I do being born down with the weight of mortal flesh , and diuers internal afflictions , ſo that I can many times ſcarſly think on *thee* ? What should I do (I ſay) but lift vp my hart, with my hands as it were by main force, ſometimes by words , and ſometimes by writing vnto *thee* , which I ☞ do not do as to one that is farr of from me, but as to one who is more neere to me then I am to my-ſelf, and of *whoſe Goodnes , whoſe Wiſedom, whoſe Beawty , whoſe Mercy , and moſt abſolut and incomparable greatnes*, I am more aſſured of , then I am of any thing I ſee with my corporal eyes. O who would not *loue this Godnes, this Maieſty* , and ſubmit them-ſelues to *this moſt amiable beloued* of our ſouls? If any comfort , or happines were to be found out of *him* , we were ſomthing excuſable in neg'ecting and forgetting our *chief good* ; But ſeeing we cannot euen in this mortal life find any content , but by *louing*, praising, and truly seeking and seru-ing *him* , we are too miserable and too blame for loosing our-selues by resting with *loue* and inordinat affection in transitory and visible things? O far be it from *thy* spouses to set their affection vpon any thing but *thee* , or to bereaue *thee* of the affection which from al is to *thee* only due. Al that we , are and haue, is too little for *thee* ; Let vs not there-for of that little we haue, take from *thee* ! O let vs *loue thee* aboue al , and al others in and for *thee*. I do be-moan this misery aboue al miseries, y[t] those who haue dedicated them-selues to *thee* , should seek the *loue* and fauour of others , to their own and the others impediment in *thy loue* and seruice. Oftentimes we comply and correspond vnder pre-tence to get temporal means , the while neglecting *thee* , *who* feedest the birds and clothest the beasts of the earth, who neither sow , nor reap, neither are they solicitous of any

G v

thing but depend of *thy* meere
prouidence, and yet *thou* prouideſt
for them. Can we think *thou* wilt
haue leſs care of vs that haue left
al the world for *thee*, then of the
vnreaſonnable creatues made only for our ſeruices ? Haſt not
thou ſaid by the *Spirit* of al *truth*,
that *firſt ſeek for the Kingdom of
God, and his iuſtice, al things els*
ſhal be added to you? O let vs therefor leaue al things truly, that we
may confide in *thee*, caſting our care
vpon *thee*, *who wilt* nourish our ſouls,
and bodies, if we wil but faithfully
and conſtantly adhere vnto *thee* our
ſupreame and only *Good*. Let vs leaue
pretending any thing, but *thee*. For
often euen vnder the pretence of
getting praiers of others, we poure
out our-ſelues, in the meane time,
neglecting to haue relation to *thee*,
who wouldſt more willingly giue,
then we could ask, if we would but
truly, and faithfully adhere to *thee*,
and not ſtray out of our ſelues,
hindering both our ſelues, and o-

Mat.
6.33.

thers from adhering to *thee*, to *whom*
we owe al we are, and can do, and
and therefor are greatly to blame,
when we do not endeauour to *loue*
thee with al our foul, with al our
mind and al our ftrength, which
grant for *thy own fake* we may endeauour to do, to *thy* honour and glory,
who be praifed, *loued*, and adored
for al eternity. *Amen.*

_____   _____   _____   _____

THE XLVIII. CONFESSION.

SHAL not my *foul be fubieſt to God?*
O my *Lord*, far be it from me
to wil, or defire any thing but according to *thy diuine wil*, which is
only holy; Let me neuer refift *thy*
wil, fignified to me by any means
whatfoeuer. Let my foul be wholy
turned into a flame of *diuine loue*,
that I may afpire and tend to nothing els but *thy-felf* alone; Blot out
my fins that my foul may return to
thee by *loue*, from *whom* by fin it hath

I vj

strayed! O let nothing but this defir
of *thee* , my *God* , poffes my hart; Let
that be my folace in labours, pains,
temptations , defolations , and al
afflictions of body , or mind ! Let
not my hart (drawn by *thee* to feek
after nothing but *loue*) be fo bafe as
to couet, defir, and reft in any thing
but *thee*. *Thou* art my life, my choice,
and my only beloued. When I hear
thee but named , my *Lord God* , it forcible draweth me into my-felf, that
I may attend vnto *thee* , forgetting
my-felf, and whatfoeuer els befids
thee , for which benefit be *thou* infinitly praifed. *Amen.*

THE XLIX. CONFESSION.

OMNIS fpiritus laudet Dominum.
Benedicite omnia opera Domini Do-
mino ; laudate & fuper exaltate eum in
fæcula. Let euery fpirit praife our Lord;
Bleffe our Lord al the works of our Lord,
praife and exalt him for euer. O my
God that I were able with a pure foul

and *louing* hart to extol *thy* praiſe.
But alas, *thy praiſe is not ſeemly in the*
mouth of a ſinner. But ſhal I for this
hold my peace? If I do, yet permit
me this comfort for *thine* own ſake,
yt I may inuite others more worthy,
to ſing and ſet forth the praiſe of
thy diuine Maieſty, with *whom* yet as
the laſt, and leaſt, my ſoul ſhal ioin
in the praiſe of *thee* our deare *Creator*;
and in that which is ſo worthily poſſeſſed by *thy* ſweet *Goodnes*, I wil rejoice with al the forces of my hart
and ſoul ! O my holy and *deare de-*
light, what a moſt harmonious melo-
dy would reſound ouer al the earth,
if *thy wil*, and iuſt diſpoſition took
place in al things. Behold al *thy* works
praiſe *thee*, euery one in their kind;
only man (for whoſe help and comfort al other things on earth were
created) peruerteth the order of *thy*
Iuſtice, by miſuſing that noble *free*
wil, which *thou* gaueſt him, to chooſe,
and *loue thee with* ! O what couldſt
thou haue done more, then with ſuch
a noble gift to haue endued vs ! Cer-

Eccli.
15. 9.

teinly if we would intend *thee* in al,
and haue relation to *thee* in al, *who*
art more present to our souls, then
we are to our selues, we should hear
thee giuing answers . sometimes by
others., sometimes by *thy self* , and
sometimes by the words of holy
Scriptures , and' ancient. Fathers;
and subiects would be tractable to
Superiors rather gouerning by *thee*
then by themselues ; what *thou*
wouldst commaund , they would
commend ; and in al not seeking
their own glory, or exaltation, would
glory in *thee*, not in their own power;
and what were done by *thee* , they
would then accompt only wel done;
but what they did of themselues,
they would accompt little profitable, as to the aduancement of souls;
☞ Then they would be able to se what
were fit for euery soul vnder their
chardg , and when *thou* permittedst
this not to be so cleer to them , they
would humble themselues acknowledging it happened for their vn-
woithines, beseeching *thee* to do that

by *thy-self* which could not be done
by them ; and if *thou* shouldst perhaps let another (though their subiect) to see and discern what were fit
in that case, or cases though he were
but the last and lowest, and of the
least esteeme in the Conuent , yet
certeinly such Superiors would not
accompt it to derogate from their
authority, that suchan one should
supply their place, and Offifice vpon occasions; becaus they seek *thy honour*, and not their own; and though
thou hadst giuen them power to command , yet no otherwise would they
vse it , then according to such maner and in such cases as *thou* dost require they should; In this maner
gouerning with relation to *thee* and
regard of *thy wil* , and with indifferency what *thou* wilt do by them,
what by others, and what by *thy-self*,
whose spirit breatheth where it pleases.
Then the sensual loue, and friendship between the Superiors and their
subiects would ceafe; then sincerity,
and reason would take place both in

Io. 3.
8.

the commander, and in the obeyer,
both thinking al their *loue* and labour to be too little for *thy Godnes*;
then would be *peace* on al fids , and
the imperfections of al, would turn
to the aduancement, not to the preiudice of any ; then as they defired
the friendship , or fauour of none,
but in al things willingly and gladly depending of *thy prouidence* , fo
they would be friends with al *thy*
friends, and pitty,and pray for (from
the bottom of their fouls) thofe that
are *thine* enemies , amongft which
they vould verily beleeue they
fhould haue been the greateft ; if
thou of *thy fweet Mercy* hadft not preuented them. Alfo inferiors that
truly liue to *thee* and defiring nothing els but *thee* , though *thou* didft
teach, and inftruct them about the
vfe of indifferent things by an internal *light* which difcerneth between
cuftome and true reafon , between
their natural defirs and *thy true Iuftice*,
which only ought to take place in
al things, yet they accounting them-

selues wholy vnworthy of being instructed by *thee* most willingly hear
thy wil and commaunds , not only
from Superiors , but from any creature whatsoeuer , accounting it sufficient for them that it was signifi-
ed to them , that it was *thy wil*, the
which we ought to follow as doth a
shaddow the the body , or els of
little worth is any thing we do. For
thou rewardest no works but *thine
own.* O if al creatures would serue
thee according to their capacities and
states , where a resemblance would
this life haue with heauen! No person , no state can pretend to be ex-
cused from being able to serue and
please *thee* , who hast made our hart
for *thy-self* , and it can neuer haue
true rest and repose but in *thee* the
Center of our souls. What creature
is so little , or contemptible that doth
not in some sort inuite vs in its kind
to *loue* and praise *thee* my *Lord God?*
If we would *loue thee*, they would not
fail to serue vs , til we could serue
thee without them. But alas as it is

affirmed, and that moſt truly, that *order is the life of things*, ſo man being out of order by ſeeking himſelf more then *thee*, and by doing that which may redound rather to his own honour then to *thine*, hath made al *thy* other creatures refuſe that obedience wᶜʰ they owed to man, iftat he were truly obedient to *thee*. Our defect in this towards *thee* puts al out of order. For how can ſubiects be pliable to the wil of Superiors, if firſt they be not in the way of obeying *thee* with relation of their obediences to man as to *thee* and meerly for an according to *thy wil* ? And how can we be at *peace* with others, if firſt we be not by true reſignation in a way to haue *peace* with *thee* in our own ſouls? Where is the Obedience due to *thee*; and others for *thee*, ſince oftentimes out of blindnes we giue Cæſar that whi ch was *Gods*, and deny to him, that which was due to him by the *wil of God* ? As alſo if Superiors and Prieſts ſhould ſtand vpon points vſurping that to themſelues which *thou* haft referued to *thy felf* ; what shal become of fubiects? Certainly they wil not wel know what to do vnles it be very right between them and *thee.* But alas, *Si fal euanuerit in quo falietur? If the falt loofe its vertue in what shal it be falted?* Happy are they that light vpon a good Superior; but much more happy are they, who by true *light* in *Humility* and Abnega-tion are inftructed by *thee*, *who* art the only true teacher of *Humility*, true obedience and perfect *Pryer.* O my *Lord*, when shal it be faid, that the multitude of beleiuers are of one hart and foul ? When shal al be vnited in the bonds of true *peace?* Neuer til our Charity beginning in *thee* do fpread it felf to al others for *thee.* For there is no true friendship but that which thou knitteft between fuch as *loue* al in and for *thee* , and *thee* aboue al that can be imagined or defired. O when shal thy Iuftice and *Truth* in all things take place, that the earth may breath forth no-thing but *thy* Praife? Then we should

Mat. 3.15.

be in paine, and not feeme to fuffer; fo fweet or pleafing would the pain be ; we should liue on earth, (not as being ftrangers) in heauen; and liuing heer should more liue with *thee* our *beloued* , then where we of neceffity liued. For then *thy wil* being dône in earth as in heauen; the earth would refemble heauen, wherby the pain and grief of our banishment would be fweetned with a comfort almoft heauenly, and that together with refigning our felues to *thy holy wil* to be contented to be denyed for a time til *thy* wil might thereby be wholy accomplished; and after that come to fee *thy* glorious face and enjoy *thee* as *thou* art in *thy-felf* , *who* is our only happines, the expectation wherof would make this world tolerable to vs , and we should then feek *thy* glory and the fulfilling of *thy* luftice in al things, and not our own comfort , and honour. Verily, al thy difpofitions are fo iuft , that al things would happen to our greateft good , if

we with humility and confidence
in *thee* would proceed in al things;
And not any ſtate, condition, or corporal complexion is there, wherein
thou haſt not been ſerued in a perfect maner by ſome, or other. And
if we run through al degrees from
the Pope to the ſimple Religious,
and from the greateſt Monarch to
the pooreſt begger, in al we ſhal find
ſome that haue faitfully ſerued and
praiſed *thee*. And as for natural com-
plexions, or diſpoſitions, the moſt
wicked|haue brought forth children
prouing Saints; and others who haue
liued (as to al maner of ſins) ſo il,
that whole Contreys haue fared the
worſe for them, and diuers ſouls
periſhed by their means, yet by
humility haue become ſo pleaſing to
thee, O *Lord*, that *thou* madſt them
thy booſom friends; And no trade
nor occupation, if it be lawful, but
hath of it Saints, to the end to ſhew
thou deſpiſeſt nothing that *thou* haſt
made, how contemptible ſoeuer it
ſeeme in the eyes of men. Why

therefor do we not *loue thee* , seeing al things on *thy* part concur to this end? We may pretend what excuse we wil ; but nothing wil excuse vs before *thee* , *who* had no other end in creating vs, but that we should be partakers of that glory which *thou* prepared for those that truly *loue thee* ; and in that country of al happines, we shal receaue al good things, and aboue al shal enioy *thee* the beginning and fountain of al *good* , without *whom* al things are as nothing as to the contenting and satisfying of our souls. And seeing meerly *thou* createdst vs for our good, *thou* being infinitly happy of *thy-self* before *thou* createdst any thing, why shal we lay the fault of our not profiting or euerlasting perishing vpon *thee* ? If there had been any thing wanting of *thy* part , we might iustly complain to *thee* ; and if there were any thing yet meerly necessary , we requiring it humbly of *thee* . *thou* couldst not (so infinit *good* art *thou*) deny it vs. But seeing *thou* createdst man in the state of innocency, and after his fal redeemedst him with the pretious Bloud of *thy ouly begotten Son*, and hast giuen vs a Law vnder which we are to walk, and by means of our holy Mother the Church hast and dost determine of al things as certainly as if that *thou thy-felf* wert stil corporally present to giue answers in al things necessary to saluation, how worthily are we to be condemned if we do not correspond and satisfy such *thy* most gratious wil, and prouision about vs ? Besids we haue *thee* within vs, to haue recourse vnto vpon al occasions, the which that we may do with the les impediments *thou* hast ordained the ouerlooking and solicitude ouer vs of the Superiors *thy* Vicegerents, who gouern vs heer by *thy* appointment, and *whom* to resist in any thing so it do not derogate from *thy* own authority immediatly to *thy-felf)* were highly to offend and displease *thee.* For by these thy Substituts *thou* dost

iudg, and determin of *Spirits* and
of the *verity* and *goodnes* of them and
of their exercifes, and doings; as
whether they proceed from *thee* and
thy motions, or no; and by them
declareft what in general is to be
done, or omitted; and in particular
as there is occafion, in feculars partly by feculars powers, and in Religious by their Paftours and Superiours, that thus being in fome certeinty of fubordination, and good
exterior order, we may freely attend to *thee* in our fouls, without
going forth but of meere neceffity.

THE L. CONFESSION.

WHO *would feek*, *or loue* any
thing but *thee* my *God*, *who* art
exceeding great, and of *thy goodnes*,
there is no end? Who would loofe
thee for nothing, and depart from
the fountain of life, for to drink
out of a Ceftern, that is ful of fil-
thy,

thy, and muddy water! What are
al things, but *thy felf,* for the fatisfying of our fouls? If thou diedſt
as thou diedſt for vs, that we might
liue ouly to *thee*, can we think it
much, if heauens, earth, fea, and
al contained in them, rife vp againſt
vs forgetting and neglecting *thy Mercy*? O let vs *loue thee*, and al things
wil be at *peace* with vs, and we at *peace*
with our felues. Is it not a shame for
vs to fee the birds praife *thee*, and
al creatures in their kind to giue the
honour, and yet we only capable
of *thy* loue forgetful and vngrateful to *thee*? What is there is this
world but it calleth vpon vs to feek
thee in fincerity of hart, and to liue
to *thee* alone, and to make vfe of
them euery one in their kind, to
the end we may concur with them
to the praife of *thee* our *Lord*, and
Creator, to *whom* al *loue* and honour is only due? The Angels moſt
humbly affiſt vs, and pitty vs offending *thee*, which willingly to do is fo
hainous a thing in their eyes that

they are amazed to fee vs ftray from true reafon. But alas man was in honour , and knew it not ; he was compared to beafts and became like vnto them. In this my mifery I figh and groane to my *God* , *who* in this my affliction is only able to help and comfort me. O how can we find in our hart to offend *thee* ? *That*, and *that* alone is to be efteemed truly a *mifery*. But yet are we finners without comfort ? No , no , my *God* , feeing *thou* canft forgiue more then we can offend , and it wil redound to *thine honour* and praife for euer and euer , that *thou* haft pardoned fo many and greiuous fins and finners. In which *thy glory* I exult from the bottom of my foul ; becaus feeing I haue offended , for which I am hartily forry , yet wil my *God* be extolled by al creatures for forgiuing it, for al eternity. O *thou who* art *thine own praife* fupply in this and in al other things, the defect that is in al vs *thy* creatures to praife *thee* as *thy* iuftice requireth *thou*

fo shouldſt be magnifyed by vs al,
who without *thee* are nothing but a
ſack full of filth, and the map of al
miſery.

THE LI. CONFESSION.

O Lord, *my deare God*, if we that
are created to *thine own image*
and *liknes*, and whoſe happines doth
conſiſt in *louing*, pleaſing, praiſing,
and enioying *thee*! If we (I ſay) did
ſeek and deſir only *thee*, how wel
would it go in this world? If we
were faithful to *thee*, al things would
be ſo to vs. When I ſee any of *thy*
creatures abuſe the nobility of their
ſoul by ſtraying from *thee*, or at leaſt
by looſing their time which is ſo pre-
cious, in labouring and taking great
pains to obtain the fauour of men,
or ſomething els as litle to the purpoſe how can it but wound my very hart? ſeeing *thou* art neglected,
and they take great pains for what
they cannot poſſible obtain; in the

meane time forgetting to seek after *thy* sweet *loue* , which might be
obtained euen for nothing, in comparison of what they sustain by labouring for that which perhaps if they
do get , or obtain , they are farther
from being satisfyed then they were
before. It is true the more we *loue*
thee, the more we desire to *loue thee*;
And the more we *loue* , the more
able we are to *loue*, and the more easy
it is to *loue*; and *loue* making al pains,
confusions, difficulties, and afflictions sweet, what is there left to suffer? Only indeed the hiding of *thy*
face and denying vs fully to enioy
thee ; this only remains to pearce
our harts with, if we truly *loue*; and
☞ yet *thy iust wil* is a consolation euen
in the greatest extremity of this difficulty. Who would therefor not
loue thee , wholy forgetting themselues and their own profit , and
commodity either for time or eternity? Certainly the Prophets, Mar-
tyrs, Confessors , and Virgins that
loued thee more then their liues,

found torments, bannishments, im-
prifonments, and perfecutions fweeter by reafon of their *loue* to *thee*, and
of their defiring to be faithful to *thy*
amiable *Maiefty* , then al the pleafures, contentments, riches honours,
and glory of the world did euer yet
yeald to thofe that haue moft abounded therewith fince the beginning
of the world. O if we could ask
Salomon (for al the aboundance
he liued in) and S. Francis in his
pouerty , or S. Laurence vpon his
Gridiron; and certainly both by his
acknowledgment and theirs , their
pouerty, and pain through *loue*, were
fweeter then al his delights euen in
this world ; yea euen Iob fitting vpon the Dunghil and faying; *God gaue,
and God hath taken away, as it pleafeth
our Lord fo let it be , his name be bleffed
for euer* enioyed more comfort and
true peace in foul , then al the comforts and pleafures of this world
could giue , or haue caufed to him.
For only fubmiffion to *thee*, my deare *God*, bringeth true comfort to our

souls! O if we did truly humble our
selues, how greatly would *thy goodnes* be exalted in our souls? If we
did seek *thee*, not *thy* gifts, graces,
and comforts, how then should we
go out of our selues and therby enter into *thee*? O if we were truly
humble; how much wouldst *thou* be
pleased to be serued by vs? and how
many do fare the better for *thy humble ones*, though they be hidden and
vnknown for such to the world?
Certeinly the humble are so deare
to *thee*, that *thou* seemest not willing,
or able to do any thing without
them. For while vnmindful of al
but *thee*, they forget themselues,
thou in the meane time enrichest
them with *thine* own works, that
they may merit more grace, glory
and fauour before *thee* in al things
thou dost or permittest, to which
to the vttermost of their power they
concurre by *humble resignation*, if
they can do no more, which is sufficient to satisfy *thee*, *who* needest not
our works, or labours; but it is our

harts, *souls*, and *loues* that *thou* requirest, and by which *thou* wilt do *good*
to vs, or by vs. What *thou* thinkest
meet for vs to do, or to be able to
do, ought to be indifferent to vs,
who should haue no wil but *thine*,
nor any election but of *thee*. Wel
may it be said, that where *Humility*
is, there is also *Wisedom*. For the truly *humble* being guided by *thy interior Truth* and Iustice more then
by human wisedom, surpasse the
weaknes of their own folly; for so
al wisedom may be esteemed, that
is not from *thee* and in *thy light*, by
which *light* only we can discern the
glorious *truth* and not by the natural light of our weak vnderstanding,
that is not able without a beame
of *thy Grace* to discouer such *truth*,
so blind is our soul of it-self without *thee*; and it is only true *humility* that maketh vs capable of this *thy
light*. And yet if a soul had been with
S. Paul in the third Heauen, if she
should leaue the way of *Humility*,
she would return to her former

blindnes , and the more she by v-
furping *thy* gifts and graces to her-
felf did puff vp her felf, the more
al true *light* and *difcretion* would depart from her foul , and the more
het folly would appeare to heauen,
and earth to her great confufion
both in this life and in the next
if she did not return and come to
know her own *nothing*. For as it is
truly faid; *The corruption of the beft, is
the worft*. O Lord deliuer al from this
accurfed fin of pride , which turned Angels into moft vgly diuels,
and hath been the canfe of the fe-
paration of fo many fouls (created
by *thee* to enioy eternal felicity)
from *thee* my *God* ; But efpecially
deliuer thofe from this moft odious
vice who haue had the means by the
mercy of *thy fweet Goodnes* , to come
to fome *true* knowledg of *thee* and
themfelues. For if we knew al, and
☞ could difcourfe with al the wit and
eloquence of the Philofophers, Ora-
tors , and Diuines of the caufes and
effects of al natural and fupernatu-

ral things , yet if we did no tknow
thee by endeauouring truly to *loue*
thee , we might truly be faid to know
nothing. For only by *louing thee* and
knowing our felues is *true Wifedom*
obtained. And how can it but peruert al true Iuftice , that *thou* art by
fo few (in comparifon of the whole
world) fought with a *pure intention* ?
If we being almoft to death benum-
ed with cold fhould for remedy go
forth into the bluftering and far
colder wind , or in the fcortching
heat of fommer fhould for mitiga-
tion therof to our body go to an
hot flaming fire , who would not
iudg vs euen out of our witts for
our fo doing ? Euen fo we when wanting fupernatural *light* that is *true*
light and neceffary for the guidance
of vs in the way towards *thee* , we
in lieu of feeking after that *light* and
of taking the means to come by it,
do betake vs on'y to our natural
light , the which as to the faid fupernatural end is but meere blindnes , and darknes, and thus proceed.

K v

ing in aſſuming for our means the
contrary of that we ſhould , we prof,
per both in our practice and in our
end accordingly. The things which
we practiſe as vertues being indeed
no *true* vertues for want of the *diſcretion* that it neceſſary for the perfection of them , and the which *diſcretion* is but the ſelf ſame as the *light*
had from *thee* , wherby often-times
our pretended vertues come to haue
more of vices then of true vertues
in them, ſuch defect proceeding out
of this , that indeed in our *inward*
and *ſecret* conſciences we think that
we are able to do that which is right
and profitable of our own ſelues,and
without *light*, and ability for it from
thee. And when harm falleth to vs,
or to others by ſuch our blind proceedings we lay the fault of it vpon *thee* where it is not , and not vpon our ſelues, where indeed it is. O
let this folly alſo be far from vs !.for
thou art iuſt , O my *Lord* , and thy
judgments are equity , how hidden ſoeuer thy meaning in them be

to our fouls. I for my part defire to adore *thee* in al *thou* difpofeft, and do moft gladly acknowledg, that al *thou* haft made is good, if it be put for that vfe for which *thou* madft it. Do not we fee that euen Spiders, and Serpents do draw the venom from the earth both for the purging it, and alfo for a farther vfe that man therof maks, and yet thefe to our feeming are of the leaft worth as to good among *thy* creatures. But it is our mif vfing, abufing, and mif-applying *thy* creatures that makes the world turn vpfide down. The hail thunder ftorms, rain, & fnow, did the three Children in the furnace inuite to praife *thee* as good in themfelues being made by *thee*. But nothing is fo good in this world, but it may be peruerted and abufed. For if man whofe foul was made by *thee* in fuch purity, by fin becometh fo foul, how can this choofe but breed diforder in the world, al things therein being giuen by *thee* to be difpofed by him, and vfed by him as

helps to ſerue *thee* while we liue heer?
But ô my *God* , I wil ſpeak to *thee*,
and I wil cal vpon *thee* who art *Wiſe-*
dom it-ſelf ; If *thou* ſmile at my folly,
yet behold me ſinner, and inſtruct
me in *thy* Law, which is ſweet aboue
al delights of the world ; and to ſerue
thee for *loue* , is that which I only
deſire. In al my miſeries and afflictions of body and ſoul *thou* deſpiſeſt not any ſoul flying to *thee* , and
dilating my-ſelf to *thee* , I do comfort and ſtrengthen my hart, which
aſpireth to nothing , as *thou* knowſt by this my ſpeaking to *thee*, but
to eaſe my ſoul by begging help of
thee , and declaring to *thee* my only
friend , my ſins and miſeries. For if
we fly from *t'ee* whither go we, but
out of one darknes into another ?
Who can diſcouer our wounds to
vs, but *thy-ſelf*, who when we acknowledge them , doſt alſo cure the lan-
guiſhing diſeaſes of our very ſouls?
O in *thy light* let me ſee *light* , that
ſo al impediments may be remoued
between *thy Godnes* and my ſoul? My

soul can neuer return to *thee*, til it be purged and purifyed by *thy grace* and Mercy. Of my-selfI can do nothing. *Thou* therefor that madst and redeemedst me, saue me, who euery moment should perish, if I were not assisted by *thee*. I see nothing, or hear any thing, but it giueth me new cause to praise *thee*, and to seek *thee* aboue al gifts, graces, and creatures; Grant me therefor to serue *thee* in that maner *thou* wouldst be serued by me· For I am not able to do any thing good of my self. Let me by *Humility* and true obedience return to *thee*, from *whom* for my sins I deserue to be separated with the diuels eternally; but *thy Mercy*, which is aboue al *thy* works, pardon me, and giue me *Grace* to liue better heerafter. O my *God*, me thinks some times I haue so liuely a feeling of my own *nothing*, and see so plainly that we depend wholy of *thy grace*, and Mercy, that I wonder how it is possible I should any more be able to presume of my-self in any

thing whatfoeuer. But alas this paffeth away;and like duft carried away
with the winde , fo is my foul with
vanity ; In which my fin , and mifery I groan to *thee* from the bottom of my foul , *who* art my *helper*
and my *deliuerer* from al mine enemies , wherof the greateft is my felf;
and to *thee* I declare my iniquities
which are without end , or meafure,
to the end I may glorify *thee* the
more *who* sheweft mercy to me , and
reiecteft not the moft difloyal of al
thy Maiefties feruants. For which let
heauen ,and earth praife *thee*, feeing
I am not able by any thing to shew
gratitude to *thee*. For I cã do nothing
but declare *thy Mercy* , and befeech
thyfelf to fupply my defect in praifing
thee. For *thou* only canft do it , as I
defire it should be done. The very
Seraphins are too short of being
able according to *thy* worth to praife
thee and al *thy* Angels and Saints accompt themfelues, as dumb in comparifon of *thy* deferts from them
For al *thy fweet Mercy* be *thou* there.

for by al, not as able, but as willing to praiſe *thee*, magnifyed for euer and euer. *Amen.*

THE XLII. CONFESSION.

O *My Lord, and my God*; If none haue much forgiuen them, but thoſe that *loue much*, what wil become of me? This day we read in our Office, that Saint Marie Magdalen coming to *thy* feet (which ſhe watered with her teares) heard that comfortable anſwer from *thee*, to wit; *Go in peace, thy ſinnes are forgiuen thee*; but it was out of this regard that ſhe *loued much*. This anſwer *thou* madſt to her (whoſe hart in ſilence ſpoak vnto *thee*) doth much comfort my ſinful ſoul. But yet when I remember how void I am of that which was the neceſſary diſpoſition for her ſoul to hear thoſe comfortable words, *thy ſins are forgiuen thee, go in peace*, it draweth teares from mine eyes to ſee how far my ſoul is de-

Luk 9. 5.

stitute of that pure *loue* which pre-
uaileth with *thy diuine Maiesty*. What
shal I say ? What shal I do ? Or
wherein shal I hope ? I am not fit to
plead for my-self, my sinnes, indeed are so many and so great ; and
as for the *loue* which only *thou* desirest, behold my soul is destitute of it.
For if I haue any towards *thee*, my
God it is but a sensible, childish
loue, which is a loue little beseem-
ing the bestowing vpon such a *God*,
who is al *Good*, Beawty, Wisedom,
yea euen *Goodnes* and *Loue it-self* ; to
whom is due a *loue* which is able to
suffer al things for this *loue* is a strong
loue, more strong *then death* it-self,
the which kind of *loue* is far from
me, who am blown down with the
least blast of temptation, and cannot endure any disgrace, desolation, or difficulty whatsoeuer, as it
beseems a true *louer* of *his*. But notwithstanding my pouerty, and misery, yet I wil hope in *him* and wil
approach to *his* feet, *who* is *Mercy it-*
self. There, my *Lord*, and my *God*,

I wil in filence figh and weep both
for my finnes and for my defect in
louing thee, who art worthy o f al *loue*
and Praife whatfoeuer. There I wil
beg this *loue* fo much to be defired.
There I wil wish and long for it, and
from *thy* feet I wil not depart til
thou denounce to me; *thy fins are forgiuen thee*, and faieft to my foul, *go
in peace.* This voice I long to hear
in my hart, that I may with the voice
of exaltation praife *thee* for euer.
Amen.

THE LIII. CONFESSION.

A *Men, Amen, dico vobis; quia rece-
perunt mercedem fuam.* (Math.6.,
*Amen, Amen I fay vnto you they haue
receiued their reward.* Thefe *thy* words
my *Lord* and my *God* come into my
mind fo often as my thoughts dare
to think of hauing deferued a. reward at *thy* hands, and ferue as a
motiue to fubiect my foul totally to
thy diuine Maiefty, before whom now

I do professe, and acknowledg that my desirs, and endeauours are so defectiue in comparison of what is to *thee* due from me ; that I may, and do euen say to my soul; *Peace; be humble and subiect in al to thy God, whom thou art not worthy so much as to name with thy defiled mouth.* Indeed my *Lord*, *whose* power and *Maiesty* prostrate I acknowledg and adore, with al mine hart and soul ; if I should , neither in this , nor in the next world, receaue any other reward but what already *thou* hast bestowed on me, which I haue (I must needs confesse) receaued *gratis of thy Mercy* without any desert of mine owne, yet that which *thou* hast so already done for me , is sufficient to declare to Heauen , and earth the superaboundance of *thy mercy* and clemency to a sinful, and contemptible creature. I wil there for sing vnto *thee mercy* , *and iudgment* al the days of my life , wishing always that *thy wil*, which is Iustice it-self, may be wholy and perfectly accom-

Shee dyed presently heerevpon.

plished in me, *thy* finful feruant Let
me liue as-long as it pleafeth *thee*,
or dy in the very beginning of
thefe my defires to *loue* ; fend fick-
nes , or health ; fuddain or lingring
death ; pouerty , or aboundance,
good fame or that I be by al the
world defpifed; and in fine in al do
with me as it is moft for *thine honour.*
For in this I place al my comfort
and happines , faithfully to ferue
thee , and to be little or great in
thine eyes, as feemeth beft to *thee.*
For I accompt it a fufficient reward
for al that euer I shal be able to do,
or fuffer , that *thou* haft admitted me
vnworthy wretch , into a place of
liuing where I may know and euen
fee with mine eyes how to ferue and
pleafe *thee* ; this (I fay) is more then
can be deferued by me For to ferue
thee is an *honour* aboue al that can be
imagined by me ; yet without any
regard of recompence it is due to
thee, that I ferue, and *loue thee* with
al the forces of my body and foul,
which grant I may now begin to do

and perſeuer therin til my end, that I may for *thy own ſake* obtain the happines eternally to praiſe *thee*. O remoue al impediments between my ſoul and *thee;* Let me dy to al created things that I may liue alone to *thee l* O let al creatures be to me, as if they were not, to the end I may more fully attend to *thee* in the bottome of my ſoul , where I wil in ſilence harken to *thee* ! Speak *Peace* to my ſoul , that I may be capable of *thy* voice more ſweet then al things whatſoeuer. Speak to my hart; but ſpeak ſo as I may hear *thee.* Teach me how to practiſe to *thy* honour thoſe diuine vertues which make ſouls ſo pleaſing to '*thee*; to wit Charity, Humility, Obedience, Patience, and *Diſcretion* , which iudgeth between cuſtome and true reaſon; between opinion and *thy* true Iuſtice, which manifeſteth it ſelf to thoſe ſouls , who ſeek only to *loue* and praiſe *thee.*

THIS *pious soul hauing written thus far went no farther, being surprised with a bodily indisposition* vpon *the* 29. *or* 30. *of* Iuly 1633. *which proued to be her last sicknes that brought her to a happy death* vpon *the* 17. *of* August *following. The last of these* Confessions *saue one, she began (as there appeareth)* vpon *S.* Mary Magdalens *day, being the* 22. *of* Iuly *next before her death*

HEERE FOLLOVV SOME
other Sentences, and Sayings of the same pious Soul found in some others papers of hers.

THE *interior*, or Spiritual disposition of man, is of that great, and infinit worth, and moment; that so it be wel, al other matters wil also go wel, and be in good plight. And the good state of the *interior* (and therby also of the exterior) proceedeth from the harkning to and following of the *Diuine interior Cal, or inspiration*, the which to a soul capable of an internal life is, or ought to be as *al in al.*

And wo to such a soul who ouercome by
threats or perswasions from without, or
by temptations within her, or other occasions whatsoeuer, giueth ouer her prosecu-
tion of *Mental prayer*, by meanes wherof
only is she capable of discerning and following the *diuine wil*, and *Cal*. And therefor ô you souls that are capable of *internal
prayer*, do you accordingly prosecute it,
and be grateful to *God* for the *grace* of it.
For it causeth the greatest happines that is
to be gotten in this life, and an answarable
happines in the future. For by it in this life
one passeth through al things how hard,
and paineful soeuer they be. By it we become familiar euen with *God him-self*, and
to haue *our conuersation in Heauen*. By it al
impediments wil be remoued between *God*
and the soul : By it you shal receaue *light*
and *grace* for al that *God* would do by you,
By it we shal come to regard *God* in al
things, and profitably neglect our selues.
By it we shal know how to conuerse on
earth without preiudice to our souls: Aud
in fine by it we shal praise *God*, and become so vnited to *him*, that nothing shal
be able to separate vs for time, or eternity
from his sweet *Goodnes*. And let him be *al
in al* to vs, *who* only can satisfy our souls.
He is *his* own Praise, iu which and by
which we are infinitly happy, though of

ſar ſelues we ate able to praiſe and *loue him*,
but in a very poore maner. who can ſay
(that deſire nothing but to *loue* and praiſe
him) that they are poor, ſeeing he *who* is
more theirs then they are their owne, is ſo
rich, ond to *whom* nothing is wanting that
ſhould make *him* an infinit happines ? in
this let vs ioy, in this iet vs glory without
intermiſſion. when we are not able to attend vnto *him* and praiſe *him* as we would,
let vs commend our hart and ſoul to the
Saints in Heauen, who without ceaſing
praiſe our *Lord* : Let vs do that by them,
which we are not able to do by our ſelue :
yea let vs deſire *him*, *who* is *his* own praiſe,
and only is able to do it as he deſerueth to
haue it done, to ſupply what he deſireth we
ſhould wiſh *him*. Let vs ſeek no other
cöfort but to be able without al comfort to
be *true* to *him*, Let vs reſt in *him* alone, and
and not in any thing that is or can be created. Let vs not ſeeke the gift, but the *giuer*.
O how little is al the *loue* we can giue *him*,
in compariſon of that he deſerueth from
vs ? where, therefor ſhal there be room
for any created thing in our ſouls ? Let vs
wiſh and deſire. and (as far as it lyes in vs)
procure that al *loue* be giuen to *him*. Let
him haue al *Glory*, al Honour, and al Praiſe.
Let vs deſire the fauour of none, but *him*
alone, to *whoſe* free diſpoſition, let vs ſtand

for time and eternity, as abſolutly by our wil, as if we neuer had any other freedom of wil in vs. Nothing we do or ſuffer, let vs eſteeme great : for our ſinnes deſerue much more. Let our whole care tend to the magnifying of *him.* Let *his honour* be ours, and let vs ſeek nothing, but to be whoiy *his*, who is moſt worthy to be that that *hee* is If it is *his* delight be to be with the children of men, what ſhould comfort vs, but to praiſe aud *loue him* ? Thoſe that ſeeke *him* ſhal find *him* With al their heart, O who would ſeek any thing beſids *him*, ſeeing *he* is not more willing to giue vs any thing, then his own ſelf, heer by *grace*, and heerafter in Heauen by glory. Let vs adore *him* in *ſpirit* and *truth.* Al we can giue *him* is nothing, vnles we entierly giue *him* onr ſelues, and that alſo cannot add to his greatnes, and glory : yet if we doe this, ſo much doth *his diuine Maieſty* eſteem of this gift, that for it and in requital of it, *he* wil giue vs *his own ſelf* : al *his* gifts, and graces are a meanes for the preparing of vs for this end, if we vſe them rightly with *Humility*, and according to the iuſt *wil* of Almighty *God.* Let vs extend our wil to ſerue, *loue*, praiſe, pleaſe, and magnify our *Lord* to the vttermoſt we are able, yea wthout al limits or bounds. Let vs deſire *his* honour, til ſuch time as we

may

may be fwallowed vp in the bottomles
Ocean of al *loue*, and praife *God in him-*
felf, in *Whom* and by and in *Whom* only, we
can praife *him* as we ought. Let vs *loue him*
as far as we are poffible able, without regard of our felues, either for time, or eternity. This is the humble *loue* that feeleth
no burden. This is the *loue* that knoweth
not how to attribute any thing it doth or
fuffereth, to it-felf. It choofeth not wherin *God* shal make vfe of her, but accom-
modateth her-felf in al things to *his diuine*
pleafure. If it were *his* wil to haue it fo, she
would rather for euer be picking vp chips
or ftraws, then out of her own election, to
be doing that which is moft admired, or
might feeme to her to procure her the
greateft reward. O you fouls that *God* beftoweth *his loue* vpon, think it not much to
beare the burthen, not only of your felues,
but alfo of al that you liue with : for *God*
beareth you vp in al, more then you can cō-
ceaue or imagin, Beware aboue al things of
pride, For that caft euen Angels out of heauen. A foul of *prayer* as-long as she keeps
Humility, is in no peril of going out of her
way.

It *is certainly true*, that *God* giueth *him-*
felf to them, who forfake *al* : I fay, *al* and
not by halfs, with referuing what we pleafe
to our felues, but to al that forfake *al*, he

giueth *himſelf*, without exception of perſons, and he that pleaſeth our *Lord* needeth
not feare al the diuels in hel.

It is a wonderful thing to ſee the variety
of opinions that are, or may be about the
beſt vſe of thoſe things that of themſelues
are indifferent, or at leaſt are not euil, one
holding this, and another that, euery man
according to his fancy, and (as Saint Paul
saith) *abounding in his own ſenſe.* No wonder then that thoſe that liue, and conuerſe
with others, and namely in a Religious
Community, do eaſily fal into occaſion of
iars, and differences with others, whilſt
euery one pretends the truth, and the beſt
to be of her ſide, howſoeuer it be indeed;
and therefor ones nature wil eaſily take
occaſion of iarring with others, if it be not
mortifyed by reſtraint from what it is in-
clining to by ſuch occaſions. It is only the
diuine vertue of *true diſcretion* that is able to
diſcern and iudg for ones own practiſe
what is good, better, or beſt of al in the
vſe of thoſe indifferent things. The more
truly mortifyed the ſoul is, the cleerer is
ſuch *light of diſcretion* in her, and wil increaſe in her, if ſhe be ſtil ſolicitous more
and more to liue to *God* in her *interior*, and
to dy to her-ſelf, and to al created things
by ſimply regarding *God* in al ſhe doth, or
omitteth, & intending *him* alone in al things.

Rom.
14. 3.

It is a true prouerbe that it is an easier matter to corrupt the mind of one, then of a
great many. Wherefor we must remember
that it is a good, and happy thing for Bre-
thren to dwel in One, or rather (by *true loue
and charity*) in that *One* Which is truly necessary, to wit, in *God.* For no *loue* is true,
but that which is in *him*, and for *him*, and
without impediment to his *loue.* Al other
loues are false, slippery, peruerse and vaine,
as not being founded in *God* the ground of
al true, and happy *loue*, nor being referred
to *him* and *his loue.* But the true *loue*, which
is the *diuine*, wil make al others deare vnto
vs for *his sake*, and none deare but in *him*
and for *him.* It wil make vs incapable of accounting any to be our enemies how hardly
soeuer they treat vs, because in al things
we wil regard *God*, that permitteth such
difficulties to happen to vs, to the end our
fidelity to *him* may therby be tried and so
not regard (with any auersion) the party
who afflicteth vs: And it wil be sufficient
for vs towards the pacification of our soul
vpon the hard, or bitter vsadge offred vs,
that we remember that he hath suffred it to
happen to vs for our good, *who* only knoweth what is best for the humbling of vs and
the abating of our pride, the which must
be done if wil be pleasing to *God*, to *whom*
now, and euer I commit my-self. *Amen.*

Vnum sit mihi totum, id est, *omnia in omnibus. Let one be al to to me, that is , Al in
Al.*This was a Poesy bestowed on me and
my Parteners by another, the *truth* wherof
I pray God may answerably be in the harts,
and *loues* of vs, and of al other souls whatsoeuer.

The *simple exercise* of the wil being faithfully and perseuerarly prosecuted (through
Gods concurring grace), remoueth in time
al impediments between our soul and *God;*
and the soul by *loue* cometh so to transcend
al created things, yea euen her own self,
that al creatures are to her as if they were
not, as to any hurtful distraction they cause
to her, or as to any other impediment between her and *God*, the which can be only
by inordinate adhering in affection to those
creatures.

A *true spiritual internal life* is so priuate
and secret between God and the soul, that
others cannot easily discerne it , no not by
by the external effects of it. For in her exterior cariadge she is common, and general
as hating singularity ; by meanes wherof,
she euoideth much occasion of pride, and
walketh the more seeurly between God and
her.

Those that liue an internal life do so withdraw al natural inordinate affection from
creatures,that they often therfor are censu-

red by superiors & equals to neglect others
out of pride. But they abhorring to haue
special interest in any, do proceed so far as
they can, according to true charity, and
mind not what others iudg of them, they
desiring only in al to dischardg their duty
to *God*, *whom* they regard in al things; and
as they haue interest in none, so not any
hath interest in them. In that which they
propose to Supe iors they proceed (as in
al things els) with al sincerity, detesting
the contrary practise euen with those that
are most aduerse, and contrary to them,
much more with Superiors; and whatsoeuer they desi e to do, they do it with such
an indifferency, th.t what euent soeuer
come of it, they remain in *peace*, embracing
it as *Gods wil, whose wil* is their law. If that
which they propose, either for the common good and *peace* of the house, or for
their own good, do not seeme fit in true
Iustice, or reason to Super ors to be granted, they impo tune no farther, nor desire
the fauour of being condescended to in
their motion, but rather (remaining themselues indifferent) that they determine and
p oceed in it, to whom it apperta neth.

A Superior hath gre t reason to take heed
of putting a soul from the exercise of her
internal Prayer, or so ouerchardging her
with labourss, or solicitudes, that she can-

not become recollected In her daily *praier*,
it being a foul that hath aptnes in her to
make fpiritual progreffe by *prayer*, and the
other exercifes of a Contemplatiue life;
yea not only the foul her-felf wil feel the
vnfpeakable dammage that wil come
to her therby, but alfo the Superior him-
felf in the Obedtence which he expecteth,
and is due to him from her, wil fee the
harme and looffe that come.h by fuch be-
reauing of the foul of her *prayer*. For fhe
who would by *difcreet*,profecuting a courfe
of *mental praier* haue become fubiect (if
it were neceffary) euen to the creature that
is of the leaft efteeme, or worth in the
world, becometh now for want of that
ftrength and help which is gotten by fuch
prayer; to be almoft impoffible to be ruled
by the wifeft man in the world. For liuing
in Religion (as I can fpeak by experience)
if one be not in a right courfe of *prayer* and
other exercifes, between *God* and our foul,
ones nature groweth much worfe then
euer it would haue been if fhe had liued in
the world. For pride and felf-loue, which
are rooted in our foul by finne, findeth
means to ftrengthen it felf exceedingly in
one in Religion, if fhe be not in a courfe
that may teach her and procure her true
Humility. For by the corrections and contradictions of the *wil* (which cannot by

any be auoided, but wil be, liuing in a Religious Community) I found my hart grown, as I may fay, as hard as a ftone, and nothing would haue been able to haue mollified it, but by being put into a courfe of *prayer*, by which a foul tendeth towards *God*, and learneth of *him* the leffon of truly *humbling*, herfelf; In which courfe being placed, and euer tending to the increafe of *Humility*, euen the defects and errors she committeth either out of frailty or ignorance, do turn to her gaine, as giuing her occafion of the greater *humbling* of her-felf to and vnder *God*; and *Humility*, and the *loue* of *God* (wherein al her good confifteth) do each of them increafe the one the other, for they are infeparable companions.

It is the grace of God and tending to *him* by way of *loue*, that only can fo enable a foul, that no difficulty, or difgrace can happen, which she is not prepared for, and therefor is able willingly to embrace the fame. Verily I can affirme this by mine own experience, that a croffe word, or flight reprehenfion before I got into this *fpiritual* cours, was more infupportable to me, and did more difquiet my mind, then al the difficulties or difgraces, which fince haue faln vpon me, haue done. For now me thinks though I be neglected by al the world, yet by flying to our *Lord he* eafeth

me of al my burthen ; and as I haue defired
to haue no other friend, or comforter but
him ſo it pleaſeth *him* neither in doubts,
feares, paines, diſgraces, nor in any other
miſeries (whereunto this life of ours is ſo
ſubiect) to reiect me; Only *he* exacts of me
that in al the contradictions of *wil he* ſends
me, or permits to fal on me , I wil humble
my-ſelf and be confident in *his* help.; Of
Which, if I do ſo , I ſhal be much more
ſure, then if in mine own hands I had a
moſt abſolut power.

None are able to preſecute the waye of the
Diuine Loue, but they who are reſolued to
to deny themſelues in al things, and who
willingly and wittingly adhere to no created thing ; For if the ſoul do willingly retain an affection to any ſuch thing, ſhe is at
a ſtop , and can go no farther. For *God*
muſt be ſought and *loued* wholy, if we deſire to arriue to *Perfection.*

Shee ſpeaking of the Sanctity of the old
    Orders in old time , when they were in
    their beſt caſe, or in the Prime of their
    good Spirits *, writeth and ſayeth as*
    as followeth , viz.

THEN *only the honour of God* was ſin-
    cearly, without intermingling of human

ends, or interefts, intended and fought, and
al Orders with one confent of hart did concurre to the aduancement of that alone, they
then applied themfelues to feueral exercifes
in the exterior euery one according to his
Inftitute, fome more eafy and fome more
ftrict, fome of more action, and fome of
leffe; yet *interiorly* their principal end was
alone, and that was to find and enjoy *God*
in their fouls; and out of that perfect *Charity* which efpecially by thofe their internal
exercifes did gro in them, they did euery
one as *God* did require and enable them,
imploy part of their time in gaining, or
doing good to other fouls. Then there
was no great care or folicitude about tem-
porallities, *God* taking care, and being as
it were folicitous of them; Then there was
indeed al fincere and real proceedings between them; Then there was perfect *amity*
without proper intereft or fond affection
to the impediment of their *louing* and feeking after *God* alone; who is that *One thing*
which only is *neceffary*; Then there was no
acceptation of perfons, but they were contented, fo *Gods* honour were aduanced, not
caring though it were done by any other
Order as wel as by themfelues. O *Lord my
God*, if this *Spirit* might be reuiued againe,
how much would my foul rejoice? If Saint
Benets his, S. Francis his, S. Ignatius his, &c.

L v

children were perfectly, as this life wil permit, vnited together, and with one hart,
and consent seek and labour to aduance
thy honour and praise, as our founders do
in Heauen, which if we did then would the
Spirit of the primitiue Church flourish,
and *thy* torn and mangled members be
healed and perfectly set againe together;
Then heretiks and sinners would easily be
conuerted by them to *thee* ; Then there
would be another *learning*, then now there
doth flourish in our Order; and *thou* by
them wouldst speak, *who makest the tongues of infants eloquent* ; Then they by
prayer conuersing in a familiar and tender
maner with *thee*, would speak so, that none
would be able to resist *thee* in them, Then
their iudgment would be so cleered that
they would vnderstand most hidden mysteries ; Then an hower of *praier* would
instruct them more fully, then fifty
years study can do, they hauing by the
meane of such *prayer* (in al things) relation to *thee* the only true *wisedom*, and
in *whose light* only is *true light* to be seen.
By *louing thee* and dying to themselues in
al things they would become maisters of
themselues, and al the world would then
nothing moue them, nor would any thing
affright them, becaus *thou* wouldst be their
stay and comfort in al things.

Wis. 10

If we wil *do* as we ought and as is best for ys, we must be subiect to the *wil* of *God* in al things without exception ; And this is the benefit of an *internal life*, that it makes one capable of seeing and knowing *Gods wil* , and also most ready to performe it, Which way soeuer he signify it to them; which makes them obey as readily , and willingly (meerly for *Gods fake* and out of obedience to *him*) a simple or imperfect Superior , as they would an Angel, or the Wisest creature in the world; yea if it were possible that a worme, or any other creature were ordained by *God* to rule ouer them, rhey would with al their harts embrace *his wil* by them. For without this total subiection to *God* , it is impossible to become truly *Spiritual*. For if we resist *his wil* in our Superiors ; in vaine do we pretend to please *him* ? This vertue therefor of Obedience , we must learn of *him*, the which must be grounded vpon true Humility, that must be our stay in al things. And those two vertues of *Humility* and *Obedience* , together with the diuine vertue of *Discretion*, he wil teach vs , if we do our parts in seeking to become more & more humble , and subiect to *him*. For seeing it is *his wil* we should obey and become truly *Humble*, how can we doubt but he wil giue vs the *grace*, if we *Humbly* and

perſeuerantly beg it of *Him*, and practiſe
thoſe vertues vpon occaſions as wel as we
can ? For *he himſelf* hath ſaid ; *wh n we aske
our father bread, he doth not giue a ſtone, nor
if we aske him fiſh, wil he giue a ſerpert;*
much leſſe wil *he* deny vs what is neceſſary
to make vs pleaſing to *him*, and we ſeeking,
or deſiring nothing but by true *loue* to be
faithful to *him. O Praier, praier,* able to obtaine al things! O how cometh it to paſſe my
Lord, that this *Omnipotent* thing (as ſome of
thy deare ſeruãts tearme it) *praier* ſhould be
ſo vnknown, yea and euen to them whom
thou tearmeſt the Salt of the earth, contemned, (I meane *Mental praier)* at leaſt for
the practiſe of poore ſimple women, for
whom they hold it aboue al things moſt
dangerous, euen to my own knowledg, as
I haue known affirmed by Superiors of
ſeueral Orders ! O miſery to be truly lamented by al that haue or may haue taſt i ı
praier, and by the effect thereof know how
ſweet a thing it is to attend only, and wholy to the praiſe, and *loue of God.* Surely the
want of the *wiſedom,* which by *praier* the
Saints did gaine, is the cauſe why cúſtome
and opinion do take place for the moſt part
in this world of true reaſon. Surely neuer
was the world reformed of its ſins and errours ; but it muſt be by the *wiſedom* which
cometh from *God,* and is farre different

Luk
11.12,

from that which is accounted Wiſedom by 1. *Cor.*
the world, which as S. Paul ſaith; *is folly* 3.19.
before God.

CERTAIN OTHER DEVO-
tions of the ſame deuot Soul D. Gertrude
More , which she left written in her
Breuiary.

In the fore part of her Breuiary she
had framed and written the en-
ſuing praier for her due performance of the diuine Office, viz:

Al you that bleſſe our Lord , exalt him
al you can ; for he is greater then al
your praiſes.

OMNIS SPIRITVS LAVDET
Dominum. Let euery ſpirit praiſe the
Lord.

AND I thy poore *creature* , who am not
worthy to name *thee* (my *Lord* my
God, and al my *good*) do heer in the preſence of al thy Celeſtial Court deſire to
peːform this my Office with al diligence,

and with an *amourous* affections towards *thee* my *Cod*, *who* haſt impoſed this ſweet and moſt to be deſired obligation vpon me ſinner, who doth not deſerue any ſuch ho-nour, or comfort from *thee* as to be admit-ted to ioine my cold and frozen praiſes with al thoſe who praiſe *thee* either on earth or in heauen where al to my comfort do with-out ceaſing continually praiſe *thee*. And for what is wanting in me for the performance thereof, as I ſhould and ought to do, ſup-ply it out of the ſuperaboundance of *thy merits* and *mercy*; I deſire to ſay it with al my hart according to the intntion of our holy Mother the Catholick Church ; of which I deſire through *thy grace* to liue, and dy a true member ; be *thou* according to her deſir, Adored, Bleſſed, Magnified, and ſupreamly Superexalted by *it*; Let it be to the honour of *thy* al Immaculate Mother the Lady and Queen of Angels, and Saints; to theſe in a patticular maner; (viz) to my good Angel, our moſt holy Father S. *Benet*, S. *Scholaſtica*, S. *Ioſeph*, S. *Peter and* S. *Paul*, S. *Iohn Enangcliſt*, S. *Iohn Baptiſt*, S. *Thomas*; and my deare S. *Auguſtin*, S. *Mary Mag-dalen*, S. *Gertrude*; and in fine, al that are in Heauen haue by it to them exhibited by *thee* what *thou*, willeſt and deſireſt ſhould be; I beſeech *thee* alſo that I may by it pray to *thee* for al afflicted, pained, tempted, and troubled, that they may pleafe and praife *thee* in thofe their miferies and ouercome them to their comfort and *thy glory*; I alfo offer to *thy fweet Mercy* al thofe fouls who by deadly fin are enemies to *thee*, which is indeed the mifery of miferies; O let them return to *thee* who art our beginning and the *true Center* of our fouls, from *whom* to be feparated by fin is a moft greiuous hel, and to *whom* to be vnited *by grace* is a moft fweet *Heauen*; Conuert therefor and recal thofe fouls to *thee* for whom *thou* fparedft not *thy* moft pretious Bloud, fhedding it to the very laft drop for vs finners; I offer *thee* alfo my Parents, who haue placed me heer in *thy houfe*, where here I may euen heare and fee how to ferue *thee*, and where I may night, and day attend to *thee* and praife *thee* my amiable and moft to be defired *beloued*, whom to ferue and to be obliged to *loue*, is the only happines in this world, and to *whom* to be tyed by vowes, and other obligations of Religion is a moft fweet *feruitude* and *yoke*, and fo fweet that no liberty is to it to be compared; I offer *thee* alfo our holy Congregation, and al that euer, or fhal defire my poore vnworthy prayers; and aboue al I offer *thee* al thofe in earth, or Purgatory which thy *diuine Maiefty* would haue me pray for to *thee*, befeeching *thee*

that *thy Diuine wil*, and pleasure may be
perfectly accomplished in al creatures, and
last of al though not with the least affection, I offer to *thee* this thy Conuent, wherof though very vnworthy of such a fauour

*The
Bene-
dictin
Nouns
at Cā-
bray.*

as to liue in such a happy company I am a
poor imperfect member, beseeching *thee for
thy owne* sake, and by the *loue thou* bearest to
al such as truly seek to please *thee* alone,
that *thou* wilt mercifully enrich their souls
with the most abundant gifts of *thy grace*,
so that their whole study may be to please,
praise, and worship *thee* in *spirit* and *truth*,
and especially I offer *thee* those therein,
that haue done, do or shal heerafter, by
their patience in supporting the defects of
their Sisters, and helping them by that
meanes to beare their burthen, and by their
giuing good example in *Humility*, Obedience, and other vertues, be a meane or
helpe to the maintaining of Peace in this
thy house; towards which thou hast shewed so much Prouidence, that if we cast not
our whole care both for body and soul vpon *thee*, we shal not deserue the fauours
thou hast shewed to vs. We a e *thy* little
flock ; keepe *thou* euer possession of vs ; let
vs be of one mind, and of one hart, and
let vs al and euery one with one consent according to *thy grace* giuen vs simply intend,
and regard *thee* in al we do, think, speak,

or defire: *thou* haft called vs and gathered
vs together, fend vs a good life, and a happy death, to *thy* Praife, Honour and Glory,
who art *God* of al things, and to *whom* now
and for euer be giuen al Laud and Praife
by al creatures. *Amen. Amen.*

*Delicta iuuentutis meæ , & ignoran-
tias meas ne memineris Domine.*

*Ab occultis meis munda me Domine,
& ab alienis parce feruo tuo.*

*O Domine Spes mea; delicta quis en-
telligit?*

O my God, my deare *delight* and al my
happines: Thou knowft I groan in *fpirit*
againft my-felf, to think that I made no
more haft to couclude an euerlafting league and *peace* with *thee* my *God!*

O teach me to *loue*, or let me not liue,
thou only canft do al things, and I, as *thou*
wel knowft, can do nothing. Behold I
defire to leaue al to find *thee*, and to dy
to al created things, to the end I may liue
only in, and to *thee*. I defire only *thee*, and
to return to *thee* the beginning of al creatures and the fupreame *beloued* of al chaft
fouls?

O how powerful is thy *true loue* in a pure
foul? O purify my hart and foul, fo that
nothing but *thy loue* may liue in me!

O when shal I fee my foul vnited to *thee?*

O when by true loue shal my foul languish for *thee?*

O when shal I be wholy turned into the *loue* of *thee?*

O that I might do in al things that which is pleafing to *thee?*

O when shal my foul by tranfcending al created things become capable by Charity of embracing *thee* in the bottom of my poor foul?

O loue, loue, loue; what wonderful effects doft thou work in a foul? *Thy loue*, my *God* doth fweeten al miferies, aud maketh light al barthens, and labours.

Verily nothing in the world is fo delightful to them that loue it, and haue as much of it as they can defire, and enioy al the pleafures and contents thereof, as it is to a *louing* foul, that fincerely feeketh *thee*, to fuffer for *thy loue*.

O my God, what do we loofe euen in this life, when we wish for, loue, or defire any thing befids *thee*. It is only *loue* that draweth thee down to vs, and eleuateth vs vp to *thee*!

O who would not fuffer any thing to obtain this *loue*.

Nothing can comfort or fatisfy my foul but to *loue thee*.

When wilt thou replenish my hart with

thy pure loue, that refteth in *thee* aboue *thy* gifts , that my foul may truly adore *thee* in *fpirit* and *truth* ?

Thou knowft that no graffe doth fo wither for want of water, as doth my poor finful foul for want of *thy loue*.

O *that* without ceafing I could praife *thee* !

As the flag , or *hart* beiug tired with purfuit doth thirft and pant after a fweet Spring, fo doth my foul after *thee*, it hauing been much more tired with ftreying from *thee* then the poor *hart* can be by being chaced by his enemies, by as much more as it is more greiuous to be hurt by ones felf , then to haue it done by others.

O *when* fhal I in al things do *thy wil*, that my actions may be iuft, and pleafing to *thee* ?

O *when* fhal I fo humble my-felf that I may be worthy in fome fort to praife *thee whom* now for my pride I am not fit to name ?

Iefu Son of Dauid haue mercy on me, and of *thy* great pitty, and Charity remember me among the Whelps that expect and beg vnder thy table for one crum of *grace* from *thee*.

Where but vnder the fhaddow of *thy* wings fhal I repofe from the heat of al inordinate paffions and defires, and from that mid-day Sun that parcheth and withereth away the new fpriggs ; or leaues of my new fowen defir of *louing*, praifing, and pleafing *thee alone*, my *Lord* and my *God* ? Who but thy felf by *thy fweet grace* can preferue me from f.lling into my old fins ; and forrowes ? *Thou* therefor art my only Refnge in this day of my tribulation, and amidft the ftorms of this wor'd , to *thee* I reueale my caufe, be *thou* my ftrength and my Glory , that I may at laft laying down the burthen of this mortal flesh, be admitted into that place , where I may Praife *thee* for euer and euer. *Amen.*

O my God, when shal that time come, that I shal neuer more offend *thee* ? This is the mifery wherein I languish, and which maketh this world tedious to me : This only is truly to be tearmed an affliction and mifery, and nothing is truly to be accounted mifery, but to difpleafe *thy diuine Maiefty*, *Iefu Son of Dauid* haue mercy on my finful foul.

O how happy are thofe that *loue thee* ? O *loue*, *loue*, *loue* of my *God* , how far is my finful foul from the happines of enioying *thee*, as my foul defireth ?

Nothing is fweet to a hart that defireth to *loue* her *God*, but to figh, long, and pant after *him*.

O *who* wil giue me the wings of a Doue, that I may fly into the open wounds of my beloued?

O *my God*, my only defire, how long shal I thus be eftranged from *thee* the *God* of my hart, and my *portion* for euer?

O *the moft dearly beloued* of my foul, how long, shal I by inordinatly adhering to created things be fo far from *louing thee*, as I ought to do? O *thou who* only deferueth our *loue*, my *God* and my al!

Lord my God who alone art *good* and iuft, shal I any longer *loue* uanity, and feek after a lye? How long shal *thy* difpofitions and moft righteous ordinances be difpleafing to *thy* poore feruant? How long shal I refift *thy diuine wil*?

Verily my God, in this my mifery I figh vnto *thee*, who art my hope from my youth, and am difpleafed with my-felf for hauing been fo vngrateful to *thy* fweet mercy, acknowledging before Heauen and earth, that nothing is iuft, but that which *thou* difpofeft, and nothing is wel done, faue fo far as it is done by *thee*, fo much as any thing I do or fay is only of mine own wil and defire, fo far it iuftly deferueth punifhment, to *thee* be al glory.

In nothing is true *Peace*, but in feeking after *God* alone, and in refting in *him* aboue al *his* gifts.

O my God, when shal I be able to say:
Quis me separabit à Charitate Dei? VVho
shal separate me, from the Charity of God?
O when shal I by true *loue* become vnited
to *thee the only desire of my hart and soul?*
Vsquequo Domine obliuisceris me in finem?
Vsquequo auertis faciem tuam à me? How
long wilt thou forget me vnto the end? How
long doth thou turn away thy face from me?
wilt thou for euer be angry with *thy* poor
seruant? Behold *thou* knowst I desire no
other comfort vpon earth, then to be able
without offending *thee* to liue without al
comfort human, or diuine.

O how *little* to be esteemed is al the sola-
ces this world can afford: *The wicked haue*
been telling me of their delights, but they are
not like those of thy Law. What comfort can
any creature l uing afford a soul that sigh-
eth, and longeth after *thee alone* my *God*,
and is bannished from the *beloued* of her
soul?

Verily my God, it is only *thy-self* that can
reioyce and comfort such a soul, *thou* only art sweet, and al things compared to *thee*
are as nothing, and lesse then nothing.

O my *Lord, and my God*, tel me, is there
any thing in Heauen or on Earth that can
satisfy my soul besids *thee?* No certainly.
Why then dost *thou* permit me thus to wan-
der from *thee*, who art only worthy to be

defired and *beloued* by my foul?

O *my moſt deare* God, who can comprehend the miſery that ſoule ſuffereth, that taketh comfort or deſireth any comfort from any creature?

O *how long* ſhal I be ſubiect to this miſery of inordinatly *louing thy* creatures, ſo that it is an impediment to the *louing* of *thee* my *Creator, who* are the ſupreame *Good?* To *thee* alone is al *loue* due, and we do ſteal from *thee,* when our affection is willingly caried to any thing els whatſoeuer.

O *my God,* my Mercy, let vs *loue thee* as *thy diuine Maieſty, who* art *Lord* of al things & in *whoſe* power al things do ſtand, let me (I ſay) *loue thee* as *thou* wouldſt be *beloued* by me.

O *my Lord,* as-long as the *peace* of my ſoul dependeth of men, I can neuer repoſe in *thee,* or find *thee* in the bottom of my ſoul!

What came I into Religion for, but to *loue* and praiſe my *God,* my *Lord,* and al my *good?*

O *when* ſhal I as I deſire, *loue thee* and pleaſe *thee* my God and al my deſire?

O *my God,* how cometh it to paſſe that *thou whoſe* mercies are *ſuper omnia opera eius, Aboue al his works,* shouldſt be now tearmed to be terrible, and hard to be pleaſed? Verily I am a ſinner and the greateſt

of al sinners, and yet I haue found *thee* so
good and easily pleased , that nothing is
more pleasant then to serue *thee* for *loue* and
to beare *thy yoke from our youth:* The yoke of
sin is heauy , but *thine* is sweet aboue a the
contentments, and pleasures of this world.

    Let those that seek not *thee* , and that
desire any thing willingly but *thee*, feare,
and return to *thee*, but let the harts of them
that loue *thee* reioice, O *Lord*. But can I say
I *loue?* Verily not I. But shal I for this feare?
No my *God*, at least not so as to loose confidence , which hath in it a great remunera-
tion, For seeing by *thy grace* I desire to *loue*,
and to leaue al for *loue*, I wil hope in *thy
Mercy* , let *it* assist my extreame frailty, and
pouerty : Of my-self I am *nothing* , but in
thy power I shal be able to do al things.

    Thou knowst that I desire to leaue al
for *thy sake* , and that if I knew any thing
that I *loued* to the impediment of my
truly seruing *thee*, it would be so great
a grief to my soul, that nothing in Heauen or earth could comfort me til I see
my-self freed from that miserable bondage,
by *thy* assisting Grace, which I implore from
the bottom of my soul : Set me free, I most
humbly beseech *thee* by the multitude of
thy Mercies from the sinnes into which I
daily fal through my frailty , remoue al impediments between my soul and *thee* , for
                          I am

I am frail aboue al meafure; Let me liue to
thee, dying to al other things whatfoeuer:
Let me find and poffeffe *thee* in the bottom
of my foul : Let al creatures be filent that
thou alone maift be heard by me : And I wil
not trouble my-felf with them without,
who are puffing and blowing, and thereby
raifing vp the duft of multiplicity, into their
own and others eyes.

Let me enter into the moft retired place
of my foul , and fing *loue fongs* to *thee*,
my *Al* and only *Good*, regarding *thee* with
the *fimple* eye of my foul, and fighing out
certain vnfpeakabe groans in this pilgrimage of mine into the eares of the only *beloued* of my hart and foul : *wo* is me, that
euer I offended fuch a *God*! Be propiti-
ous, O *Lord* vnto my fin, for it is great!
O *Mercy*, which hath neither end, nor
meafure, haue pitty on me, and forgiue me
my fins. *Amen*.

O *Lord my God*! Let *thy Truth*, and not
the blindnes of my own ignorance, fpeak
to me : Speak *Lord*, for *thy* feruant heareth, or at leaft defireth to hear *thee*.

Behold I fet open the eares of my foul,
that I mny heare my *beloued* fpeak *Iuftice*
and *Peace* to my hart. *For thy voice is fweet
and thy face comely*, and there is none like
vnto *thee* in Beawty and *wifedom*.

Thou my God, the repofe of my labours

M

the ioy of my foul, and the comfort of my
hart : Be to me *al* in *al*, and aboue *al*,
which can be enioyed or defired : Let me,
O let me, reft in *thee* and in no created
thing whatfoeuer!

Simplify my foul that it may be able to
adhere to *thee* my God , tranfcending al
created things. O when fhal my foul forget al, and only be mindful of *thee*, the moft
pure *fpirit*, refting in *thee* aboue al *thy* Graces
and Gifts!

O when fhal I be by profound *Humility*
reduced to the *nothing*, which only makes a
a foul capable of *thee*, *who* art al *good* things,
who art that fimple *good*, in which nothing
is wanting?

How long fhal I glory in any created
thing, and feek my-felf to the dishonour
of *him*, with out *whom* I could neither haue
life nor being, much leffe to be able without *him* to do any thing meriting *grace* and
Saluation?

O *my God*, when wilt *thou* fet me free,
that I may glory in *thee* alone, and not by
pride exalt duft and afhes, which is blown
away with euery wind, and hath no ftability in it, but fo far as it is holpen by *thy*
meere Mercy. What flefh dareth glory in it-
felf, or prefume it is able to do any *good*?
Verily my *God*, if I had moft couragioufly
vndergon al the temptations, miferies, and

afflictions that haue been, or euer shal be by al thy seruants together, I ought not to think my-self able to suffer the least that can be imagined as of my-self, but iustly ought to feare mine own frailty. Let them that *glory* therefor *glory* in *thee*, and not in themselues.

O *that* some little spark of that *true light*, which true *Humility* causeth, would enter into my soul, and neuer depart out of it, til I were wholy trasformed into that *loue* which giueth *thee al*, and it-self nothing, sauing its own defectuousnes. *Thou only art Iust, thou only Holy*, and I the most vile and contemptible of al *thy* creatutes in *thine* eyes, *who* discerneth most cleerly how it stands wi:h me for my pride and other my abominable sinnes. Wash me in *thy* Bloud, and I shal yet become whiter then snow.

What would it auaile me, if I were neuer so great in the eyes of men, yea euen as great as I most vnworthy am in mine own? Could they saue me, or iustify me in *thy sight*? Is it not affirmed by the *Spirit* of al *Truth*, *Vanitas omnis homo viuens. Al liuing man is vanity*, without any exception of persons? Verily my *God*, we are indeed but as we are in *thy* sight, *who* iudgest according to the *Humility* of our hart which is hidden from the sense of man. Man may iudg that to be *Humility* which indeed is pride, and there is no pride so great as that which clotheth it-self vnder he colour of *Humility*, but *thou* canst not be deceaued by any. O happy soul that only desireth *thee* to be a witnes of her desirs, endeauours, and intentions!

Happy they that are approued by *thee* my *God*, though heer they be despised, neglected, and contemned by the whole world.

With *what face* can my soul tel my *God*, *I desire to loue him*, if I do it not more willingly, then I do, vndergo the hard censures of men? Shal I desire that which I do or say may be wel thought of by others since my *God him-self*, was thought to do al *he* did in the power of *Beelzebub*. Shal she who hath done nothing that is good, be in esteeme, when as her *beloued* who is *goodnes* and Iustice it-self, was despised and contemned? O my *God*, far be this disloyalty from my hart. Let me suffer for my sinnes, that I may become pleasing in *thy* sight, which is al my soul desireth.

O *my God*, when shal I find and possesse *thee* in the bottom of my soul? When shal the eyes of my body be so closed from beholding al vanity, that the eyes of my soul may be cleered by *thee* to the discerning of *truth*? Truly *thou* art a hidden *God* and none can walk in *thy light*, but the *peaceful*

Humble, patient, and clean of hart.

O if we did but once see in *thy light* of *truth* how little we are able to do, or suffer of our selues, we would tremble to think we were able to do any thing that were good, or to attribute any thing to our own endeauours, *Nisi Dominus ædificauerit domum, in vanum laborauerunt qui ædificant eam: Nisi Dominus custodierit ciuitatem frustra vigilat qui custodit eam. Vnles God build the house in vaine do they labour who build it. Vnles God guard the City in vaine do they watch who guard it.* It is in vaine for you to rise before light!

Psal. 126.

O *light* shine in my soul, and let not the darknes of mine own ignorance ouerwhelme me, any longer!

Let my soul loue, that it may liue in and to *thee* alone my *Lord God.*

VVhen wilt *thou* giue me the *grace* of true *Humility,* which is so much spoken of, and so hard to be known what it is indeed?

O we can neuer while we liue in this world, be secure from falling into the cursed sin of pride which maketh souls more odious to *thee,* then any o her sin whatsoeuer. O my *God* helpe me out of this snare, which laieth open the way to al other sinnes.

O who dare though hee had been rapt into the third Heauens with S. Paul, attri-

bute any gift, or grace to his owne defert?
What haue we that we haue not receaued?
and if we haue receaued it, wherof should
we glory? O how foone do we loofe the
the labour of many years in one moment
by pride? *God* protecteth vs and directeth
vs if we remain humble; but in our pride
he leaueth vs to our felues, til we fee, and
feele to our coft our own weaknes and mifery.

O *how* plaine doth it appeare to thofe
who are now fecure for al eternity in *thy*
Heauenly Kingdom, that if *thou* hadft with
drawn *thy grace* from them while they liued heer, their cafe would haue been moft
miferable? O how far are they from attri-
buting any thing to their own merits, faue
fo far as they were meerly enabled therto by
thy grace? And how far short do they efteeme their deferts to be of the *Glory*, and
Honour they receaue from thy Merciful
and bountiful hand? What pains, what labours, what fuffering of difgraces can deferue to enioy *thee*, and fee *thee* face to face
for euer and euer? Certainly thofe who
enioy this happines, haue receaued it by
the merits of thy moft bitter death and Paffion, which (*God* graunt) may bring me
wretch alfo to Saluation. *Amen.*

O *Loue, loue, loue,* when shall nothing els
liue in me but *thy* true *loue* my *God*? how long

shal I remaine deuided from *thee*? When
shal I by pure and perfect *loue* be vnited to
my *God*, al impediments being remoued?

When shal no created thing be able to
diuert my soul from attending to my *Lord
God*? When shal I be able to suffer without
offending my *God*, or being weary thereof.

O *how* little true *peace* doth that soul enioy *who* careth for the praises of men, or
feareth their dispraises; Nothing more slippery, nothing more vnconstant, nothing
more vncertain then the fauour, or friendship of man, who to day wil be thy friend
and extol *thee* to the skies; to morrow
none wil haue *thee* lesse in esteeme then he;
and what a misery then is it to place happines or security in the fauour of man?
And this ô my soul, *thy God* permits *thee* to
see, to the end *thou* shouldst adhere to *him*
alone, and not to that which is subiect to
fail. Desire the friendship of *God* alone,
and then his friends both in Heauen and
earth shal be ready to serue *thee* for thy
aduancement in *his loue* and seruice. What
can any man diminish of thy good by
his speaking, or thinking il of thee? Or
what can he add to thee indeed by highly
esteeming of thee?

Remember that al Praise is due vnto *God*,
but to thee confusion of face for thy abominable sins. Giue al Glory vnto *him*, with

ont *whom* thou couldst not so much as
haue a being. My *God*, be *thou* Adored and
Exalted by al, *who* art Blessed for euer and
euer. *Amen.*

Thou, O *sweet Iesu*, hast pronounced
with thine own blessed mouth, these words?
*Confiteor tibi Pater Domine Cæli & terræ,
quia abscondisti hæc à sapientibus & pruden-
tibus, & reuelasti ea paruulis ; Ita Pater,
quoniam sic placitum fuit ante te.* I confesse
to thee *Father Lord of Heauen and Earth,
that thou hast hid these from the wise and prudent and reuealed them to little ones. Yea Father for so it wel pleased thee.* These are the
souls to whom thy yoke is sweet and thy
burthen light these obserue and see in the
light of thy truth that al thou dost, or ordain-
est is *iust* and *true*, and that it is our sin and
ignorance only that peruerteth the order of
thy Iustice. O let vs crie out to *thee*, and
prepare our souls that in *thy light* we may
see *light*. For it is not human wisedom, or
knowledg that wil serue our turn to find
out *thee* in the bottome of our soul, for
which we were created, and for which
our soul hath such a capacity, that the very
Angels are amazed to see so great an honour
and fauour to be offered and bestowed vpon so poor and frail a creature, and yet that
we should turn a deaf eare to our *beloued,*
who saieth, his *delight is to be with the children*

of men: O how pittifully doth this most sweet and merciful *God* of ours lament our losse and misery of loosing that happines of en-ioying *him* in our soules in an extraordinary maner, yea euen in this life, if we did not cast away our *loue* and affection vpon creat-ed things, neglecting and forgetting the noble capacity wherewith the hath most bountifully endued our soules: Hear there-for what he sayeth by his Prophet; *Be ye astonished, O Heauens vpon this, and the gates thereof, be ye extreamly desolate vpon it; for two euils hath my people done, (*viz.*) They haue left and forsaken me the Fountain of liuing water, and haue dig-ged for themselues cesternes: Cesterns that are broken, that are not able to hold wa-ters.* O wo is me my *God*, that I should thus haue forsaken *thee*; What meaneth this *thy* great Mercy? I should haue la-mented mine own misery (of not on-ly neglecting to seeke after *thee* alone, but also of most miserably offending *thee* in-finit waies) and *thou* bemoanedst my case as if some preiudice were therby to come to *thee*! O what wouldst or couldst *thou* loose by my not being so happy as truly to seek after *thy loue?* truly nothing, seeing *thy Glory* cannot be added to or diminished by my misery. But *thy* infinit *Charity* which brought *thee* into the world to suffer and

Ier. 2.
13.

dy for me, is the reason of *thy* mercfful
calling vpon my poor soul, to which thou
haſt ſaid ; *I wil not the the death of a ſinner,
but rather that he be conuerted and liue.* In
the hope of this promiſe I fly to *thee : Thou
who* art able to do al th ngs ,helpe me that
can do nothing : *Thou* knowſt I¡ haue placed al my hope and comfort in *thee alone,*
and that I deteſt al that is in me which is
diſpleaſing in *thine* eyes. Far be it from me
to haue any other intention in any thing I
do or omit , but ſimply to pleaſe *thee.* I renounce al inordinate affection to al created
things whatſoeuer , and whatſoeuer I do
that is not done ſincearly for *thy loue* and
honour, I moſt willingly ſubmit my-ſelf to
any puniſhment *thy* iuſt and Merciful Iuſtice ſhal lay vpon me. Giue what *thou* com-
mandſt, and then exact what *thou* pleaſeſt.
O my *God* is it much I ſerue *thee whom* al
the world is bound to ſerue ? O what is
more ſweet then to ſerue *thee for loue,* without any pretence of our own commodity
for time, or eternity ? Truly in this lyeth
hidden the greateſt comfort that a ſoul ba-
niſhed from *thee* is capable of receauing :
To *thee who* art the ſupreame and only *true
Good* ; by al creatures be al Praiſe eternally
giuen. *Amen.*

*This which next of al followeth she there
writ, as taken out of S. Augustin,
(Viz.) I was not acquainted with that
true interior Iustice, which iudgeth not
by custome but by the righteous Law of
Almighty God.*

O My God, *apud te est fons vitæ, & in lu-
mine tuo videbimus lumen; Qui sequi-
tur me, non ambulat in tenebris.* With
thee is the fountain of life, in thy light we shal
see light, who followeth me *walketh not in
darknes,* and they that walke not in *thy light*
can neuer iudg of things according to *thy
iustice,* but iudge according to custome, or
their own sense. This *true light* is thy gift,
and Grace, which *thou* only impartest in
aboundance to the meek and humble of
hart, and to those *who* endeauour to regard
and seek *thee* alone in al their actions in
simplicity, and sincerity of hart, and *who*
intend *thee* only in al they do or omit.

*(Vnderneath the picture there annexed
of saint VVilliam Duke of Aquitain,
she had written as followeth, viz.*

O *my God* through the merits and intercession of this most glorious Saint, be mer-

L vj

ciful to me finner , and giue me grace
to *loue* , and praife *thee* with al my foul
and ftrength , and neither for time , or
eternity to feek or defire any thing , but
only *thy-felf* alone *fimply* , and purely by
fincere and perfect *loue* , refting in *thee* my
God aboue al gifts and creatures, and Ado-
ring *thee who* art *God* Bleffed for euer and
euer. *Amen. Amen.*

Mans life on earth is a continuall warfar,
and liuing but a short time, he is replenished
with many miseries. VVatch therefor and pray
that you enter not into temptation. By *Hu-*
mility and *Praier* we shal be able to paffe
through any difficulties.

(*To the image of death there annexed*
   together with other enseignes of death,
   she added thefe following words, viz.)

O how little to be efteemed , or defired
is al that paffeth away with time.

(*Thus far of her Deuotions written by*
   her in her Breuiary within the year be-
   fore she dyed.]

HEERE FOLLOVV SOME
other Deuotions of the same
pious soul D. Gertrude
More.

A short Oblation of this smal work by
the writer gatherer thereof to our
most sweet and Merciful God.

M T *GOD* to *thee* I dedicate
This *simple* work of mine,
And also with it hart and soul,
To be for euer *thine.*
No other motiue wil I haue,
Then by it *thee* to praise.
And stir vp my poor frozen soul
By *loue* it-self to raise.
O I desir neither tongue, nor pen
But to extol *Gods* praise,
In which exces le melt away
Ten thousand thousand ways,
And as one that is sick with *loue*
Engraues on euery Tree
The Name and Praise of him she loues
So shal it be with me.

I *F the glorious light of thy Church Saint*
Augustin , whose hart was so inflamed
with *loue ,* that the whole world was a

witnes thereof (and euer wil be to *thine* honour from *whom* proceedeth al *good.*) If he (I fay) ſtood need of gathering out of *thy* Soly Scriptures and the writings of holy Saints, ſomewhat that might eleuate his mind to *thee*, when he grew more cold by reaſon of humain frailty (as he profeſſeth before his Manuel) whoſe words I wil heerafter bring in as being moſt ſweet to me) what need then hath my poor ſoul to gather together certain deuout and amou, rous words, who ſcarſely in the reading thereof can lift vp my hart to *thee*; but my hope is in *thy* Mercy, which is aboue al *thy* works, and out of which thou haſt ſaid by thy Prophet, *Men and beaſts thou wilt ſaue.* To this Mercy I fly, in this Mercy is al my comfort and conſolation, I caſt my-ſelf into the arms of this *thy* Mercy and Pitty, I haue nothing wherein I can truſt. Some haue ſuffered for *thee* in their body, others in their mind, others in both; Some for *thee* haue taken great pains, and vndergon great labours and auſterities, others by couradgiouſly ſupporting diſgraces and miſeries, haue become thereby moſt deare to *thee,* others while they were afflicted and perſecuted, praied to *thee* for their enemies, and therby procured pardon for their own ſins. But alas my *God*, as for me, when I caſt backe mine eyes vpon my life paſt, I can

Pſal. 35.

find nothing done or suffered by me wherin I càn hope , wherein I can trust. Al those things which I behold others daily to practise, are, far fromme, I haue liued in this house, (of whom I may truly say; *Hæc est generatio quærentium faciem Dei Iacob. This is the generation of those that seek the face of the God of Iacob*) vnmindful and vngrateful to the *God* of Iacob ; yea my whole life hath been ful of sin and iniquity, and without end or measure haue my offences been against *thee* ; yea iustly maist thou condemn me to the bottomlesse pitty of hel. But yet I wil hope in *thee.* I am sorry from the very bottom of my hart that euer I offended *thee,* or straied from *thee.* Behold I now consecrate my-selfa new body and soul to *thee,* take away from my soul what therein displeaseth *thee.* Al *thy* Angels, and Saints be intercessors for me , especially thy deare Mother, the faithful helper and Aduocate of vs sinners.

Psal. 23.

TO OVR BLESSED LADY
the Aduocate of sinners.

AL hail, O *Virgin,* crownd with stars, aud Moone vnder thy feet, Obtaine vs pardon of our sinnes of *Christ* our *Saviour* sweet.

For though thou art Mother of my *God*,
    yet thy Humility
Diſdaineth not this ſimple wretch,
    that flyes for helpe to thee.
Thou knowſt thou art more deare to me,
    then any can expreſſe,
And that I do congratulate
    with ioy thy happineſſe;
Who art the Queen of Heauen and earth,
    thy helping hand me lend,
That I may *loue* and praiſe my *God*,
    and haue a happy end.
And though my ſins me terrify,
    yet hoping ſtil in *thee*
I find my ſoul refreshed much
    when I vnto thee fly.
For thou moſt willingly to *God*
    petitions doſt preſent,
And doſt obtain much grace for vs
    in this our baniſhment.
The honour and the glorious praiſe
    by al be giuen to thee,
Which *Ieſus thy* beloued Son
    ordaind eternally
For thee, whom he exalts in heauen
    aboue the Angels al,
And whom we find a Patroneſſe,
    when vnto thee we cal.
         Amen.

O Mater Dei,
Memento mei. Amen.

As also my good Angel, S. Ioseph. Saint
Iohn Euangelist, S. Martin, S. Augustin,
S. Thomas of Aquin, and thou my most
holy Father S. Benet.

To our most Holy Father Saint
BENEDICT.

MOst glorious *Father* in whose School,
    I liue and hope to dye,
God grant I may obserue thy *Rule,*
    for in that al doth lye.
For no perfection can be named,
    which vs it doth not teach.
O happy she, who in her soul,
    the sense thereof doth reach!
But many praise Obedience,
    and thy humility,
And yet conceaue not as they should,
    what either of them be.
The simple humble *louing* souls
    only the sense find out
Of any discret obedient *Rule,*
    and these are void of doubt.
Yea vnder shadow of thy wings
    they vp to heauen, fly,
And tast heere in this vaile of teares
    what perfect *peace* doth lye,
Hid in performance of thy *Rule*
    that leadeth vnto heauen;

O happy souls who it performe,
   the ways so sweet and euen!
By Prayer and Patience its fulfilled,
   Charity, Obedience,
By seeking after *God* alone,
   and giuing none offence.
The more I looke vpon thy *Rule*,
   the more in it I find,
O do to me the sense vnfold,
   For letter makes vs blind!
And blessed, yea a thousand times,
   Be thou who it hast writ,
And thy sweet blessings giue to them,
   who truly performe it.
For those are they which wil conserue
   this house in perfect *peace*,
Without which al we do, is loft,
   and al thats good wil cease.
And praised be our glorious *God*,
   who gaue to thee such grace,
Not only *him* thy self to seeke,
   but also out to trace
A way so easy and secure,
   if we wil but thee heare,
To haue relation to our *God*,
   who is to vs so neere,
For at this thou dost chiefly aime,
   that *God* our souls do teach.
O if we did truly obey,
   he would by al things preach
His wil to vs by euery thing

that did to vs befal;
And then as thou defirst it should
   he would be *al in al-*
O pray deare *Father* that he euer be,
   our only *loue* and *al* eternally. *Amen.*

Saint Scholaftica, S. Gertrude, and in
fine al in heauen, or on earth that are pleafing to *thee*, be pleafed to make me partaker of their merits and praiers ; and
aboue al wash me in *thy* pretious Bloud,
one drop whereof had been fufficient to
haue redemed a thoufand worlds. In this
is my hope and confidence, by this I hope
to be enriched with al that *is* wanting in
me : For, in *that thou art* and *poffeffeft,*
I more reioyce and exult , then if I had
whatfoeuer in earth, or in heauen I could
defire at my command. In this ioy I cry
out withal my hart, with al my foul, and
with al my ftrengh : *O how much good,
and happines do I poffeffe , feeing my God,
(who is more my-felf then I my-felf am)
doth poffeffe fo infinit Glory , Maiefty, and
fo infinit good things: for indeed I haue, and
hold him more mine own, then any thing that
euer I had , or held heertofore.* This is the
comfott of my pouerty and the repofe of
my labour. This my moft delightful, moft
amiable , moft bright and beawtiful, and
moft Glorious *God,* is always prefent with

me , to heare my praiſes and receaue my
petitions. In *him* I am rich, though in my
felf I am poore and contemptible. To *him*
my moſt *louing God* , be giuen now and
euer al Laud and Praiſe, and Glory by al
in heauen and earth for euer and euer.
Amen.

Theſe Collections once more I offer to
thee my God, and thoſe that in peruſing
thereof are moued thereby to *lowe* and
praiſe *thee* be they my (*God*) mindful of
me in their holy prayers , which are moſt
pleaſing to *thee*. And I alſo defire that
ſome wil out of their Charity reade theſe
things to me which heerafter follow, when
ſicke to death i ſhal be becompaſſed with
thoſe fears and terrors which ordinarily
accompany that dreadful hower ; at which
time , as al other , be *thou* my helper and
Protector, and in the Bowels of *thy* Mercy
Good Father , remember me poor begger,
and from heauen ſend me now and at my
departure *thy Grace* which may bring me
to *thee* where I may with al thy Elect,
Praiſe, Adore and worſhip *thee* for euer
and euer.

An acte of Contrition, partly taken out of the words of bleſſed S. Auguſtin.

1. O LORD I *confeſſe* I haue ſinned aboue the ſands of the Sea in number, yet ſuch is the greiſe which I take thereat, that I wil not refuſe to ſuffer any kind of puniſhment for the ſame. *O Ieſus,* whatſoeuer *thy* wil ſhal be that I ſhould do, I deſire to performe it according to *thy* holy wil. I haue nothing to offer vnto *thee*, but a *hart willing to do* whatſoeuer *thou* wouldſt haue me.

2. Heer I offer my-ſelf bound both hand, and foot, and I lye proſtrate at *thy* feet crauing pardon for my abominable ſins and offences.

3. I fly not away, I appeale not from thy ſentence, otherwiſe then from *thy* Iuſtice to *thy* Mercy which we ſinners do daily experience to be aboue al *thy* works.

4. I do not plead to be releaſed of any puniſhment, but rather that thou maiſt iudge me according to thine own *Bleſſed Wil*, only let me not be *ſeparated from thee.*

O thou thy-ſelf doſt ſay to vs: *Thou wilt net ſinners death,*

But that we do conuert and liue
   euen while our ſouls haue breath,
And no more then to ceaſe to be
   canſt thou (O *God*) refuſe
To pardon humble penitents
   that do themſelues accuſe,
Being no accepter of perſons
   al hauing coſt *thee* deare,
Yea euen *thy* very life; it-ſelf
   how can I therefor fear?
If euer yet *he* did diſdain
   ſinners that fled to him,
Then had I little cauſe of hope
   but this was neuer ſeen.
Fot if they doe return to *thee*,
   thy hart thou wilt not cloſe,
As witnes can my wretched ſoul,
   who was ſo like to loſe
Al grace and goodnes (if thou hadſt
   not me with helpe preuented)
By ſins that would with bloudy teares,
   be while I liue lamented,
If I as grateful were to *thee*,
   as *thou* deſerueſt I ſhould,
Or as another in my caſe
   vuto *thy* mercy would.
But *thou* whiles that thou liuedſt heer,
   by tokens plain didſt ſhew,
That none ſhould be refuſed by *thee*,
   who doſt in mercy flow.
And that my wicked hart did proue,

who after fins fo many
Hath found much fauour in *thine* eys,
  without deferuing any.
O bleſſed euer be my *God*,
  for this preuenting grace,
Which I vnworthy haue receaud
  in this moſt happy place.
I fled-from *thee* by many fins,
  and *thou* didſt follow me,
As if my ruin would haue cauſd
  ſome detriment to *thee*.
How can this chooſe but wound my hart,
  when I remember it,
And euer ſerue to humble me,
  while at *thy* feet I fit?
From whence my *Lord*, my *God*, and al,
  permit me not to rife,
til I do *loue thee* as thou wouldſt,
  the which doth al compriſe.

5. I know *thou* wilſt not the death of
a finner, but rather that I be conuerted
and *liue*.

6. Be pacified therefor I befeech *thee*
for thine own fake, and receaue me into
thy fauour, looke vpon *thine* own wounds,
and let them plead my pardon; *do not for
euer blot me out of the book of life*, but rather giue me *grace*, faithfully heerafter to
ſerue and pleaſe *thee*.

7. I know it is reaſon, that one who

hath been so vngratefull to *thy* Supreame *Maiesty*, as I haue been should *humbled, despise and willingly abase himself euen at the feet* of al creatures, which *thy* sweet *Goodnes* grant me to do, that I may heerafter *find fauour in thine eyes*, who be blessed and praised by al for euer. Amen.

O sweet Iesus to *whom* nothing is impossible but not to be mercifull to the miserable; forgiue me mine offence; I am sorry from the bottom of my hart that euer I offended *thee*, or contradicted *thy holy wil*; but I know *thou* canst forgiue more then I can offend, which maketh me confident of being receaued into *thy* fauour, though *thy* most aboundant Mercy; to *whom* my *God* be giuen al Laud, Honour, and Praise, by al creatures in heauen and in earth for euer and euer. *Amen.*

O amiable Iesus behold al *thy* creatures do inuite and exhort me to yeald *thee* praises for al *thy* benefits, which haue been (I must ackowledgt) without end or measure towards me *thy* vnworthy creature. Euery creature doth in their kind sing and set forth *thy* great *Goodnes*, inuiting me to *loue* only *thee*; and yet behold how cold and dul I am in Louing, Praising, and Exalting *thee*! O what shal I say? but cry out to *thee*, *who* art my hope, my help, my *Loue*, my life and *Al*; yea my Father, my

Spouse,

Spoufe, and my *God*, to grant *thy* Grace may not be void in me after fo many infinit benefits! O be *thou* heerafter the only defire and ioy of my foul. Let me look after nothing but *thee*, *loue* nothing but *thee*, let me night and day figh and long after *thee* my *beloued*, Let it fuffice me to haue my inteutions and proceedings only approued by *thee*. O let me honour, and refpeƈ al for *thy* fake, howfoeuer they treate me; for my ingratitude hath been fo great to *thee*, that al creatures as wel good as bad, may iuftly defpife me, and do *thee* great *honour* thereby. I offer *thee* therefor thine own merits feeing I haue none of mine own, for thofe that fhal any way reuenge *thy* quarrel by afflicting her, who deferueth nothing but hel for hauing fo often offended *thee*.

After fomething which she had collect-
ed out of the following of Chrift concern-
ing Prayer. she writ as followeth.

O MY *Lord God*, how much do *thy* Saints praife and commend the holy Exercife of *Praier*. O how happy are thofe that haue no other ftudy, or care, then how to extol, and praife *thy Diuine Maiefty*, and in *Humility* of hart to make their neceffities knowen vnto *thee*, *who* art the Father of Mercies , & *Deus totius conſolationis , qui conſolatur nos in omni tribulatione noſtra.* And the God of al conſolation, *who comforts vs in al our tribulation.* To *whom* should we ſinners fly, but to *thee* my *God ?* who didſt *thou* euer reiect that lamented and was ſory for their ſinnes ? Nay did not publicans, and harlots finde *thee* more willing to forgiue, thē they could be toaske for pardon ? *Thou who* forgaueſt S. Peter, S. Mary Magdalen, S. Auguſtin and infinit others their ſinnes and offences, be merciful to me, who groaneth in *ſpirit* againſt my-ſelf, to ſee, and remember that I haue made no more haſt to conclude an euer-laſting *peace* and league with *thee,* O my *God !*

To thee now al the powers of my ſcat-tered , defiled, and deformed ſoul, doth aſpire.

Behold I do extol now *thy* deare ſeruice to the skie ; profeſsing and proteſting that there is no liberty ſo ſweet, as to be bound and obliged by vowes to ſerue *thee* for *loue.*

Thou true and moſt bleſſed *God,* how didſt *thou* with a moſt ſweet and ſeuere kind of Mercy, receaue, chek, and conuince me, ſtraying, and flying from *thee,* by ſhame-fully ſeeking that in *thy* creatures, which is only to be found in *thee,* to wit, comfort, and *peace ?*

O Lord , I am *thy* seruant; say vnto my soul, I *am thy Saluation*, and al that is within me shal say; *Quis similis tibi, Deus meus. VVho is like vnto thee my Lord God.*

Behold, I haue had an auersion from al that which *thou louest*, and an inclination to al which *thou* hatest : *But thou hast broken my bands, and I wil offer thee a Sacrifice of Praise* , submitting henceforth my stif neck to *thine easy* yoke, and my shoulders to *thy light* butthen.

Vnderneath a picture of B. Iohn de Cruce, she *writ as followeth,* viz.

O Blessed and pure Saint, pray for me sinful wretch , who am not worthy to cal vpon *thee*, yet confiding in thine inflamed charity , I commit and commend my-self to thy sweet protection now and at the dreadful howre of my death, remember me I beseech thee. *Amen.*

(To some Collections which she *drew out of S. Augustins Confessions,* she *added as followeth.*)

Good God be merciful to mine iniquities for this deare Saints sake of thine, whose *Humility* doth so astonish me , that I cannot choose but cry with a loud voice in my hart, *O how admirable art thou in thy Saints* ? What are his whole Books of Conꞏ feſſions, but a profound acknowledgment of his ſinnes, which he doth not only confeſſe to *thee*, but to al the world, to the end that al may perpetually praiſe *thy* Mercy ? But O my *God* for this *Humility* of his, *thou* haſt highly exalted him : for which be *thou* eternally magnified and praiſed by al creatures. He was one of thoſe ſinners for whoſe conuerſation, *There was more ioy in Heauen, then vpon ninty nine Iuſt* ; and not without great cauſe , ſeeing he was to be a chief pillar in *thy* Church , and one who might and did draw infinit ſinners by his words and writings out of the mire and dreggs of ſinne, and taught them to ſubmit themſelues to *thine* eaſy yoke, and to ſerue *thee* for *loue*, and to glory in nothing but *thee*. Yea what is wanting in his words, that may inuite our ſouls to *loue thee* with al our harts , with al our ſtrengths , and our neighbour as our ſelues ? Who can ſpeaꞏe in the words of thine own Oracles more comfortably to ſinners then he hath done ? In fine hꞏs words are ſo amorouſly ſweet in *thy* Praiſes, that euen my frozen ſoul had been melted thereꞏ by into *thy* praiſe. He for *thy* ſake be an Aduocate and Interceſſor to *thee* for me, the moſt ſinful, and contemptible of al *thy* ſeruants, he I ſay, *to whom* many *ſinnes* wꞏre

forgiuen, becaufe *he loued* much, whom I
defire together with al the Celeftial Court,
to Adore, and Praife *thee* for me, who am
not worthy to name *thee who* be euer bleffed. *Amen.*

In a Collection which she was making
out of the Booke of Pfalmes, she added
to fome verfes as followeth.

Pfal. 23. verf. 6.

THis is the *generation of them that feeke*
h m: of them that feek the face of the God
of Jacob (I pray God it may proue fo with
vs to *his* Honour and Glory)

Pfal. 31. verf. 0.

I wil giue thee vnderftanding : and wil
inftruct thee in the way that thou shalt go, I
wil faften mine eyes vpon thee. (who is not
wholy inflamed with a defire to feeke after
God alone, to heare fuch a promife from
his own mellifluous mouth.)

Pfal. 35. verf. 10.

Becaufe with thee is the fountain of life :
and in thy light we shal fee light. (I befeech
al thofe deuout fouls that shal perufe *this*
book, to labour carefully for that light
which the Prophet heer fpeaketh of; which
proceedeth from *loue*, and not frcm human
wifedom. This *light*, (by which we shal
difcerne *truth* from falshood) is gotten by

conuersing with Almighty *God*, and humbling our selues vnder his mighty hand.
This *light* hath taught many their way to
God, that could neither write nor read.
Sweet Iesus make vs of the number of these
little ones to whom this *light* is reuealed
which is hidden from the wise and prudent; which is bestowed vpon those that
faithfully adhere to *God*, and not on those
that glory rather in themselues them in *him*.
He be Blessed and Praised by al, for euer
and euer. *Amen.*

Psal. 86. vers. 5.

*Reueale thy way to our Lord and hope in
him: and he wil do it.* (A comfortable saying for those that *God* permits stil to remain
(do what they can) in their imperfections.

℣. 7. *Haue no emulation in him that appeareth in his way* : ℣. 6. *Be subiect to our
Lord and pray him.*   (*Note this wel.*)

℣. 11. *The meeke shal inherit the land:
and shal be delighted in multitude of peace.*
(If we truly labour for this *peace*, (which
is in much Patience) the *God* of *Peace* wil
be amongst vs.)

℣. 25. *When he shal fal he shal not be brui-
sed, because our Lord putteth his hand vnder.*
(O what an incouradgment is this to a
poore frail soul ; Let vs notwithstanding
our imperfections, confidently, and amo-
rously when we fail, hope in *his Mercy*, and

then *He* wil heal and helpe vs, *who* makes
vs fo many fweet promifes. *VVho* be bleffed by al creatutes for euer and euer. *Amen.*

℣. 26. *I haue been yong (*for I am old*)
and I haue not feene the iuft forfaken,* nor his
feed feeking bread. (Why do we diftruct
then, who haue dedicated our felues wholy to *God*, fearing ro depend] only of *his
diuine Prouidence,* which is the greateft happines in this world, and fo much to be defired if we had fo much *loue*, and couradge
as we should.

Pfal. 38. ℣. 8.

*Doubtles al things are vanity euery man
liuing* O my poor foul, take good notice of
this verfe; Adhere to our *Lord whofe* years
neuer fail, and *whofe* helpe is alwaies at
hand Giue that to *God* that is Gods, and
that to Cæfar that is Cæfars: marke what
the Prophet faith in the fame Pfalme, viz.
*And now what is my Expectation, is it not
our Lord?* and *my fubftance is with thee.*

Pfal. 39. *verf.* 15.

*But thou O Lord make not thy confiderati-
ons far from me : thy Mercy and thy truth
haue alwayes receaued me.* (O be thou euer
bleffed for it by al creatures, my *God* and
Al. Amen.

Pfal. 40. *verf.* 1.

*Bleffed is the man that vnderftandeth con-
cerning the needy and the poor: in the euil day*

N iiij

our Lord wil deliuer him. (O my poor soul,
though thou hast not wherewith to releeue
the poor in th ir húger & thirst; yet dispaire
not to gaine this blessing that our *Lord* wil
protect thee in the euil day , which thou
standest so much need off. For , to pray for
those that afflict thee , and render good for
euil to those that molest thee , and being a
comfort in al thou canst imagin, to those
that are afflicted either in body or in m nd
without exception of persons , is included
in the gaining of that most to be desired
promise. Remember with ioy , and imitate
the best thou art able, the happy example of
the late blessed Bishop of Geneua, of whom
it is reported, that one in his diocese exceed-
inly molesting, afflicting, and persecuting
this holy Saint , yét he vsed him with al.
loue, gentlenes, and respect; yea more then
any other person. At which patient proceeding of his one of his subiects wond-
ring at , and speaking to him of it , asked
him how he could vse that man so mildly,
who neuer requited him with other then il
turnes for al the grace he shewed him, being as it were top ful of bitternes against
him To which the Saint humbly answeer-
ed , O saith he, if he should *put out one of*
mine eyes I woul smile vpon him with the other.
I beseech *thee* my *God for thy own sake*, grāt
thy vnworthiest seruant grace to imitate this

example; though to speake truly, none can
do her an iniury, who deserueth so much
in punishment for her sinnes.

Psal. 41. vers. 6. and 7.

*VVhy art thou sorrowful my soul? and why
dost thou trouble me? Hope in God; because yet
I wil confesse to him: the saluation of my countenance, and my God.* (O my soul, hope in
thy God, *who* can do al things! O blessed
Hope and *Confidence*, which is able to obtain al things, and ouercome al things.

℣. 11. *In the day our Lord hath commanded
his Mercy: and in the night a song of him.*
Dost thou not hear my soul, *thy Lord* doth
require of thee? Mercy towards thy euen
Christian, for that *he* sheweth to thee.
And that night and day thou wilt sing *his*
Praise. But *Lord thou* knowst that *thy* Praise
is not seemly in the mouth of a sinner. What
then shal I do? O, hope in *thy* Mercy!

*Certaine comfortable sayings, taken out
of the holy Scripture; for the encou-
radgment of those that desire with all
their harts to* Loue *and please our
most merciful God, and first out of the
Prophet Isaie. Chap. the first.*

*Verse
16.* WASH *you, be cleane: take
away the euil of your cogita-
tions from mine eyes: Cease to do peruersly,*

N w

17. *Learne to do good: Seek iudgment, succour the oppressed, iudge for pupil, defend the widow. And come, and accuse me, saith our Lord.*

18. *If your sins shal be as scarlet, they shal be made as whit as snow: and if they be as red as vermilion, they shal be whit as wool.*

19. *If you be willing: and wil hear me, you shal eat the good things of the earth.*

22. *Thy siluer is turned into drosse: thy wine is mingled with water.* (But hear what followeth, O my soul, and therefor be not discomforted though al thou dost and sufferest be very imperfect; yet behold what he promiseth *who* can do al things. If *he* wil, *he* can make thee clean. If he command, the wind and sea wil be stil, and there wil *ensue a calme*. Commit thy self to *him*, and *he* wil helpe thee when *he* thinketh fit. O *God, thy wil* be done therefor in me for euer and euer. *Amen*.

25. *I wil turn my hand to thee. and boyle out thy drosse til it be pure: and wil take away al thy tinne.*

26. *After these things thou shalt be called the Iust, a faithful City.*

(Shal I feare to be forsaken by *thee* my *God*, after al these sweet promises? No, I wil hope in the multitude of *thy* Mercies. Though I haue hitherto sinned against Heauen and before *thee*, so that I am not worthy to be called *thy child* ; yet let **me** eat of the *crumes* which fal from *my Maisters* table , that I may grow stronger heerafter in resisting that which maketh me displeasing in *thy pure eyes.* Hear , my *Lord* the voyce of a sinner , which would faine *loue thee* , aud with her hart and soul as greatly please *the as euer she hath offended thee.* Let me either *loue,* or not *liue.* I know *thy Mercies* are so great , that *thou* hast admitted those to eat of the bread of Angels, which hertofore fed of *Huskes* like swine; yea S. *Gertrude* saith , that the more base, vile , and contemptible the creature is to whom thou shewest mercy , the more extolled art *thou* by al *thine* Angels, and Saints in Heauen. I wil therefore hope in *thee,* and beseech al *thy* Saints to pray for me, and praise *thee* for taking pitty of me, who am not worthy to cast vp'mine eyes to Heauen much les to thinke vpon , or praise *thee.* To *thee* O my *God* and al my desire be giuen perpetual Praise and Adoration for al eternity by al creatures ! *Amen.*

CHAP. II.

Verse COme let vs go vp to the *Mount* of 3. our *Lord* , and to the *house of the God of Iacob :* and he wil teach vs his *waies* and we shal walke in his *pathes.*

5. *House of Iacob come ye : aud let vs*

walke in the light of our Lord. (O my *God*,
happy are they that walke in this *light*. In
this *light* none walke but the *Humble* and
cleane of hart , and those that serue *thee*
for *loue* , whose ioy *thou thy-self* art , and
who sing with the Prophet: *Renuit consolari
anima mea. My soul refused to be comforted.*
These do in some sorte more or lesse as
thou pleasest , find how sweet and happy a
thing it is to seeke, and sigh after *thee alone*.
Return , my soul, to *thy* beloued ; return,
seek for no consolation, but put *thy* hope
in *God*. Commit *thy-self* vnto God , and let
him do with *thee* what pleaseth *him*. Neuer
seeke thine owne glory; neuer desire thy
wil may be done : but in al things intend,
loue, and preferre the Glory and wil of *God*.
If any come vnto *him* , he shal not return
empty, because *he* willngly giueth water to
the thirsty. In the bowels of *thy* Mercy my
God, remember me poor begger , born and
liuing in blindnes. Grant me that I may see
and walke in *thy light*, that my soul may become truly pleasing to *thee*, O my Lord *God*,
whom only I desire to *loue*, *serue and praise*,
make me in al things conformable to *thy*
holy *wil*, *who* be blessed for euer and euer.
Amen. Amen. Amen.

Scio cui credidi , & certus sum. I know
whom I hane trusted and am secure, saith
S. Paul. O glorious S. Augustin my deare

Patron, whom from my infancy (in my
poor mauer) I haue honoured in a particular maner, and who haft been alwaies
ready to affift me in calling vpon thee, I befeech thee for the loue of *him*, by *whofe loue*
thy hart was fo inflamed, to affift me at the
hour of my death, and obtaine for me of
cur *Lord*, that liuing and dying I may be
wholy conformable to *his Bleffed wil*; neither defiting for time, or eternity any other
thing, then that his diuine pleafure be perfectly accomplifhed in me, *his* vnworthy,
& vngrateful creature. And in that dreadful
houre of my death, obtain for me wretched
finner, confidence in his Mercies which are
(as *thou* knowft) aboue al h.s works. I am
not worthy to *loue*: but *he* is worthy of al
loue and Adoration. I cannot without great
ioy remember thefe following words of
the Prophet Ifaie; hoping his Goodnes wil
for his own fake giue me leaue to apply
them to me poor and finful foul, though
I defetue nothing of my-felf; neuer hauing
done *him* any faithful feruice in al my life.

Chap 43. *v*. 1. And now thus faith our
Lord that created thee and formed thee:
*Feare not, becaufe I haue redeemed thee, and
called thee by thy name, Thou art mine.*

2. *When thou shalt paffe through the waters
I wil be with thee, and the flouds shal not couer
thee: When thou shalt walke in fire, thou shalt
not be burned, and the flame shal not burn inr*

thee. (O bleſſed Saint make interceſſion for
me, that I may be confident in him, *who*
thus aboundeth with Mercy. *Amen.*)

3. *Becauſe I am the Lord thy God the Holy
one of Iſrael thy Sauiour.*

4. *Since thou becameſt honourable in mine
eyes and glorious I haue loued thee.*

5. *Feare not, becaus I am with thee.*

6. *And euery one that innocateth my name
for my glory I haue created him, formed him,
and made him.*

8. *Bring forth the blind people, and hauing
eyes, the deaf and he that hath eares:*

9. *Let them giue their witnes & be iuſtified.*

10. *In very deed you are my witnes ſaith our
Lord, and my ſeruants whom I haue choſen,
that you may know and beleeue me and vnderſtand that I my ſelf am.*

11. *I am, I am the Lord, and there is no
Sauiour beſide me, and there is not that
can deliuer out of my hand.*

16. *Thou ſaith our Lord that gaue away
in the Sea, and a path in the vehement waters.*

18. *Remember not former things, and looke
not on things of old. I am he that takes cleane
away thine iniquities for mine own ſake, and
I wil not remember thy ſins.*

26. *Bring me into remembrance, and let vs
be iudged together. Tel me if thou haue any
thing that maieſt be iuſtified.*

Hetherto the words of the Prophet Iſaie.

S. Iohn 2. ℣. 12. I writ to you litle children,

*becaus your sins are forgiuen you for his name.
And now my children abid in him, that when
he shal appeare we may haue confidence and
not be confounded of him in his coming. My
dearest beleeue not euery spirit; and euery spirit
that dissolueth Iesus is not of God.*

*Feare is not Charity, but perfect Charity
casteth out feare. Let vs therefore loue God :
becaus God loued vs. This is the Charity of
God that we keep his Commandments : and
his Commandments are not heauty.*

O infinit Goodnes, who art Charity it-self,
powre *thy Grace* aboundantly into my poor
soul. I inuoke *thee* my *God*, by the merits,
and intercession of al *thy* Saints in Heauen,
and seruants on earth; to haue mercy on me
now in this my last extreamity. Al I desire
is, that in life and death I may be disposed
of according to the multitude of *thy* most
aboundant Mercies a fountain neuer drawn
dry; Al my ioy is in that *thou* art, my *God*,
and that I am at *thy* disposing. Though I am
poor in al vertues, yet I am confident to be
partaker of *thy* Merits, ó sweet *Iesus* which
thou liberally bestowest, according to *thy*
wil and pleasure ! O be *thou* blessed in al *thou*
disposest ! O my *God*, who art al I desire.
Into *thy* hands I commend my *spirit*, who
art blessed for euer. *Amen.*

The most learned of D. S. Augustin saith.
Ait eruditissimus Doctorum Augustinus.

O eternal Truth , and true Charity, and
O æterna veritas & vera Charitas,
Deare Eternity. Thou art my *God* to *thee*
& chara Eternitas. Tu es Deus meus,
I suspire day and night ! This is that subliue
Tibi suspiro die ac nocte. Hic est sublimis ille.
Contemplatiue Auguftine.
Contemplator Augustinus.
Cuius cor Charitas Christi vulnerauerat:
Whose hart the Charity of Christ had wounded.
O my deare Saint, whose great *Humility,*
I can neuer to much praise and admire :
pray for her to whom thou haft been in her
greateft afflictions and miseries euen as a
Father and Mother ; for which be exhibited honouur to thee by the most sweet-hart
of *I E S V S* our Sauiour, the Son of the
liuing *God* : by which and from which
doth most aboundant sweetnes flow to al
the elect. In the power that *he* gaue thee,
being one by whom he bound, and loosed
finners , giue an aboundant benediction to
thy poore seruant , and beg of my *God* that
I may neuer seek or intend any thing for
time or eternity, but his honour and Glory
and that I may so humble and subiect my-
self vnder *his* mighty hand , that for *his loue*
I may willingly submit my-self in what
maner *he* pleases to al creatures. Let me
commit, and commend my-self to *thy* protection , who art a careful receauer of al my
petitions , and who art one who in a most.

particular maner *God* hath giuen me confidence in, in al the neceffities wherein my
foul doth ftand need of an Aduocat and
friend. O happy change to leaue al friends
on earth to find the more certaiu & affured
friends and Interceffors in Heauen, who
are neuer abfent, neuer vncertain, nor euer
do they fail as thofe in this world are fubiect to do! Be therefor mindful of me I befeech *thee*, in my life & alfo in my laft extremity; and remember, that when affrighted
with the multitude and greiuoufnes of my
finnes and imperfections, I durft fcarfely
caft vp mine eyes to Heauen, or cal vpon
God and *his* Bleffed Mother, *who* might
iuftly difdain fo vngrateful and contemptible a creature; Yet by thy meanes,
and being incouradged by thy example,
and reading thy life and books fo ful of
Confidence and fweetnes; I found my hart
lightned, and my *fpirit* refreshed, and my
foul exceedingly comforted, finding in thee
and by thee expreffed, what a good *God*
we haue, and that as *his* Mercies are aboue
al his works, fo *he* is able to forgiue more
then we can offend. Thou knoweft, thy
very name, when I am fad and afflicted,
doth refresh me to behold it, and feemeth
to fmile vpon me in my miferies, affuring
me of thy helpe in al my foul ftandeth
need of thee, in this my pilgrimage and
ban shment from my *God*, who is my only

loue, life, deſire, and al my happines. To *Whom* fot euer be al Glory, Honour, and Adoration, by al as wel on earth, as in Heauen, and *whom*, by his ſweet Mercy and thy interceſſion, I deſire and hope to *loue*, and ſeruè for euer and euer, *Amen*.

Omnes qui habebant infirmos ducebant illos ad Ieſum, & ſanabantur. Al that had diſeaſed brought them to Ieſus, and they were cured. To whom therefor ſhould I fly in my manifold infirmities, but to *thee* my *Ieſus*, my God, and my *Sauiour*? Who is worthy of our loues, our thoughts, our harts, and our ſouls, but thy own ſelf my *Lord*, who made vs for this alone, that by true ſincere affection we ſhould adhre to thee, the chiefe and ſupreame Good? O woe is me, if for any intention, or for any creatures ſake whatſoeuer; I ſhould do any thing with other intention willingly, then to pleaſe and become inwardly in the bottom of my ſoul vnited to *thee*, heer by *grace*, and in Heauen for al eternity. Al things and creatures fail, only *thy ſelf* art conſtant, *thou* art always preſent, alwaies willing to helpe *thy* poor ſeruants, & euer ready to cure our wounds, which through human frailty by ſin we daily cauſe in our ſouls.

Let vs who haue been greiuous ſinners, and do ſo aboundantly experience *thy* Mercy, giue great and continual praiſe to *thee* our *God*, who hath ſweetly redeemed vs to

Luk 4.40.

thy-felf in the Bloud of *Iefus thy* Sonne the immaculate Lambe, giuing vs therby hope of remiffion of our innumerable fins. Great art *thou O Lord*, and exceeding worthy of al Praife. O let al things Adore and Exalt my *God*, with al their foul, and *ftrength*. What other ftudy, what other endeauour, or what other defire, fhal poffeffe my foul willingly day, or night; but that I may in al, and aboue al things, praife, and *loue* my God. As nothing is fuperior to a foul but *thy felf*, fo nothing but *thou* can fatisfy and fatiat our foules in Heauet or earth; nothing I fay but *thy-felf*, to *whom* ouly let my hart tende, and only in al things intend. *Thou* being the only *true* and proper *(enter* of our hart and foul, what can make this miferable banifhment (whereto my greife I daily offend *thee*) tolerable to me, but only to afpire to *thee* by fighs, defires, and vnfpeakable groanes, in my hart and foul? O let *true loue* vnite me to *thee*, *who* art by al Adored and Praifed for al eternity in thy Heauenly contrey. *Amen.*

Some fpeeches *of heathen Confuls and Philo-fophers, which fhew Chriftians their duty & alfo their happines in knowing how to make good vfe of their knowledge to their Salua-tion, in which thofe Heathens perifhed, be-cans they did not beleeue and acknowledg our* Lord God; *but vanifh away in their*

oẇn cogitations . by ſeeking only fame , ho-
nour, and applauſe of the people, &c. Which
yet in their Ẇiſedom they ſaẇ to be but an
vncertain vanity.

A_ND firſt_ The anſwer of one of the
greateſt and wiſeſt of them ; when he
was offered power , and honour , and ſacri-
fice , according to their cuſtome of vſing
ſuch as for wiſedome nobility , and couradg deſerued it in their eyes.

The more (ſaith he) I conſider with my-
ſelf of things done both in old and later times , the more the vncertainties and vani-
ties of fortune in al moral affaires occurie
to my rememhranee, and the more plainly
doth their vanity appeare vnto me. (O my _God_,
what a definition is heer of a heathen, which
did not ſo much as know _thee_, or for what
end this vncertainty was in them permitted
by _thee_. What a ſhame is it, if we who are not
only Chriſtians but religious ſhould eſteem
or ſeek after any thing but _thee_, in _whom_ alone is ſtability to be found and enioyed? _One_
☞ _hing is neceſſary._ Let chance, fortun, & power (where it is giuen by _thee_) diſpoſe of al
things as they wil, as for me, I wil ſing in al
occurrences ; _It is good for me to adhere to my_
Lord God, the only deſire and _beloued_ of my
ſoul and hart. I wil haue no care or ſtudy, but
how I may in al chances ſpend my whole
forces and ſtrength in _his_ Praiſe , _who_ be

Adored proſtrat by al creatures for euer and
euer. *Amen. Amen.*

A NOTHER SAID.

*Such as ſtand iu feare, are irreſolute in al
their determinations.* (He ſpoake it of thoſe
who out of feare to diſpleaſe, and deſire to
pleaſe for human reſpects, became thereby
a ſlaue to euery ones humour, and keept not
their freedom and liberty, which was got
by ſuppreſſing of natural paſſions.

Another ſpeaking in a controuerſy where
one was to be iudg of two accuſing on another, and defending themſelues before the
Senate, ſaith, The truth or thing beleeued,
and wreſted to the worſt, are eaſily to be diſ-
cerned by one iudg if he be viſe, vpright,
and iuſt, and not interreſted in neither ſide.

Alſo another ſaid. That the diſloyal are
odious euen to thoſe whoſe inſtrumēts they
are: Of a little beginning, comes often great
incōuenience, which might be preuented by
doing as one of the Heathens did, who ex-
celled moſt of his time in Nobility, wiſedom
and al moral vertues, who had ſo great temper ouer his affections and paſſions, that neither for honour (as being offered to be made
a King) nor for gain, would he be falſe to his
Prince, who yet fauoured him ſo little by
reaſon he was ſo much honoured by al the
common wealth, that he gaue way to haue
him poiſoned at thirty years of age, he being alſo his own father that was Cæſar. He

was so iust, that in matters of the greatest controuersy he alwaies did true Iustice, and his enemy whom he knew sought his death, he honoured as his Partner, being yet in nobility much his inferior, but boare rule with him at Cæsars command. This enemy being once at a bãquet with him where most of the Nobility were present, he vttered such disgraceful words and speaches of him to his face, that al were amazed to see him not so much as change his countenance at him. And after this, hearing he was in distresse at Sea, he sent his own Conuoy to deliuer him from drowning, though he knew his iourney was to accuse him to Cæsar and the Senat, and also to plot his death, which indeed he at last achiued, *being both at one Bancquet not lõg after: which example* sheweth vs how amiable vertue is euen in the very Heathens, in whom it was but moral, how much ought we to practise it, in whom by Charity it becometh *Diuine?* O how truly glorious are they my *God,* who indeed posses thy *loue,* wᶜʰ so worthily by holy Scripture is tearmed, most *Honourable wisedome?* But alas to humain frailty it is hard to putvp iniuries, much more to do good for euil, at least nature suggesteth to vs, that it is vnpleasant, and therefore vrgeth vs, not to put vp this, or that, least those who are contrary to vs do add difficulty vpon difficulty, seeing we put it vp so quietly. But this pretence of nature is so

fals and oft, euen in humain respects, so in-
conuenient, whilst we by disputing, resisting, or in the like maner requiting, do draw
grater incōueniences vpon our selues, where
as quietly letting it passe, it would soon come
to nothing. Nay farther I wil speak & add this
to the honour of my *Lord God, whose* way of
vertue and the *Cross* is so sweet in cōparison
of the way of sin, and yealding to our passions that if *he* had neuer intended other reward for those that *Humbly* practise vertue,
and go the way of *Resignation,* but that they
receaue in this life ; *he* could not haue been
taxed of too sleightly rewarding their labour.
For certainly the *peace* that followeth doing
good, for euil, and yeelding sweet, (for bitter, and passing al difficulties *humbly* and patiently ouer, is much more pleasant, then by
hauing ful power to do vpon such occasions
the quite contrary. Such is the very natūre
of al *his* exactions and ordinations, that euen
the very effect of them, maketh thē worthy
to be *loued* desired, ond practised. For who
can consider of al vertues, nad not see how
great a happines lieth hid in the *true practise*
of thē euen in this life? As for exāple, Iustice,
Patience, Benignity, Longanimity, Charity,
and true *Discretion* accompanied with vnfai-
ned *humility,* who doth not see that these &
the like vertues, make vs pleasing to God,
and man, & that the not *practising* thē doth
make vs troublesom to others, and aboue al

to our ſelues? Giue vs, O my *God*, al thoſe vertues which make ſouls ſo pleaſing in *thy diuine eyes*! Let not the very Infidels & Heathés be our accuſers, who practiſed that out of the light of nature wᶜʰ we omit in this haᵖy time of *Grace*. hal they contemn the world, and shal we deſire the baſe pleaſures and cótentments thereof? Shal they fly into dens, & caues to get wiſdom & learning, & shal not we be contented to be forgotten by al the world? Shal they do good for euil, & we do euil for good, and put vp nothing for *loue* of *thee*? Shal they ſubdue their paſſions and affections to become maiſters of their ſouls, and shal not we do it, who by it may come to haue the freer acceſſe to *thee* in our ſouls? O no, far be it from vs, my *Lord* & my *God*, but rather let our ſouls draw no breath but to aſpire to *thee* by true *loue*. Let vs adhere to *thee*, and to no created thing whatſoeuer, that we may for euer & euer be vnited to *thee*, who created vs for that end, for wᶜʰ be *thou* Bleſſed and Praiſed eternally. *Amen*.

Thus wrote our pious ſoul D. Gertrude More, vpon theſe ſayings and doings of thoſe Heathen Philoſophers.

FINIS.

L A V S   D E O.